Privatizing Criminal Justice

Sage Contemporary Criminology

Series editors

John Lea ● Roger Matthews ● Geoffrey Pearson ● Jock Young
Centre for Criminology, Middlesex Polytechnic

Sage Contemporary Criminology draws on the best of current work in criminology and socio-legal studies, both in Britain and internationally, to provide lecturers, students and policy-makers with the latest research on the functioning of the criminal justice and legal systems. Individual titles will cover a wide span of issues such as new developments in informal justice; changing forms of policing and crime prevention; the impact of crime in the inner city; and the role of the legal system in relation to social divisions by gender and race. Throughout, the series will relate theoretical problems in the social analysis of deviancy and social control to the practical and policy-related issues in criminology and law.

Already published

Jeanne Gregory, *Sex, Race and the Law: Legislating for Equality*
John Pitts, *The Politics of Juvenile Crime*
Roger Matthews (ed.), *Informal Justice?*
Nigel South, *Policing for Profit: The Private Security Sector*

Privatizing Criminal Justice

edited by
Roger Matthews

165101

⑤ SAGE Publications
London • Newbury Park • New Delhi

First published 1989

SAGE Publications Ltd
1 Olivers Yard, 55 City Road
London EC1Y 1SP

SAGE Publications Inc
2455 Teller Road
Thousand Oaks, California 91320

SAGE Publications India Pvt Ltd
B-42 Panchsheel Enclave
PO Box 4109
New Dehli 110 017

British Library Cataloguing in Publication data

Privatizing criminal justice. — (Sage contemporary
 criminology)
 1. Criminal law. Justice. Administration.
 Privatisation
 I. Matthews, Roger, *1948–*
 364

ISBN 0–8039–8240–2   ISBN-13 978-0-8039-8240-6
ISBN 0–8039–8241–0 Pbk   ISBN-13 978-0-8039-8241-3 (pbk)

Library of Congress catalog card number 89-62597

Typeset by Fakenham Photosetting Ltd, Fakenham, Norfolk
Printed in Great Britain by Billing and Sons Ltd, Worcester

Contents

We already have a considerable degree of privatization in the area of criminal justice – we call it *crime*.

Denis Healey MP

Notes on the Contributors

Bonnie Berry is Associate Professor at Indiana University. She is interested in the operation of multiple social control systems and in the role of advanced technology in the control of individual deviance. She gained her doctorate from Ohio State University, and has studied and worked in the University of Miami, the University of California Los Angeles and the University of Washington.

Roger Matthews is a Senior Lecturer in Criminology and a member of the Centre for Criminology at Middlesex Polytechnic. He is co-editor (with Jock Young) of *Confronting Crime* (1986) and editor of *Informal Justice?* (1988).

Rob Mawby is Principal Lecturer in Social Policy at Plymouth Polytechnic. His main interests are in victim services, policing, and the role of the voluntary sector in the criminal justice system. His recent books, written with Martin Gill, are *Crime Victims* (1987), *Volunteers in the Criminal Justice System* (forthcoming, 1990) and *A Special Kind of Constable?* (forthcoming, 1990); he is currently completing a text on *Comparative Policing Issues* (forthcoming, 1990).

Mike Nellis is a Lecturer in Social Work (Criminal Justice) at Sheffield University, with a long-standing interest in juvenile crime. He has previously been an Intermediate Treatment Officer, and is associated with Radical Alternatives to Prison. He is currently working on a thesis on the historical development of Intermediate Treatment in England and Wales.

Ken Pease is Reader in Criminology at Manchester University. He is a former Principal Research Officer in what is now the Home Office Research and Planning Unit, and a member of the Parole Board. He was Head of the School of Sociology and Social Policy at Ulster Polytechnic. He has also worked intermittently as consultant to the United Nations Crime Branch in Vienna, and has been involved in analysis of the second and third United Nations World Crime Surveys.

Mick Ryan is Principal Lecturer in Humanities at Thames Polytechnic, and author of *The Acceptable Pressure Group: A Case Study of the Howard League and RAP* (1978) and *The Politics of Penal Reform* (1983). With Tony Ward he is co-author of *Privatization and the Penal System: The American Experience and the Debate in Britain* (1989).

Nigel South is a Research Associate of the Centre for Criminology, Middlesex Polytechnic. He has published a number of articles on aspects of private security, private justice and on the irregular economy, and has also written widely on drug-related issues. He is author of *Policing for Profit: The Private Security Sector* (1988), and co-editor (with N. Dorn) of *A Land Fit for Heroin?* (1987).

Max Taylor is Professor of Applied Psychology at University College Cork, and before that was Head of the School of Psychology at Ulster Polytechnic. He is author of *The Terrorist* (1988). His area of major research interest in recent years has been police training and performance, but he has also published work on burglar behaviour and on terrorism.

Tony Ward is a barrister and Joint Organizer of INQUEST and co-author, with Mick Ryan, of *Privatization and the Penal System: The American Experience and the Debate in Britain* (Open University Press, 1989). He is also the author of *Death and Disorder* (1986), and co-author, with David Downes, of *Democratic Policing* (1986). He is a part-time tutor in criminology at the Centre for Extra-Mural Studies, Birkbeck College, London.

Robert P. Weiss is Associate Professor of Sociology at the State University of New York at Plattsburgh. His research interests include the historical development of the private detective agency, and the history of punishment. His study of penology has been inspired by twenty years' work as an educator (and student) of American prisoners. His articles have appeared in the *Historical Journal*, *Social History*, *Crime and Social Justice*, and in several edited volumes.

1 Privatization in Perspective

Roger Matthews

The term 'privatization' has slipped almost imperceptibly into popular discourse over the last few years. As the buzz-word of the eighties it has become a catch-all term referring to almost any process where the State is no longer identified as the provider of particular goods and services. 'Privatization' has therefore come to be used to refer to a disparate set of processes ranging from the sale of public companies to contracting out, as well as various forms of deregulation.

Within the fields of health care, education, transport and communications, in the post-war period, the State has come to be seen — in Britain at least — as the natural provider. Not surprisingly, therefore, the recent attempts to privatize these 'public' services have elicited a range of powerful responses ranging from messianic acclamation on one side to violent resistance on the other. The severity of these responses reflects the degree to which the process of privatization signals a major transformation in the nature of contemporary social and political relations.

In contrast, proposals to privatize parts of the criminal justice system have elicited a peculiar set of responses. Although there have been some heated exchanges there has been a widespread sense of bemused disbelief. That is, it is widely assumed that whatever may have been implemented in other areas of social life, the provision of laws, punishment and crime control constitute a unique and privileged realm of activity that should be provided by the State. For, it is argued, one of the essential characteristics of the State is its claim to exercise a monopoly over the use of legitimate force. The dispersal of this coercive power amongst private agencies is seen as threatening the impartiality and universality of law enforcement and thereby undermining normative structures. The exercise of coercive power and the distribution of punishment are held to have profound social and symbolic implications which cannot be safely discharged to private and particularistic interests.

But the belief that 'it could not happen here' has been dispelled — or at least moderated — by two basic realizations. The first is that there already exists a significant degree of 'privatization' within the criminal justice system. Even a cursory examination of the principal agencies involved reveals that they already incorporate personnel who are not directly in the employment of the State. Most notable is the significant degree of 'private policing' which is carried out on both sides of the Atlantic. The number of private security police in Britain, America and Canada is estimated to exceed the number of public police (Shearing and Stenning, 1981; South, 1988). Within the ambit of criminal justice too there is already an impressive variety of voluntary, non-profit-making and private agencies who between them provide a range of services — particularly for juveniles — which complement and compete with State provision (Lindquist, 1980).

The second major shift in thinking which has occurred involves the recognition that there exists an important distinction between the *provision* and the *administration* of goods and services. It had been widely assumed that, wherever possible, the State should both supply *and* take responsibility for the implementation of criminal justice, and that its failure to perform either of these functions to the full would undermine its legitimacy. But it is becoming apparent that many services can be readily provided by a range of non-State agencies without necessarily impairing the legitimacy of the State. The rapid growth of the voluntary sector in recent years has not noticeably undermined or threatened the operation of the professionalized statutory agencies (see the chapters by Mawby and by Nellis in this volume); while the contracting out of youth services has not destabilized the juvenile justice system. On the contrary, the incorporation and expansion of these semi-autonomous agencies appears to have extended both the range and depth of State authority. Thus it appears that as long as the State exercises ultimate responsibility, it can effectively disengage from the immediate provision of certain services within the criminal justice system without necessarily incurring any significant disadvantages.

There is a continuous range of goods and services which are supplied by non-State agencies to the public sector. Within the criminal justice system an elaborate range of commodities are furnished daily. One American report indicates some of the specialist items which are available:

> Inside prisons the corporate world includes Aerko International's Mister Clear Out ('The state of the art in tear gas hand grenades especially designed for indoor use'); the Peerless Handcuff ('A major breakthrough in cuff design'); Disposable Waste Systems Muffin Monster ('It will grind up into small pieces all the things that inmates put down toilets'); Servomation, a food distribution company ('Justice is served') and Coca Cola ('Time goes better with Coke'). (Kroll, 1984: 19)

Related to the already extensive use of private agencies and providers within the criminal justice system is the discovery that many of the central functions now carried out by the State were carried out by private profit-making agencies in the not too distant past (McConville, 1987). We should, therefore, strictly speaking refer to the process of *re*-privatization. However, it would be a mistake to believe that the current movement towards privatization is simply a return to the past. For as Santos has argued, where private activities are taken over and rationalized by the State they do not re-emerge in the original form, but are invariably transformed in the process (Santos, 1980). These transformed processes also re-emerge within a new and distinctly different set of social relations.

What we are now experiencing is a departure whose significance cannot be grasped by examining previous epochs, but rather needs to be understood within the network of contemporary social relations. As Ascher notes, the change in the nature of privatization in recent years is characterized by a change from specialized to generalized provision, from backdrop services to front-line provision, and from local authority based schemes of contracting out to the decentralization and erosion of State monopolies (Ascher, 1987).

In the field of criminal justice some of these changes are exemplified by the shift in the relation between public and private policing. Thus Shearing and Stenning have pointed out that

> The major change has been the rapid growth since the early 1960s of policing provided on a contract basis for profit, by private enterprise. This has established private security as a readily available alternative to public police for those with the means to afford it, and it has made private security a much more visible contributor to policing than it has been hitherto. The result has been an unobtrusive but significant restructuring of our institutions for the maintenance of order and a substantial erosion by the private sector of the State's assumed monopoly over policing and by implication justice. (Shearing and Stenning, 1981: 496)

The movement towards privatization within criminal justice also includes an extension of the existing localized and limited forms of contracting out of specialist services to the wholesale transfer of provision to private profit-making and non-profit-making agencies: the transformation of private prisons for use with exceptional offenders to their adoption for use with 'normal' offenders; the expansion of the voluntary sector; and greater use made of civilian staff within State agencies, as well as the expansion of various forms of 'private justice' (Camp and Camp, 1985; Lerman, 1984; Henry, 1983; South, 1984).

The major support for privatization has come from the New Right as well as a growing number of disenchanted liberals who see the expansion of State provision as more of a problem than a solution (Young, 1987). The supporters of privatization have also been able to draw freely upon the general critiques of State provision mounted by the left throughout the sixties and seventies. The State-sponsored criminal justice system, it had been forcibly argued, was grossly inefficient, overly centralized, discriminatory and often ineffective (Hall et al., 1978; Quinney, 1977; and Ryan and Ward, this volume).

Prisons in particular have become a focal point of concern (see Immarigeon, 1987). Whilst right-wing governments have maintained a commitment to an expansionist policy of prison building, they have not been entirely deaf to critics who claim that it would be difficult to devise a less accountable and less effective system of punishment than the existing prison system (Fitzgerald and Sim, 1979; Stern, 1987; Rutherford, 1984). Against the background of these forceful critiques and escalating costs even the opponents of privatization found it difficult to argue that privatization, in the penal sphere at least, could make the situation any worse (Shaw, 1987). Even the spectre of some people making profit out of other people's misery has not been sufficient to mobilize a broadly based anti-privatization campaign.

Privatization is also prompted by hard-line conservatives who believe that it offers the possibility of achieving the twin aims of expanding the control apparatus while reducing the level of State expenditure. The possibilities of a more comprehensive system of crime control at reduced cost has also, no doubt, a broad popular political appeal. For it is the poor and powerless, in particular, who not only suffer disproportionate levels of victimization but also carry a disproportionate percentage of the financial costs of maintaining an increasingly costly criminal justice system. Despite the attempts to reduce the overall level of State expenditure, the 'law and order budget' has increased enormously in recent years. Between 1976 and 1986, for example, the total expenditure on prisons in England and Wales alone increased about five-fold from £163 million to £786 million (HMSO, 1987); and the current prison building programme will cost the British taxpayer in excess of £1 billion by the time it is completed in the mid-1990s. Similarly increases have occurred in the USA, where the expenditure for civil and criminal justice has increased by 75 per cent between 1979 and 1985 and where the total expenditure for fiscal year 1985 reached a staggering $45.6 billion (Bureau of Justice, 1987). Against this background any strategy to reduce the level of expenditure on 'law and order' begins to look politically attractive.

However, the belief that privatization will automatically reduce costs, particularly in the penal sphere, has been repeatedly questioned (Borna, 1986; Ericson et al., 1987). Comparisons between the costs of public and private institutions are extremely difficult to evaluate. The division of labour between public and private agencies, and the differences in roles, level of training and range of functions, make direct comparisons difficult. Also, there may be critical functions which are not amenable to quantification (for example, of rehabilitation, or crime prevention). There are also problems of evaluating short-term and long-term costs as well as the hidden costs of monitoring private providers.

But in cases where it might be possible to make comparable costings we find that the existing State agencies often lack any meaningful controls that would allow the evaluation of service delivery or efficiency. The recent establishment of the National Audit Office in Britain to investigate the operation of public agencies like the prisons and the police has drawn attention to the remarkable lack of accounting procedures and the absence of the kind of financial controls that might allow these agencies to be properly assessed (National Audit Office, 1985).

The uncertainty of the cost-effectiveness of privatization has forced its advocates to stress other possible advantages. They have come increasingly to suggest that its real advantages may lie in its increased flexibility, its ability to realize objectives that might be difficult or impossible to achieve in the public sector and its ability to quickly mobilize facilities to meet pressing needs; or that it might encourage experimentation and the introduction of innovative practices. Further, the advocates of privatization have argued that it increases competition, reduces the power of the unions and opens up new managerial possibilities, as well as generating new forms of public participation.

As Kay and Thompson have argued, there appears to be a continuously shifting series of justifications which have become associated with privatization, with various objectives being substituted for those which are discarded.

> However, the fact that a policy has a variety of objectives, and that many of these at times conflict, is not in itself criticism of that policy. But the reality behind the apparent multiplicity of objectives is not that the policy has a rather sophisticated rationale, but rather that it is lacking any clear analysis of purpose or effects, and hence any objective which seems achievable is seized as justification. The outcome is that no objectives are effectively attained, and that in particular economic efficiency — which is at once the most important of these and the most difficult to attain — has systematically been subordinated to other goals. (Kay and Thompson, 1986: 20)

If privatization fails to decrease the level of public expenditure it will, however, involve strategic shifts in the distribution of power and resources. There will no doubt be specific areas in which, in the short term at least, some savings will be made, but it is more likely that privatization will involve shifts in the processes of financial and political decision-making. It is probable that specific savings or advantages will be gained for a particular department only for increased costs to be incurred elsewhere. Privatization may also involve changes in the distribution of costs and responsibility between central and local State agencies; for although the privatization movement is often associated with decentralization, it may simultaneously involve reciprocal centralizing processes.

The most immediate example of this complex relation associated with the return of privatization is the interest in deinstitutionalization and the expansion of community care. In the field of juvenile justice in particular, there is a continual struggle for the control of the 'body of the delinquent' between locally based 'inclusive' welfare-orientated programmes and centrally organized 'segregative' custodial programmes. But since the privatization of decentralized alternatives to custody may well end up by feeding the custodial institutions with ever expanded populations as a result of the process of 'net-widening', the long-term cost of this expanding welfare–punishment continuum may be substantial. Alternatively, the private sector may form part of an expanded welfare–punishment–privatization matrix as has occurred in the USA, resulting in an expanding, increasingly 'hidden', and impenetrable juvenile justice system (Schwartz et al., 1986; Lerman, 1982). Reflecting on the experience in USA, researchers found that:

> It should be noted that the growth of the private sector was actively advocated by juvenile justice reformers of the early 1970s. It was argued that smaller, privately operated programs could provide improved care to troubled youth. Indeed, the deinstitionalization movement resulting in many youth, particularly female status offenders, being shifted from public training schools to private residential programs. Some now question whether this development represented significant progress. For example, private facilities traditionally spend less per youth than public facilities and youth reside in private programs much longer than in public facilities. Most important, the growth in the private correctional admissions did not offset growth in the public sector. (Krisberg et al., 1986: 28)

Despite the generally negative evaluations of aspects of privatization its advocates remain undeterred. For many, privatization has become elevated to the level of theology, such that testing its claims against the apparent reality is not taken as conclusive. Among its more enthusiastic advocates, privatization represents more than a policy which offers specific tangible benefits; rather, it represents a vision of a different society. The 'hidden hand' of the market mechanism is held to be the only viable organizational and distributional mechanism (Heald and Thomas, 1986).

In contrast to those who have adopted privatization as the new theology the political opposition have identified it as a new form of demonology, whose inflated rhetoric masks the introduction of more invidious forms of personal acquisition, individualism and egoism. For opponents, privatization represents an instrument for reducing social provision, for justifying neglect of the poor and needy and for undermining organized resistance to governmental policy, and it must therefore be actively resisted.

But the debate between the supporters and critics — broadly the right and the left — has become increasingly polarized around what are seen as exclusive oppositions — the State and the market, the public and private realms. However, even among the most ardent supporters of privatization there is an awareness that if the market mechanisms were left to their own devices, they would in a relatively short time result in large concentrations of power that would, in turn, threaten the very basis of the democratic process itself. Historically, the inherent instability and vagaries of the market mechanism have themselves fostered the increased socialization of production and necessitated increased State involvement in the regulation of the social economy. On the other hand, even ardent statists find it difficult to imagine any functioning society which does not involve some form of market mechanism or recognize the dangers of an all-embracing State apparatus. Rather than focusing upon unworkable and unrealistic oppositions,

> A pragmatic public policy must recognise when private alternatives might work better and by the same token where new forms of public provision may ameliorate the endemic shortcomings of the market. Most of all it must recognise that the markets are not natural creations, they are always legally and politically structured. Hence the choice is not public or private but which of many public–private structures works best. And 'best' cannot mean only most efficient, for a reasonable appraisal of alternatives needs to weigh concerns of justice, security and citizenship. (Starr, 1987: 198)

Thus the major significance of the privatization debate lies not so much in privileging the market over the State or vice versa, but rather lies in its invitation to examine alternative State–market relations in relation to the central concerns of justice, security and citizenship. This requires moving away from abstract polemics and replacing it with a more detailed analysis of the specific effects of the different alignments that constitute the criminal justice system.

But the initial problem that immediately confronts those who want to expand the range of non-State influences which operate in relation to the criminal justice process is that we know very little about the actual demand for services. That is, the interests of the general public are conspicuously absent from the debate. Instead, the discussion about the costs and benefits of privatization is predominently 'supply' orientated. The shift towards privatization will, it could be argued, represent a shift towards the 'demand' side of the equation. However, the likelihood is that, even where this takes place, it will be a response to 'effective' demand (that is, towards those who can actually afford to pay for services) rather than a response to general demand. This problem is complicated even more by the peculiarly symbiotic relationship between demand and supply within particular areas of criminal justice. The demand for public policing, for example, is inextricably linked to public perceptions of police effectiveness. Thus in considering the relation between public and private provision it is necessary to locate the issue in strategic and contextual terms.

It makes a great deal of difference, for example, in reducing the level of State policing, whether the private alternative is adequate and affordable. If not, the result may well be the extension of choice for those who can afford or want a more commercialized service, with little or nothing left for the rest. This is in a sense what has happened to the legal process in Britain, since in real terms the costs and organization of legal action are such that something in the region of 40 per cent of the population are effectively barred from its use. In this area there seem to be compelling reasons for providing a much higher degree of legal aid and for moderating the inflated costs of legal services.

There is no reason, of course, why a shift towards privatization in one sphere cannot be accompanied by greater State intervention in another. This in one sense is occurring continuously, but at present there seems to be little in the way of any clear guidelines for determining the appropriate combination of State and market forces. Decisions seem to be largely guided by political expediences and contingencies. But if we are interested in developing a more adequate response then it would seem necessary to try to formulate some rational criteria by which decisions could be made.

This question is not unfamiliar to social policy analysts (Savas, 1982). A general distinction has been made between 'public goods' such as national defence that are seen as necessarily supplied by the State, and other private goods that can most effectively be supplied by non-State agencies. But these distinctions are only applicable to a limited range of goods and services, and they do not provide an adequate framework for deciding the most appropriate mode of provision in the vast majority of cases.

One of the most startling aspects of recent developments is the extremely wide range of goods and services which are open to some form of privatization; and that even such seemingly classic examples of 'public goods' as incarceration or crime prevention are amenable to privatization. The difficulty of making decisions about the most appropriate public–private relation in each of these areas is that it is a three-dimensional problem. As indicated above, there are two dimensions of provision and administration and a third dimension of effectiveness. These three dimensions require further examination.

The mode of provision

Clearly, many of the services currently provided by the State in the field of criminal justice are open to some form of privatization. But the alternative to State provision is not only the introduction of private profit-making agencies. Between these two modalities are various combinations of alternatives ranging from community action, to private non-profit making organizations, to voluntary organizations, as well as various combinations of these options. However, the profoundly social nature of much crime control activity makes the establishment of a predominance of private profit-making agencies that are only accountable to their direct employers' difficulty to justify. For individually focused forms of intervention can lead to displacement, and the intensification of problems elsewhere.

A broad definition of privatization can encompass a variety of individual and community responses including self-help schemes, forms of individual protection (for example, the purchase and carrying of weapons), citizen patrols and vigilante groups (Lavrakas, 1985; Smith and Uchida, 1988). The growing emphasis upon individual responsibility in crime control has served to remind us that the vast majority of conflicts and crimes are dealt with in the community. The advantages of increased community participation are seen to lie not only in the possibility of reducing crime, but also the possibilities of reducing the fear of crime and generating an increased sense of security and social cohesion (Clarke, 1987; Skogan, 1987). But, as Denis Rosenbaum has pointed out, some forms of community or citizen response can actually serve to intensify the situation, because

> The problem as research suggests, is that neighbourhoods that need the most help (i.e. have the most serious crime problems) will be the least receptive to such programmes because these residential areas are characterized by suspicion, distrust, hostility, and lack of shared norms regarding appropriate public behaviour. (Rosenbaum, 1987: 115)

It is normally, however, where community involvement is most difficult to mobilize that the problem of crime is most acute. This is because 'crime' often signifies the failure of self-help and community strategies to manage particular sets of conflicts. For formal legal intervention arises in many cases at the point at which 'problematic situations' cannot be adequately dealt with by the available informal networks (Lea, 1987; Hulsman, 1986).

The shift from formal to informal regulation can also include those forms of privatization generally referred to as 'community care', in which the locus of control is moved into the family or the neighbourhood. This form of 'privatization' has become most evident in the area of juvenile control, and has been highlighted in relation to the decarceration of mental patients, the aged and the disabled (Scull, 1977). The shift from the public to the private sector may involve unforeseen consequences, for

> Privatisation is likely to exploit the informal sector of care further by assuming that care will be provided in the absence of payment. Thus like cuts in some public services, it will be more economic simply because it is inadequate. (LeGrand and Robinson, 1984: 37)

The expansion of 'community care' is likely to shift the burden disproportionately on to the shoulders of the female members of the household, and in some cases the removal of State intervention may result in forms of 'benign neglect' in which 'problem populations' are left to take care of themselves or to eke out a meagre existence in the ghettos of the inner city. Alternatively, the encouragement of 'active citizenship' in relation to crime control can all too easily lead to vigilantism, the growth of interpersonal violence and the re-emergence of the 'law of the jungle'. Apart from the growing emphasis upon 'self-help' and community action there has been a substantial expansion of voluntary organizations that are currently becoming an important, but often neglected, feature within the criminal justice system.

Explaining the role and recent expansion of the voluntary sector has proved difficult. For it does not fit neatly into the State–market opposition and raises problems for conventional economic theory. The essence of the problem, according to Sugden, is that 'the voluntary sector appears to be principally engaged in the provision of public goods to an extent which is quite inconsistent with standard theory' (Sugden, 1984: 707).

The novelty of the voluntary sector lies in its ability to draw in both public and private sources of funding, while mixing formal and informal responsibilities in new ways; it has also opened up new channels of training and recruitment (Lawrence, 1983). Its critics have suggested that it substitutes unskilled and unorganized labour for professional agencies. Its advocates, on the other hand, argue that it offers a unique response to people's immediate and unmet needs. Importantly, in fact, it provides the possibility of different styles of provision and intervention. It can also foster active pressure groups capable of responding to the needs and fears of those sections of the population whose voice is seldom heard.

Services in criminal justice may also be provided by private non-profit-making organizations. Particularly in the USA and Canada, these play a role in the organization of prisons and in the provision of probation and supervisory activities. The provision of services by non-profit-making organizations using voluntary or professional labour allows organizations to operate to meet 'specific' needs, and permits private firms to pay a greater contribution to the mainten-ance of the criminal justice system through forms of sponsorship or through the expression of social responsibility. Although not all private firms involved in providing services in the criminal justice system are profit-making, there has been little emphasis in Britain, in particular, on encouraging private industry to carry a larger share of the burden of financing the criminal justice system (Matthews, 1988a). One of the spin-offs of introducing business interests into the operation of the criminal justice system is that they may enhance its political viability. Thus between State and private provision aimed at profit maximization there are a number of alternative modes of provision.

The forms of administration

It is in the administration of these various modes of provision that some of the more dramatic and far-reaching changes have occurred. New techniques of administration have been developed as the emphasis has moved towards different styles of regulation within the criminal justice area. Increasingly, there has been a shift towards contracting out, the use of subsidies and licensing, and the growth of regulatory agencies.

The contracting out of certain forms of provision — particularly services including medical, educational, and addiction treatment services — has become a widely used method of administering pro-vision to non-State agencies. Probably the best known example of contracting out followed the closure of the Massachusetts juvenile reformatories in the early 1970s (Miller, 1973). Contracting out of youth services was seen as a way of providing more appropriate and cost-effective non-custodial facilities for a substantial number of juveniles in trouble. Although a considerable level of deinstitutiona-lization was achieved, however, the 'privatization' initiative did not succeed in reducing costs or the level of recidivism (Serrill, 1975).

Nevertheless, contracting out certain services within the criminal justice system continues to be attractive to administrators who relish the flexibility which it promises. But there are real problems with the monitoring and administration of contractual services. Contracting out faces major problems in developing adequate criteria for the implementation of contracts. Competitive tendering does not ensure the most effective or required results — particularly over the long term. There are problems concerning measurement, the establishment of clear comparative criteria between the performance of competing agencies, the development of procedures for monitoring contract compliance, and in enforcing sanctions for non-compliance (see Weiss, this volume). As Taylor and Pease (this volume) argue, there is an urgent need to develop more stringent and clear-cut criteria if non-State agencies are to be invited to provide an increasing range of front-line services (see also Gentry, 1986).

An alternative mode of administration is available through the use of subsidies. By this means it is possible to increase the profitability of those agencies that the state wants to encourage. Subsidies can work in a number of ways, but normally take one of two forms. Either they consist of fixed amounts issued over a specified period, or they involve payments made to particular agencies in relation to the realization or pursuit of specified goals. Examples of the second form of subsidy can be drawn from the probation subsidy programmes which have been set up in the USA — particularly those in Minnesota and California. Although both these programmes are designed to give counties incentives to reduce the number of persons committed to state correctional facilities they operate in slightly different ways. In the Minnesota programme, financial penalties were inflicted upon county authorities for individuals sentenced from their jurisdictions to terms of imprisonment of five years or less in a state correctional facility; whereas in California, counties which did not reduce state commitments did not receive the subsidy money (McSparron, 1980).

Evaluation of these and similar programmes has produced mixed results. For whereas the California programme saved money, the Minnesota programme did not. Instead, the latter created a system of 'double tracking', involving the establishment of a parallel system of punishment, and encouraged a process of 'transcarceration', whereby offenders were moved from one institution to another rather than deinstitutionalized.

Although subsidies provides the real possibility of directing the operation of non-State agencies in effective ways they can also create their own problems. For where the level of subsidy is fixed, there is always the possibility that the availability of subsidies may encourage a stream of new agencies into an area, thus lowering the original level of individual subsidy and creating problems of profitability for existing agencies. Also, as in the cases of Minnesota and California, where there is a shift from federal to local state organizations, there is a possibility — particularly in periods of hardship — that local state agencies may be encouraged to take on problems which might be better dealt with in other ways.

A less noticeable, but arguably more significant, aspect of privatization that has occurred as a result of the shift in emphasis from direct State provision towards a more administrative stance is the development of regulatory agencies. Their development has underlined the growing realization that the law is only one of a number of regulatory mechanisms, and that its symbolic or back-up role may in some instances be more appropriate than its direct and immediate implementation.

Certain areas of personal and social life are coming to be seen as more properly regulated by relatively independent bodies or governed by some form of 'self-regulation'. In the areas of work, housing and transport, agencies have emerged which have shifted the onus of regulation away from what are considered as relatively ineffective or inappropriate State agencies (Wilson, 1980). A range of mechanisms, including franchising and licensing, are intended to control both the quantity and quality of provision. By setting minimum standards and by monitoring the operation of the agencies concerned, the State can minimize its own level of involvement while maintaining sanctions to ensure compliance.

The licensing of private security police, for example, has minimized many of the initial problems associated with the operation of private security companies, while the agencies themselves have benefited from increased professionalization and the restriction of competition in the industry (Scott and McPherson, 1971; Marx, 1987; South, 1988).

Probably the most telling example of the use of regulatory agencies has been in relation to the control of corporate crime. Purely legal regulation of corporate crime has been widely seen as ineffective and even counterproductive. Because of the problems of locating responsibility within corporate entities and of developing effective forms of accountability, corporations have resisted direct legal regulation. The general problem that has been identified is that

> Organisations are so different that any unrealistic approach to controlling them will encounter difficulty. Inevitably, models of accountability just like models of rule creation are pushed towards particularism. There may be less injustice and better protection of the public by making private justice systems more explicit and giving them public recognition than by imposing universalistic laws upon organisational situations with which these laws are out of line. (Braithwaite and Fisse, 1985: 335)

This form of analysis suggests that different types of crime are better dealt with by different combinations of state and private agencies, and implies a distancing from a legal-centric view of control. It also raises the question of whether there are particular sets of activities which may be more reasonably regulated by universalistic legal rules than others.

But like contracting out, regulatory agencies experience serious problems of monitoring and the enforcement of rules. In particular, they face the danger of co-option by large powerful organizations. Whether regulatory agencies are effective or not will depend upon the levels of sanctions that they can ultimately mobilize and the degree of critical autonomy that they can maintain from the organization being monitored. Unfortunately, those who are interested in promoting regulatory agencies are often those who are least likely to want to enact strict enforcement. As a result, within these agencies and as with contractual services, there has been a considerable gap between promise and performance. As David Heald argues,

> Questions will increasingly be asked about the costs and benefits of the regulatory systems which will be replacing public ownership in key sectors. Momentum, which the programme certainly has, is not a substitute for forethought because decisions now will close future options and may be prohibitively costly or difficult to unwind. Quite apart from the detail of regulating criteria there are prior questions about the viability and independence of the regulatory bodies themselves. (Heald, 1985: 19–20)

These new and expanding modes of administration have effected a simultaneous decentralization and centralizaton of control. Whatever the complexity of the relation between State and non-State agencies in terms of the actual provision of services, these changes have produced new centralizing tendencies and have encouraged new departures in the exercise of power (see Fitzpatrick, 1988).

The level of effectiveness

The first two dimensions of analysis are concerned with the provision and administration of goods and services, while the third dimension refers to more instrumental questions about the effectiveness of these different combinations of public and private responses. Unravelling the complexities of the issue involves investigating the relation between form and content.

I have discussed the question of reducing costs through privatization and have suggested that although important it is only one of a number of possible criteria of effectiveness that need to be calculated when making assessments. Other critical indicators of effectiveness include the possibilities of increased flexibility, increased quality of service, wider forms of accountability, increased security and the enhancement of justice.

Where the aim is to overcome the inertia that characterizes the existing criminal justice system, or to move away from entrenched and fixed practices, privatization could provide a much-needed catalyst to change by introducing new personnel and methods. Although

> Given the multiple (and often conflicting) ambitions attached to the privatisation of corrections it is tempting to conclude at the outset that someone is bound to be disappointed. The notion that private organisations can provide more for less is undeniably attractive, but probably unrealistic. The greatest promise of the private sector may instead lie in its capacity to satisfy objectives that might be difficult if not impossible to achieve in the public sector — introducing public sector managers to the principles of competitive business, quickly mobilising facilities and manpower to meet immediate needs, rapidly adapting services to changing market circumstances, experimenting with new practices, in satisfying special needs with an economy of scale not possible in a single public sector jurisdiction. (Mullen, 1985)

Where the need for flexibility is paramount, privatization may offer possibilities. However, it is the case that flexibility, efficiency and choice for the user may mean disruption, stress and uncertainty for the producer. Significantly, the already extensive involvement of the private sector in the criminal justice system has provided relatively little in the way of innovative or progressive practices. Where the operations of the private sector have been substituted for those of the public sector they tend to look remarkably similar. On the other hand, where the desired aim is to increase the quality of service privatization may be relevant. If, for example, the aim is to enhance the levels of rehabilitation of offenders, privatization could be useful (Hall, 1986). Where the private sector can provide facilities with greater rehabilitative value, then its adoption would probably receive a significant degree of public support (Cullen and Gilbert, 1982).

The prospect of improving prison conditions is undeniably attractive. And it certainly is the case that some of the new private prisons compare on a physical level at least very favourably with the existing State institutions. However, it has been argued that the first wave of private prisons are 'loss leaders', and that it is the quality of long-term provision which is problematic. It may be that

> Much of the attraction of the private sector depends upon its marginality. To the extent that the private sector replaces the public sector, there is a risk that it may also reproduce its weaknesses, its rigidities, its unresponsiveness and its administrative costs — with the bureaucracy of regulation taking the place of the bureaucracy of management. (Klein, 1984: 28)

It was certainly true in the case of British Telecom and British Gas that where huge public companies were replaced by huge private companies the same types of inflexibility and unresponsiveness were evident in both cases. There has been no reduction in costs to the consumer and no noticeable improvement in service. This point has also been made in relation to the voluntary sector, whose flexibility and effectiveness derives to a significant degree from the pre-existence of a wide range of general State provision necessary for its operation (Brenton, 1985).

A recurring criticism of the existing system is the serious lack of accountability. From the closed fortress of the prison to the shrouded courtrooms across the country, the level of accountability is notoriously low. One important and often repeated justification for privatization is that the market opens up entirely different structures of accountability. The introduction of elements of competition and public choice is identified as one of the major advantages of introducing or expanding market principles. The systems of accountability in the non-State sector are seen as being more direct and precise than the generally diffuse systems of accountability that operate in the State sector. Where elected representatives and permanent officers are both responsible for providing and monitoring services, there is an inevitable tension which normally encourages a reduced flow of information, lower visibility and minimum degrees of access.

The possibility of encouraging a greater number of independent and autonomous agencies to run and monitor the criminal justice process offers the prospect of opening up parts of the system to greater degrees of public scrutiny and of introducing new forms of decision-making and awareness. The danger is, of course, that where privatization is linked directly to the pursuit of profit the politicization of decision-making through democratic processes may be viewed as a disposable impediment to profit maximization. For this reason, some free market advocates see those kinds of authoritarian government which attempt to disengage polity from economy as more acceptable than their libertarian rhetoric might suggest (Heald and Thomas, 1986). The growing involvement of the private sector may indeed serve to reduce accountability and restrict democratic debate. By exercising undue pressure on criminal justice policy, private interests might be able to shape policies in ways which further their own specific interests.

Aligned to the question of accountability is that of security: it is often claimed by politicians that accountability has to be curtailed in order to maximize the level of social and personal security. Open access to police operations, for example, will, it is claimed, reduce police effectiveness and impair their ability to protect the public. Many have found these arguments persuasive as their own demands for social and personal security have grown. But this opposition between accountability and effectiveness has been shown to be largely erroneous — at least in the case of the public police. For the reporting of crime and the flow of information to the police is crucially dependent upon the levels of trust and public confidence that the police can maintain (Kinsey et al., 1986). But the increased demands for security have encouraged various forms of privatization, ranging from the 'locks and bolts' approach to household security, to the use of concierges and private policing agencies, and have also generated pressure for the development of more effective and appropriate forms of punishment (Clotfelter, 1977).

The organization of personal and social security is identified as one of the primary responsibilities of the State, and the encouragement of privatized alternatives is seen as both an indictment of State intervention and as a convenient way of shifting the burden away from the government and on to individual citizens or communities. It raises fundamental questions of legitimacy and authority and brings into question the essential nature and role of the State itself (Berki, 1986).

Victimization surveys indicate an exceedingly high level of insecurity among particular sections of the population. And it is often those who can least afford a private alternative to state provision who are most vulnerable (Jones et al., 1986). Thus the shift towards privatized forms of crime control could have profound effects upon the distribution of crime, in that it could result in the increased prevention of crime in some areas while changing the relative vulnerability of some sections of the population, leading to the increased incidence of multiple victimization. Moreover, there is a growing recognition of the relationship between the general social level of cohesion and public order in particular areas and its effects upon personal security. The signs of social neglect may signal that a particular area and its inhabitants are legitimate targets for predatory crime (Kelling, 1987).

The question of security therefore raises the problem of the relation between personal and social forms of provision as well as the relation between social deprivation and crime. It also raises questions about the nature and administration of justice. Like the organization of security, the administration of justice is widely seen as one of those functions where public administration is essential to its operation. In the administration of justice as well as the exercise of coercive power, the symbolic element is of paramount importance. Meting out justice is a communicative act with profound social consequences (Starr, 1987).

The pursuit of justice as a universalistic process has normally been thought to involve the state in compensating for the inequalities of the market and the differentials of power and resources. The realization of social and distributive justice is seen as dependent upon concerted state intervention while its administration is seen to require a body of loyal and incorruptible administrators to ensure equal treatment. But, as Stuart Henry has pointed out, there is a great deal of law and justice carried on outside the formal legal apparatus (Henry, 1983). Although there is a necessary interdependence between public and private realms, the private mechanisms display a significant degree of autonomy from the public apparatuses. The focus upon these developing forms of 'private' and 'informal' justice indicates the pluralistic nature of legal regulation, and the existence of various spheres of legality and quasi-legality through which conflicts, crimes and disputes are processed. These emerging forms of dispute resolution may well prove capable of dealing with cases that would normally fall outside the formal legal mechanisms. In this way they may offer an extension of justice rather than its dilution (Matthews, 1988b).

Thus there are a number of criteria of effectiveness which need to be considered in any thorough discussion of privatization. These may be in conflict or may reinforce each other. For example, the aim of maximizing accountability by extending forms of privatization may increase costs. On the other hand, increased accountability and flow of information through privatization may simultaneously improve the administration of justice (Pepinsky, 1987). Ultimately, it is therefore a question of prioritizing certain goals within the criminal justice system and then developing the most appropriate mode of provision and administration which will maximize the possibility of realizing those goals (Hann, 1985).

To date much of the debate has been preoccupied with the question of cost. It is, however, necessary to weigh costs against other criteria and thus to widen the basis of evaluation. But even in relation to cost the question has been narrowly conceived. The focus has been — particularly in Britain — on attempting to reduce state costs by encouraging private profit-making organizations to take over the functions. But little attention has been given to reducing the costs of law and order by shifting the focus of crime control to incorporate more lucrative forms of white-collar crime, or to finding ways to encourage private industry to bear a much larger percentage of the cost for maintaining 'law and order' programmes. Nor has much serious attention been paid to increasing the democratization of decision-making within the criminal justice system. Where privatization has been advocated, and even where citizens have been encouraged to take greater responsibility for crime control, it normally falls far short of effective participation in top-level decision-making within State institutions. An effective and comprehensive privatization programme in the field of criminal justice requires establishing the conditions for all people to freely act in the market and by implication requires forms of political participation which go beyond buying, selling and voting. Between the bureaucratic state and the atomized market there is a need to give voice to an 'objective' public interest, based upon open access to information, that can engage in meaningful decision-making processes.

In attempting to move beyond the public–private dichotomy there is an urgent need to develop a more pluralistic vision that can accommodate these new relations and possibilities, and simultaneously delineate a more effective and accountable system of decision-making. The strategic choices we make will be necessarily linked to political priorities and programmes, but in general our choices may have more to do with the style of the public–private relation and whether or not 'privatization' operates as an extension to, or runs parallel to, or alternatively replaces, State provision. As John Gandy expresses it, our choices may be between the 'extension ladder' model, the 'parallel bars' model and the 'public agent' model:

> The 'extension ladder' model is one in which private agencies provide services that are supplementary to those provided by government. Voluntary non-profit organisations have traditionally provided these services, particularly in community programmes designed to assist offenders in their reintegration into the community. In the 'parallel bars' model the private organisations provide programmes or services comparable to those provided by the government. However, the private organisation is expected to be an innovator, setter of standards, monitor and advocate. The use of voluntary non-profit organisations to provide pre-release counselling, operate half-way houses, and intensive community supervision are examples of the implementation of this model. The 'public agent' model involves channeling of public funds to the private sector through the purchase of services or grants for programmes and services such as probation, parole, health, and psychological services. In this model the government controls the private sector through regulation. (Gandy, 1985: xii)

Conclusion

There is an obvious danger when focusing upon the question of privatization of exaggerating its significance and overestimating its impact. But there can be no doubt that some of the changes which have occurred recently in relation to privatization are dramatic and wide-ranging. The movement appears to be gaining momentum and has injected a new dynamic into criminal justice concerns (Shackleton, 1986).

However, the response to these changes, particularly by the leading agencies involved, has been largely defensive or negative. The contradictory nature of this movement and the possibilities which it opens up have hardly been explored. Since the presentation of the privatization programme, particularly in relation to the area of criminal justice, has been fairly narrowly portrayed and often badly thought out, public debate has become unnecessarily restricted (Morgan and King, 1987). One of the major reasons for this is that the debate itself remains polarized within a State–market dichotomy. Also, many government initiatives to date appear unsystematic or unworkable, often directed by immediate narrow pragmatic concerns, myopic vision and personal interest.

There is no intrinsic reason why developing certain forms of privatization should not in the sphere of criminal justice — as elsewhere — lead to the improvement of services and even facilitate the creation of a more pluralistic and equal society. That much of the recent pressure towards privatization has led to inequalities is not an inevitable consequence of privatization itself. Rather it is the product of the political and social values that have recently intensified the pressures towards privatization (O'Higgins, 1987).

On the other hand, a great deal has been said about the liberalizing potential of privatization, although the experience across the board indicates that there is no necessary relation between increased privatization and liberalization. Where privatization becomes an end in itself, the possibilities of effecting greater liberalization within the State sector can be disregarded. As a consequence, the blind pursuit of privatization may further decrease the possibilities of making constructive interventions in the State sector, whose institutions and agencies are further devalued. In this way, privatization could considerably accelerate rather than remedy the problems associated with our decaying and debilitating institutions; privatization could become something of a distraction by providing further justification for not reforming and improving existing State agencies. For some, the basic message of privatization is that the failures and limitations of criminal justice agencies and institutions is not one of implementation or design, but signal a deeper series of flaws within the formation of the public enterprises themselves (Heald, 1985).

One positive outcome of the continuing preoccupation with cost-effectiveness has been the instigation of more systematic forms of auditing State agencies. This, in turn, has encouraged a more detailed consideration of how costs in the State sector might be reduced, management practices improved, and services extended. Further, the extent of the changes that have occurred under the banner of privatization over the past decade or so has clearly shown that rapid and radical change is possible within the criminal justice system and gives the lie to those forms of impossibilism which claim that significant change is not achievable and that all reforms are inconsequential.

At its most constructive, the privatization debate may encourage a re-evaluation of the operation of specific practices as well as inviting a critical re-examination of the relationship between the various agencies involved. This, in turn, could encourage new alignments and generate new practices that may possibly overcome the inertia that has characterized the criminal justice system for so long.

Finally, the enduring paradox of privatization is that its original political supporters conceived it as a form of depoliticization, and as a strategy for removing the encumbrances of democratic decision-making processes into the 'free' realm of the market. However, the focus upon privatization has served to sensitize many observers and practitioners to the range of market inequalities in different spheres and has led them to argue for extended and improved state control to compensate for these inequalities. By the same token, the debate around privatization invites us to rethink some of our basic assumptions about the provision, the administration and the effectiveness of the whole criminal justice enterprise.

References

Ascher, K. (1987) *The Politics of Privatisation*. Macmillan.

Berki, R. (1986) *Security and Society*. Dent.

Borna, S. (1986) 'Free Enterprise goes to Prison', *British Journal of Criminology*, 26 (4): 321–34.

Braithwaite, J. and Fisse, B. (1985) 'Varieties of Responsibility and Organised Crime', *Law and Policing*, 7 (3): 315–43.

Brenton, M. (1985) *The Voluntary Sector in British Social Services*. Longman.

Bureau of Justice (1987) *Justice Expenditure and Employment 1985*. NCL 104460. Washington DC: BJ.

Camp, C. and Camp, G. (1985) 'Correctional Privatisation in Perspective', *Prison Journal*, 62 (2): 14–31.

Clarke, M. (1987) 'Citizenship, Community and the Management of Crime', *British Journal of Criminology*, 27 (4): 384–400.

Clotfelter, C. (1977) 'Public Services, Private Substitutes and the Demand for Protection against Crime', *American Economic Review*, 67 (5): 867–77.

Cullen, F. (1986) 'The Privatisation of Treatment: Prison Reform in the 1980's', *Federal Probation*, 50: 8–16.

Cullen, F. and Gilbert, K. (1982) *Reaffirming Rehabilitation*. Anderson Publishing Co.

Ericson, R., McMahon, M. and Evans, D. (1987) 'Punishing for Profit: Reflection on the Revival of Privatisation in Corrections', *Canadian Journal of Criminology*, 29 (4): 355–87.

Fitzgerald, M. and Sim, J. (1979) *British Prisons*. Basil Blackwell.

Fitzpatrick, P. (1988) 'The Rise and Rise of Informalism', in R. Matthews (ed.), *Informal Justice?* Sage.

Gandy, J. (1985) *Privatization of Correctional Services for Adults*. Report to Ministry of Solicitor General of Canada.

Gandy, J. and Hurl, L. (1987) 'Private Sector Involvement in Prison Industries; Options and Issues', *Canadian Journal of Criminology*, 29 (2): 185–204.

Gentry, J. (1986) 'The Panopticon Revisited: The Problem Monitoring Private Prisons', *Yale Law Journal*, 96 (2): 353–75.

Hall, R. (1986) 'Privatising Prisons', *Public Policy and Administration*, 1 (1): 50–60.

Hall, S. et al. (1978) *Policing the Crisis*. Macmillan.

Heald, D. (1985) 'Will the Privatisation of Public Enterprises Solve the Problem of Control?' *Public Administration*, 63: 7–22.

Heald, D. and Thomas, D. (1986) 'Privatisation as Theology', *Public Policy and Administration*, 1 (2): 49–66.

Henry, S. (1983) *Private Justice*. Routledge & Kegan Paul.

HMSO (1987) *Prison Statistics: England and Wales*. HMSO, London.

Hulsman, L. (1986) 'Critical Criminology and the Concept of Crime', in H. Bianchi and R. Van Swaaningen (eds), *Abolitionism: Towards a Non-Repressive Approach to Crime*. Free University Press.

Immarigeon, R. (1987) 'Privatising Adult Imprisonment in the U.S. A Bibliography', *Criminal Justice Abstracts*, 19 (1): 123–39.

Jones, T., Maclean, B. and Young, J. (1986) *The Islington Crime Survey*. Gower.

Kay, J. and Thompson, D. (1986) 'Privatisation: A Policy in Search of a Rationale', *Economic Journal*, 96: 18–32.

Kelling, G. (1987) 'Acquiring a Taste for Order: The Community and the Police', *Crime and Delinquency*, 23 (1): 90–103.

Kinsey, R., Lea, J. and Young, J. (1986) *Losing the Fight against Crime*. Basil Blackwell.

Klein, R. (1984) 'Privatisation and the Welfare State', *Lloyds Bank Review* (Jan.): 12–29.

Krisberg, B. et al. (1986) 'The Watershed of Juvenile Justice Reform', *Crime and Delinquency*, 32 (1): 5–39.

Kroll, N. (1984) 'Prisons for Profit', *The Progressive*, September: 18–22.

Lavrakas, P. (1985) 'Citizen Self-Help and Neighbourhood Crime Prevention Policy, in L. Curtis (ed.), *American Violence and Public Policy*. Yale Univ. Press.

Lawrence, R. (1983) 'Voluntary Action: A Stalking Horse for the Right?', *Critical Social Policy*, 2 (3): 14–31.

LeGrand, J. and Robinson, R. (1984) *Privatisation and the Welfare State*. George Allen & Unwin.

Lea, J. (1987) 'Left Realism: A Defense', *Contemporary Crisis*, 11: 280–371.

Lerman, P. (1982) *Deinstitutionalisation and the Welfare State*. Rutgers Univ. Press.

Lerman, P. (1984) 'Child Welfare, the Private Sector and Community-Based Corrections', *Crime and Delinquency*, 30 (1): 5–38.

Lindquist, C. (1980) 'The Private Sector in Corrections: Contracting Probation Services From Community Organisations', *Federal Probation*, 44: 58–64.

McConville, S. (1987) 'Aid From Industry? Private Corrections and Prison Crowding', in S. Gottfredson and S. McConville (eds), *America's Correctional Crisis*. Greenwood Press.

McSparron, J. (1980) 'Community Corrections and Diversion', *Crime and Delinquency*, 26 (2): 226–47.

Mann, F. (1985) 'Private Arbitration and Public Polity', *Civil Justice Quarterly*, 4: 257–67.

Marx, G. (1987) 'The Interviewing of Public and Private Police in Undercover Work', in C. Shearing and P. Stenning (eds), *Private Policing*. Sage.

Matthews, R. (1988a) 'Making Crime Pay', *New Society*, 12th Feb.: 11–12.

Matthews, R. (ed.) (1988b) *Informal Justice?* Sage.

Miller, J. (1973) *Closing Correctional Institutions* (ed. Y. Bakal). Lexington, Mass.

Morgan, R. and King, R. (1987) 'Profiting from Prison', *New Society*, 23 Oct.: 21–3.

Mullen, J. (1985) 'Corrections and the Private Sector', *Prison Journal*, 62, (2): 31–73.

National Audit Office (1985) *Programme for the Provision of Prison Places*. HMSO, London.

O'Higgins, M. (1987) 'Privatisation and Social Welfare: Concepts, Analysis and The British Experience', in S,. Kamerman and A. Kahn (eds), *Privatization and Social Welfare*. Princeton University Press.

Pepinsky, H. (1987) 'Justice as Information Sharing', in J. Lowman et al. (eds), *Transcarceration: Essays in the Sociology of Social Control*. Gower.

Quinney, R. (1977) *Class State and Crime*. Longman.

Rosenbaum, D. (1987) 'The Theory behind Neighbourhood Watch: Is it a Sound Fear and Crime Reduction Strategy?' *Crime and Delinquency*, 33 (1): 103–35.

Rutherford, A. (1984) *Prisons and the Process of Justice*. Heinemann.

Santos, B. (1980) Law and Community: The Changing Nature of State Power in Late Capitalism', *International Journal of the Sociology of Law*, 8: 379–97.

Savas, E. (1982) *Privatisation and the Public Sector*. New Jersey.

Schwartz, I. et al. (1986) 'The "Hidden" System of Juvenile Control', *Crime and Delinquency*, 30 (3): 371–86.

Scott, T. and McPherson, M. (1971) 'The Development of the Private Sector of the Criminal Justice System', *Law and Society Review*, 6 (2): 267–88.

Scull, A. (1977) *Decarceration: Community Treatment and the Deviant*. Prentice-Hall.

Serrill, M. (1975) 'Juvenile Corrections in Massachusetts', *Corrections Magazine*, 2: 3–40.

Shackleton, J. (1986) 'Back to the Market', *Public Policy and Administration*, 1 (3): 20–39.

Shaw, S. (1987) 'Privatisation and Penal Reform', in *Prison Report*. Prison Reform Trust, London.

Shearing, C. and Stenning, P. (1981) 'Modern Private Security: Its growth and implications', in M. Tonry and N. Morris (eds), *Crime and Justice*, vol. 3. Chicago Univ. Press.

Shearing, C. and Stenning, P. (eds) (1987) *Private Policing*. Sage.

Skogan, W. (1987) 'The Impact of Victimisation on Fear', *Crime and Delinquency*, 33 (1): 135–55.

Smith, D. and Uchida, C. (1988). 'The Social Organization of Self-help: A Study of Defensive Weapon Ownership', *American Sociological Review*, 53: 94–102.

South, N. (1984) 'Private Security, The Division of Policing Labour and the Commercial Compromise of the State', in S. Spitzer and A. Scull (eds), *Research in Law, Deviance and Social Control*, vol,. 6. JAI Press.

South, N. (1988) *Policing for Profit: The Private Security Sector*. Sage.

Starr, P. (1987) 'The Limits of Privatisation', *Academy of Political Sciences*, 36 (3): 190–221.

Stern, V. (1987) *Bricks of Shame*. Penguin.

Sugden, R. (1984) 'Voluntary Organisations and the Welfare State', in J. Le Grand and R. Robinson (eds), *Privatisation and the Welfare State*. George Allen & Unwin.

Weiss, R. (1987) 'The Reappearance of the Ideal Factory: The Entrepreneur and Social Control in the Contemporary Prison', in J. Lowman et al. (eds), *Transcarceration*. Gower.

Wilson, J. (ed.) (1980) *The Politics of Regulation*. Basic Books.

Young, P. (1987) *The Prison Cell*. Adam Smith Institute. London.

2 PRIVATE PRISONS AND THE STATE

The continuing growth of prison populations in the post-war period and the mounting costs of incarceration have prompted governments to look increasingly towards private enterprise for solutions. Particularly in countries where governments are already committed to a broad privatization programme the idea of privatizing prisons, in various ways, has become an increasingly acceptable proposition.

The privatization of prisons can take a number of forms ranging from the building and running of penal facilities, to the contracting-out of penal services and the employment of penal labour in profit-making enterprises. The notion of fulfilling any or all of these functions through profit-making organizations appears to many contemporary observers unnatural. But as Robert Weiss points out, the organization of prisons as profit-making institutions was the norm until the middle of the nineteenth century in industrialized countries. Partly as a result of the restrictions placed upon the activities of prison labour, and partly because of the scandals and abuses which became associated with private prisons, the State took over the provisions of penal services.

The recent drive towards the (re-)privatization of prisons is, however, not simply a reversion to these nineteenth-century conditions. Rather, it is occurring within a distinctly different context. Even so, the re-emergence of private prisons does raise the question of whether prisons can be made more cost-effective and whether it is possible to develop a better division of labour between private and public agencies in the penal sphere. There are also critical issues concerning accountability, responsibility and legality which the contemporary movement towards the privatization of prisons raises.

In Britain many of these issues have been referred to in relation to the recent proposal to privatize remand prisons; these particular institutions have been identified as being the most appropriate for privatization. Privatizing remand prisons is seen to have the advantage of reducing pressure on the prison system (since they constitute one of the most densely populated sectors), and is also held to 'raise fewer difficult operational questions or issues of principle' (HMSO, 1988: 5).

But the experience of privatization in the penal sphere in the USA, as Robert Weiss points out, suggests that privatization of the kind currently envisaged in Britain is fraught with difficulties. Although there is some evidence that private firms may be able to speed up the process of prison building and may make certain savings, there are serious potential problems involved in delegating the provision or administration of prisons to private agencies. Initially, there are problems of accountability and the development of effective monitoring systems, as well as a range of legal issues. The American experience suggests that if privatization is to be pursued as a policy in the penal sphere a number of complex issues need to be thought through carefully.

Private Prisons and the State

Robert P. Weiss

The number of persons confined in US state and Federal prisons has doubled during the last decade, bringing the total at the end of 1988 to 627 402 convicts (*New York Times*, 24 April 1989). In the period 1980 to 1984 alone, the state prison population grew by more than 134 000 inmates, a 40 per cent increase (Bureau of Justice Statistics (BJS), 1985: 1). By 1985 the USA had the highest incarceration rate ever recorded: 201 per 100 000 (BJS, 1986). This Great Confinement has occurred whilst the rate of major crimes has levelled off or decreased; yet, penal commitments show no sign of abating. And, whilst a 'get tough' approach to criminal sentencing has been widely applauded, taxpayers have been less enthusiastic about funding new prison space; concurrent with increasing incarceration is a strong trend to restrict the size, scope and cost of government. Instead of keeping pace, fiscally conservative social policies have left the nations's prison and gaol systems dangerously overcrowded, anti-quated and understaffed. State prisons are operating at between 107 and 124 per cent of their capacity (BJS, 1989: 61), and, just to keep up with new admissions 1000 additional beds are required each week. As a result, prisons in two-thirds of the nations' states are under court order to correct conditions which violate the United States Constitu-tions's prohibition against cruel and unusual punishment (BJS, 1985). Corrections officials who fail to comply with court-established deadlines are threatened with contempt.[1] Several state corrections systems have been ordered to stop new admissions, under penalty of heavy fines, until they fall below their rated capacities.[2]

Federal court pressure on state departments of correction has caused a displacement of crowding from state to local lock-ups, with over 12 000 serious offenders lodged in local gaols at the end of 1988 (BJS, 1989: 61). The back-up of convicts scheduled to be transferred from local gaols to state prisons has precipitated some highly emotional confrontations between sheriffs and state authorities. In Texas, whose prison system has been ordered closed to new admis-sions nineteen times in the first eight months of 1987 (Applebome, 1987a: 11; *New York Times*, 17 August 1987), one county sheriff threatened to deliver new convicts anyway, and chain them to the state prison fence if necessary. In Dallas, Texas, scores of county prisoners have been found sleeping on gaol floors. County officials nationwide are frustrated because they have had to deal with a 41 per cent increase in prisoners from 1979 to 1984, a period when revenues shrank and living space per inmate declined 11 per cent. A record 297 092 persons were held in local gaols at the end of 1987. Not surprisingly, in 1986, 23 per cent (134) of the gaols in jurisdictions with large gaol populations were also under court order to improve conditions (BJS, 1989: 62).

State legislatures have begun to respond to the penal crisis by adding over 77 000 beds in the last five years. And officials expect to spend another US$5 billion over the next decade to increase their prison capacities by another 104 688 beds (Becker and Stanley, 1985: 729). Most observers agree, however, that this expansion will probably be insufficient, especially if the bottleneck at the criminal courts level is relieved somewhat by the hiring of more judges. The Census Bureau projects the national incarceration rate at 227 per 100 000 by 1990 (Applebome, 1987b). Prison funding will probably remain inadequate because new prison construction ordinarily is financed through the sale of tax-exempt general-obligation bonds, which require tax increases to make bondholder interest payments — something that voters have been increasingly reluctant to approve. Voter austerity has forced enterprising state officials to turn to unconventional or 'creative' financing schemes which bypass referendums. The State of Ohio, for instance, established a 'building authority', or paper agency, which raises revenues through the bond market and then leases penal facilities to other state governmental agencies (DeWitt, 1986). Similarly, New York State turned to its Building Authority for prison construction funding after voters rejected a $500 million bond issue. Officials in some states, however, are turning to an even more controversial alternative — the private sector.

Private companies have for many years made profits from the provision of auxiliary services that gaols and prisons have been unable to provide on a cost-efficient basis. Municipal and county gaols are typically poorly administered institutions, and few gaolers possess the specialized knowledge in nutrition, health care, and mental health and other areas of human welfare for which the courts are increasingly holding them accountable. Private services include food preparation, physical plant maintenance, social services, medical care and data processing. Currently, the most egregious defect is overcrowding, and private firms now advertise services that promise to help get public officials off the hook on that issue. The crime-control/fiscal-crisis contradiction is fertile ground for entrepreneurs seeking new marketing opportunities to relieve the plight of beleaguered government officials, and they are promoting a panoply of ventures that include: (1) private financing for prison construction; (2) the private operation of penal industries; (3) correctional facility management, and (4) the combined financing, design, construction and operation of entire correctional facilities. Private financing of gaols and prisons is the most popular form of privatization. Through 'lease-purchase' agreements, correctional agencies become tenants of facilities that are owned by private firms, to whom the government makes instalment payments. This allows the cost to come out of government's regular appropriation, avoiding the politically difficult step of raising debt ceilings. E. F. Hutton and Lehman Brothers Kuhn Loeb are among the respected Wall Street firms arranging financial deals.[3] Shearson Lehman/American Express, one of the more aggressive financial institutions in the business, reportedly arranged over $500 million in prison financing in just the two years 1983 to 1985 (Becker and Stanley, 1985: 727). Much of this financing went to fiscally strapped local governments.

Private industrial operations within state prisons is a second new (or, more accurately, renewed) area of profit-seeking. Since World War II, prison industries have been in decline and today America's prisons are little more than enormous warehouses on the edge of riot. Prisoner idleness is particularly troublesome in overcrowded conditions, and the reintroduction of penal industry could help discourage violence. In the fondest hopes of private industry advocates, moreover, deductions from prisoner wages could help defray room and board expenses whilst providing occupational training (also old ideas). A prominent spokesperson for the idea of turning a profit on penal labour is the former Chief Justice of the US Supreme Court, Warren Burger. In numerous speeches, he has called for the conversion of prisons into 'factories with fences'. The Federal government moved in December 1979 to facilitate the reindustrialization of prisons with legislation exempting seven 'pilot' states from laws, in effect since the Great Depression, prohibiting interstate commerce in prison-made goods. According to the original version of this programme, prisoner-workers were to be paid competitive wages from which rent and taxes could be deducted. A half-dozen private companies, from computer manufacturers to hotel chains, joined the so-called Free Venture Industries Program, and began operating branch facilities behind prison walls. Although companies are supposed to pay wages that match the 'prevailing wage' of the community in which the prison is located, in practice few prisoners earn wages comparable to their free-world counterparts (Gargan, 1983). Moreover, prisoner-workers typically labour under far more stringent shop-floor regulation (Weiss, 1987b). Their pay, nevertheless, has greatly exceeded the typical state prison industry standard, and for this reason private sector jobs are in great demand by prisoners, even though many complain of exploitation.

Private prison initiatives

> Merging the highest standards of corrections with the proven principles of free enterprise.
>
> Corrections Corporation of America Promotional Brochure

The most controversial area of privatization involves the ownership and management of prisons, the focus of this chapter. Whilst there are many descriptive articles in popular magazines and professional association and business journals, there are few scholarly treatments of the topic.[4] After a historical overview of private prisons in the USA, I will examine the supposed administrative superiority of privately operated prisons. I will then focus on a critical discussion of the legal, symbolic, political and ideological issues of delegating State power to entrepreneurs. The chapter concludes with a consideration of the implications for prisoners, guards and free-world workers of a conjunction of private penal industry and private prison administration.

The private operation of penal institutions is an old business reappearing: in eighteenth-century England about half of the gaols were privately owned. Members of the royalty and clergymen sublet their penal establishments to full-time keepers. These gaolers were not State employees but small businessmen who made their profit from inmate extortion. For example, Newgate prison had an 'entrance fee' and weekly 'rent'. Food, water, bedding, 'easement of irons', even gin — every concession had its price (Howard, 1777: 12). England's 'trade in chains' lasted until the 1790s, when transportation to Australia began. The penal entrepreneur in the USA had a better angle on profits: he exploited the convicts' labour. Largely because of black recalcitrance, Southern states after the Civil War suffered a severe labour shortage (Adamson, 1983). The 'convict-lease' and the 'contract' system of penal exploitation were created in large measure to help fill gaps in the labour market (Hindus, 1980; Adamson, 1983; Weiss, 1987a). In the former system of forced convict labour, entrepreneurs bid in a competitive market for the charge of entire county or state penal systems. Typically, convicts were removed from state property in rolling cages to work as penal slaves on railroad construction, mining, cotton plantation farming, lumbering, and other areas of production where free-labour was scarce (Barnes, 1972; Adamson, 1983). In the second form of penal slavery, the 'contract' system, companies paid the state for the labour power of the convicts, but left their maintenance and discipline to state officials. Both forms of penal labour attracted a new breed of fast-profit capitalists, 'buccaneers', who wrung handsome profits from the misery of their hapless charges.

Today's private operators appear to be more sophisticated than their predecessors. For instance, Control Data Corporation, a multi-national computer manufacturer with a reputation for liberal-minded management, is one of the leading private prison aspirants. The company is widely known for its attempt to wed profit-making with 'socially useful' projects, such as vocational training programmes for prisoners, and the popular PLATO computer educational programme, which serves the 'homebound' market. For nearly ten years, the giant manufacturer operated a successful computer disc-drive assembly production facility at the maximum-security Minnesota Correctional Facility at Stillwater (Gargan, 1983), establishing a model for other private initiatives within prisons (Benidt, 1985). RCA, another industrial giant, has been under contract with the State of Pennsylvania for educational programmes for delinquents. Its Service Corporate division operates the Weaversville Intensive Treatment Unit in Pennsylvania, a high-security facility for juveniles. Eckerd Drugstore chain operates the Okeechobee School for Boys in Florida on a non-profit basis. Below these companies lies a tier of smaller, unabashedly profit hungry, firms devoted exclusively to correctional facility management. Most aspire to both ownership and management. These companies typically are organized by former correctional administrators from the public sector, but receive financing from 'venture capitalists', many of whom have investments in other areas of public service as well.

Corrections Corporation of America (CCA) of Nashville, Tennessee, is the prototype for many independent prison-for-profit firms. CCA was established in 1983 by Tennessee real estate and insurance investor Thomas Beasley, who said he got the idea for the company during a cocktail party conversation with an executive of the Magic Chef stove company. 'He said he thought it would be a heck of a venture for a young man: To solve the prison problem and make a lot of money at the same time', Beasley recalled (Hurst, 1983). As former Chairman of the Tennessee Republican Party, Beasley sees to it that his company's interests are well known to the State's political and business figures. Beasley's venture was launched with the encouragement of Republican Governor Lamar Alexander, a close friend, and $35 million in venture capital from Nashville's Jack Massey (Hurst, 1983). The Massey Birch investment group of Nashville also owns Kentucky Fried Chicken and the Hospital Corporation of America, both successful national chain businesses (Tolchin, 1985c). Two former Tennessee State corrections officials act as chief executives at CCA, but rank-and-file security personnel are recruited mostly from the private sector.

CCA operates two detention facilities for the Immigration and Naturalization Service (INS); a treatment centre for the Federal Bureau of Prisons; a 500-bed county workhouse in Hamilton County, Tennessee; a juvenile facility in Memphis; and a 200-bed county gaol in Bay County, Florida; and a 500-bed minimum security prison in Cleveland, Texas (Belkin, 1989). CCA's most ambitious bid is its current offer to pay the State of Tennessee $250 million for a 99-year lease of the State's entire prison population (Tolchin, 1985f). This proposal has evoked a mixed response in the state capitol, however. There is considerable opposition nationwide to privatization of adult mainstream populations and, with the exception of Florida, Texas, New Mexico and Kentucky, private firms have not been successful in receiving operating contracts for state prisons.

Administrative issues
According to Logan and Rausch (1985: 312), 'profit-and-loss' incentives are superior to bureaucratic, or 'budget-based', incentives in the delivery of public services; the quest for profit makes private operators efficient. Moreover, privatization enthusiasts point out, company officials are not 'manacled' by the bureaucratic red tape that encumbers government officials. Private operators have been able to reduce labour costs and shorten programme implementation time by avoiding numerous bureaucratic regulations and procedures, including competitive bidding. Speed in facility design and construction reduces costs during inflationary periods, and helps to meet court-imposed deadlines for prison improvements. 'While local governments can often take three or four years to build a new correction center because of bureaucratic constraints, private groups have built such facilities within six months' (Tolchin, 1985c: 14), the length of time it took CCA to build a Houston detention centre for illegal aliens. RCA set up its Weaversville Unit in just ten days, after the Pennsylvania Attorney General ruled that juveniles could not be incarcerated with adult offenders. Finally, private companies are more flexible in construction and programme development than is government. Entrepreneurs have been free to convert old hospitals, apartment buildings, and even motels into penal facilities (Krajick, 1984), and can create or abandon programmes and facilities with a freedom unheard of in the public sector. CCA's Vice President for Marketing, without a hint of irony, told an audience at a recent symposium on private prisons that his company built its first prison in the design of a warehouse so that, in the event of bankruptcy, it could be easily converted to other purposes.

Private companies can point to some remarkable successes in prison management. In October 1985, when the Bay County, Florida, gaol was faced with two lawsuits charging overcrowding, fire safety violations and inadequate medical care and staffing, county commissioners decided to take control of the gaol away from the sheriff. They turned its operation over to the CCA, and it became the first large maximum-security gaol to be given to a private company. Within eight months of assuming operation of the gaol, the state dropped its lawsuit (Bean, 1986); overcrowding was reduced, major building renovations conducted, extra staff was added, inmates were provided with numerous amenities, and CCA saved the county an estimated $700 000. And all this was accomplished using most of the sheriff's original gaol staff, who received pay rises.

In an overall assessment of corporate efficiency, however, one must consider failures elsewhere which offset the Bay County accomplishment. At the Silverdale Detention centre, a workhouse for 300 men and women in Hamilton County, Tennessee, state officials reported a $200 000 cost overrun in CCA's contract during the first seven months of its operation (Tolchin, 1985e). Privatization critic Mark A. Cunniff, the executive director of the National Association of Criminal Justice Planners, attributes the overrun to a lack of experience in contracting out this kind of service. Silverdale went through three wardens in seven months (Tolchin, 1985e), for instance. Special administrative, especially legal, accounting mechanisms will be necessary. As Governor James J. Blanchard of Michigan told a 1985 National Governors Association Conference: 'The history of contracting out is that these firms get such specific contracts, they can squirm out of anything' (Tolchin, 1985f). And there are other reasons to suspect that private industry would not always be the most cost-efficient alternative. A 1985 General Accounting Office study revealed that Federal employee pay and benefits were 15 per cent lower than those of comparable private employees (Tolchin, 1986), contrary to the popular assertion that government workers are underproductive and overcompensated in comparison with industry (*New York Times*, 30 August 1987).

Logan and Rausch cast their argument for the superiority of 'private enterprise prisons' in the theoretical categories of classical liberalism, speaking of 'laws of supply and demand', 'government monopoly' and 'free market in corrections', as if competitive capitalism and laissez-faire governmental policy actually characterized contemporary reality. The authors depict a corporate dream world where 'market and economic incentives' replace government regulation. One has only to look at the US defence industry — including its documented history of payroll padding, price-fixing, bribery, inflated costs, shoddy construction, and cost overruns — to be disabused of the notion that, invariably, 'providing services under competitive free-market conditions . . . will be an improvement' over 'government monopoly', as Logan and Rausch (1985: 317) allege.

Those who argue that privately operated prisons would be administratively more efficient typically neglect to discuss the effects that adoption of the capitalist model may have on employee relations. Conspicuously absent from Logan and Rausch's classical liberal translation of penal enterprise is the adversarial language of industrial relations. In the world of commodities, where convicts become the 'products' of the 'criminal justice market', and wardens become 'executives', guards become 'workers'. This conversion, then, is not simply a change in terminology; privatization represents a fundamental change in social relations, and involves a shift in power among the structural interests of corrections. The typical 'corporate warden' is a well-paid pensioned state or Federal service retiree, recruited from the public sector by the prospect of a high-salaried second career (Krajick, 1984).[5] The occupational prospects for those lower on the professional ladder are not so bright, however. Whilst penal facility administrators and departmental bureaucrats from the public sector have an opportunity to enter the managerial ranks of private prison corporations, rank-and-file security personnel become 'proletarianized'.

In state service, conflict with management over the satisfaction of working grievances are to a large extent displaced into the political sphere, where lobbying and even picketing of state capitols by correctional worker organizations are not uncommon.[6] In the private sphere, negotiation between buyer and seller over the intensity and conditions of work raise additional points of conflict, and one can expect that correctional workers will direct their hostility toward company managers instead of the state. Robert Kuttner (1986) argues: 'Beyond a certain point, government-by-contract couples the inefficiencies of the public sector with the less savory aspects of the private sector', and these distasteful features will probably include the panoply of union-busting measures characteristic of many other service industries. And unless 'state employee' is redefined, guards for private companies — unlike state workers — will be able to strike, a possibility that many critics find troubling.

The delegation of State power

Even assuming that private contracting were cheaper, sceptics of private prisons argue that efficiency should not be the sole concern of corrections. Preoccupation with efficiency diverts attention from the more important questions concerning the legality and propriety of privatizing an activity that would seem to be a core function, indeed the *raison d'être*, of government — the administration of justice. Here, critics raise what they regard as a most important issue — the special accountability required of those responsible for imprisonment.[7] As Kuttner argues:

> In theory, contracting-out government services brings to the public realm all the virtues of the private market — flexibility, innovation, and competition. In practice, however, contracting out government begs the ancient political question: Who will watch the watchers? (Kuttner, 1986)

Will the operation of prisons become more removed from constitutional and democratic controls as a result of contracting?

Legal issues
At a recent governor's conference on the topic of privatization, New York Governor Mario Cuomo (Tolchin, 1985d) expressed a notion popular with many of those in attendance: 'It is not government's obligation to provide services, but to see that they are provided'. T. Don Hutto (Mullen, 1985: 7), vice-president of CCA, concurs: 'the administration of justice is the exclusive prerogative of government but not of government employees'. But, one could argue, a fundamental distinction needs to be made between, on the one hand, privatization that replaces public sector *means* with respect to a public function, and, on the other, privatization of the *authority* that exercises that function.[8] This is what distinguishes some mundane contractual service like solid waste collection, and even community-based corrections (whose charges are there voluntarily), from policing or imprisonment — society's penultimate sanction. Legally, only the state has the authority to derive people of liberty and to exercise force which accompanies that authority. Proponents of the private prison business argue that their work does not involve special powers. Logan and Rausch, for instance, assume a reductionist view of incarceration:

> If a prison system is broken down into its various separate activities, there are only a few aspects that do not have counterparts in the private sector. (Logan and Rausch, 1985: 311)

But critics reply that operating a total institution is more than the mere sum of its various particular activities (Wecht, 1987: 821). In its totality, imprisonment is coercion, and for this reason the actions of prison officials should require special accountability. Mike Maguire et al., in their book *Accountability and Prisons*, are worth quoting at length on this point:

> Prisons are closed and total institutions. Their populations do not consti-

tute a credible interest group; they are not consulted by or represented within management; in the last analysis, the control exercised over them is bluntly coercive; and considerations of control and security ... dictate a great degree of secrecy in their operation. Mundane aspects of their life, such as access to lawyers or relatives, communication in general, and a whole range of issues from sanitation to sexual activity, are subject to detailed regulation by prison staff. In addition to, and sometimes instead of, the criminal law, prisoners are subject to institutional disciplinary codes. Punishments such as loss of remission time ... , cellular confinement, fines or loss of privileges may be imposed by prison governors or quasi-judicial bodies. ... All these features of prison life indicate that extensive discretion is exercised over every aspect of inmates' existence. (Maguire et al., 1985: 5)

Mr Hutto, a recent president of the American Correctional Association, and former commissioner of corrections in Arkansas and Virginia, claims that CCA employees are strictly regulated in their performance of state functions: 'as representatives of government, [they] are directed and controlled by policy and personnel regulations and practice. Private management firms are controlled by law and written contract, but the government retains ultimate authority — and should do so', he continued. Yet, in practice, those who administer private detention facilities — although not state officials — exercise a great deal of discretionary authority. This was poignantly revealed in a newspaper article on private gaols, in which John S. Robinson, a CCA employee who administers a Houston detention facility for illegal aliens, was interviewed.

Mr. Robinson's job includes overseeing disciplinary cases that arise from fighting or other infractions at the Houston facility. The cases are heard by company employees. Penalties range from restriction to a dormitory to 72 hours in isolation. 'I review every disciplinary action,' Mr. Robinson said. 'I'm the Supreme Court.' (Tolchin, 1985c)

In addition to judging infractions and imposing penalties, officers of private prisons will advise parole boards on whether prisoners should be released. If they could not do so, they would lose an important source of control. Perhaps the most controversial activity, however, concerns the authority to use deadly force. On this issue, James K. Stewart, director of the National Institute of Justice and a supporter of profit-making prisons, says:

The use of force is something that bothers me, but in fact in our society we delegate it regularly to non-governmental entities — in the private security area, in stores and banks, in hospitals and psychiatric wards. (Stewart, 1985)

But the difference between a convict in the state penitentiary and a shopper at the local mall is that the latter person voluntarily enters the premises. Private security personnel, unless specially deputized, derive their police authority from the employers' right to protect private property, and they are permitted to use deadly force (or threaten to do so) only on private property.

The question of whether or not a private company is involved in 'state action' is important, according to constitutional scholar Ira P. Robbins (1985: 10), because 'the Fifth and Fourteenth Amendments to the US Constitution, which prohibit the federal government from denying federal constitutional rights and which guarantee due process of law, apply only to acts of the state and federal governments, and not to the acts of private parties or entities'. According to Robbins (1985: 10), there are two fundamental constitutional questions concerning prison privatization: '(1) whether the acts of a private entity operating a correctional institution constitute "state action", thus allowing for liability . . . and (2) whether, in any event, delegation of the corrections function to a private industry is itself constitutional'.

These questions were raised in a 1984 Federal District Court case involving another privately operated Houston detention centre for aliens. In *Medina* v. *O'Neill*, a civil rights suit was brought on behalf of sixteen alien stowaways who were incarcerated in a 12'×20' cell by a private security company, which was under contract to a shipping company but under an INS directive. Another issue involved the killing of one inmate and the serious wounding of another by a shotgun-wielding guard after an escape attempt. The INS tried to avoid liability by claiming that they delegated authority to a private authority.

> The plaintiffs claimed that they had been unconstitutionally deprived of life and liberty, arguing *inter alia,* that the INS had a duty to oversee their detention and that the defendants' failure to do so constituted state action. In opposition, the federal defendants contended that at all times the plaintiffs were in the custody of the private company, and, therefore, that the problems stemming from the plaintiffs' detention arose from purely private acts. Thus, the defendants averred that there was not state action. (Robbins, 1985: 11)

The Federal District Court ruled that there was 'obvious state action' on the part of both the private detention company and the INS. 'State action' exists, the court observed, when the state delegates to private parties a power 'traditionally exclusively reserved to the State'. Citing the 1982 Supreme Court decision in *Rendell-Baker* v. *Kohn*, the court observed that 'the relevant question is not simply whether a private group is serving a "public function" . . . the question is whether the function performed has traditionally been the exclusive prerogative of the state'. Judge John V. Singleton found that the

Medina case satisfied this 'public function' test: 'Detention is a power reserved to the government and is an exclusive prerogative of the state' (Stancill, 1984). Judge Singleton did not, however, rule in favour of the plaintiff's argument that the INS did not have the constitutional right to contract with private groups for detention. The delegation of state power is legal but the state is not relieved of liability by doing so.

The private corrections area is so new that it is still a vast legal *terra incognita*. But as Glen Richard Jeffes, Pennsylvania Commissioner of Corrections, observed: 'Any state that moves in this direction is going to have to double its legal staff, to handle all the lawsuits' (Tolchin, 1985h). What the Federal District court decided is that both the state and private prison companies are liable on the matter of deadly force. Although private employees in the role of correctional officers may legally carry weapons, provided that they meet the same standards that regulate public correctional officers, companies have several strategies with which they try to diminish their liability for the use of deadly force. According to Amanda W. Cannon,

> One method that is planned by CCA in its operation of Bay County Jail is the licensing of its operations as a private security agency. This arrangement allows for private correctional officers to receive less than 50 hours of training compared to the 320 hour curriculum currently mandated. (Cannon, 1986: 11)

And there is now at least one private policing organization entering the prison business: the Wackenhut Corporation, the nation's largest independent private security company. According to an editorial in the *Wall Street Journal* by Philip E. Fixler, Jr (1984), director of the Reason Foundation's Local Government Center, 'Wackenhut has submitted two proposals for the construction and operation of INS facilities. It is also working with several states on the possible operation of adult medium-security facilities — with Wackenhut to finance, design, construct and operate them'. More recently, Wackenhut and CCA have each contracted to build two new $12 million private prisons in Texas (Belkin, 1989).

Another method of diminishing a private vendor's liability is through deputization. Officials have been reluctant to delegate special police powers, however, and the National Sheriff's Association has officially announced its opposition to private gaol and prison management. A third, more likely, proposal for limiting liability is to intermingle private employees with public correctional officers (for instance, having the state retain perimeter security), a practice that has implications for employee relations and inmate discipline. Aside from the question of determining the relative danger of various security assignments, would two-tier pay structure develop? In other words, would differential pay for armed and unarmed security result in a segmentation of the labour market in corrections? Would lines of conflict develop around authority to oversee internal disciplinary proceedings and other issues of authority? And would state officials try to 'second guess' company employees? Manipulative prisoners, ever vigilant for opportunities to divide staff members, can be expected to work at driving a wedge between the two grades of staff.

Symbolic issues: point of contradiction?
In order to indirectly diminish the chances for lawsuit, private prison operators attempt to reduce confrontational situations in a number of ways. Most companies structure operations so as to minimize physical proximity of guards to prisoners. Promotion photos show companies which have invested heavily in high technology security devices. Guards do much of their supervision from behind bullet-proof glass observation booths, and video monitors for surveillance appear ubiquitous. But whilst the instruments of power in private prisons are unequivocally coercive, the source of their authority is left obscure.[9] Unlike private security firms, private prison companies do not have their employees assume the trappings of official governmental authority. Accordingly, they have dispensed with paramilitary uniforms and ranking; martial vocabulary and regimen, which have characterized the penal profession since the inception of the penitentiary, are no longer employed. Prison companies still want to create the illusion of legitimate authority, but a business-like image is projected instead of a pseudo-official one. At CCA-run facilities, for example, prisoners are not referred to as 'inmates' — instead, they are called 'residents', and guards are referred to as 'resident supervisors'. Dressed in camel-coloured sweaters that bear a discreet company insignia, private guards are represented as what one might call 'corporate security technicians'. It is almost as if the efficiency of means — safe, cost-effective security — is being presented to prisoners as *the basis* for company authority over them. Images of expertise should replace naked force. But the 'reference to power is rarely neutral; there are few words that produce such admiring or, in the frequent case, indignant response', according to Galbraith (1983: 11). Robbins comments on the 'hidden issue' of symbolism where private guards exercise state power:

> When it enters a judgment of conviction and imposes a sentence a court exercises its authority, both actually and symbolically. Does it weaken

that authority, however — as well as the integrity of a system of *justice* — when an inmate looks at his keeper's uniform and, instead of encountering an emblem that reads 'Federal Bureau of Prisons' or 'State Department of Corrections' he faces one that says 'Acme Corrections Company'? (Robbins, 1985: 21–2)

Private correctional businesses thus far have concentrated on the market for juveniles, undocumented aliens for short-term detention, minimum security misdemeanants, and parolees and the mentally ill in half-way houses — that is, those least able or likely to create disturbances. But, for a number of reasons, felons in long-term total institutions are more likely to bridle at private detention. Private prison companies cannot readily draw on the personal traits of their staff members — leadership, moral certainty, quality of mind — for their authority.[10] Although companies are, for the exercise of power, trying to create an alternative institutional basis to replace state organization, their guards may be forced (or may elect) instead to rely more on *personal* authority of the worst kind — threats of physical force. The private exercise of public authority will be made most problematic by the socio-economic background of those recruited by companies with a keen regard for the bottom line of profit maximization. In these cases, security personnel will probably be drawn from the same class stratum as the convicts themselves. Because labour costs account for such a high percentage of total expenditures in the prison business, when profits are squeezed, management will be tempted to economize on guard screening and training as well. Whilst private correctional managers encourage a professional demeanour in security staff, employee professionality can only exist at the level of appearances. Private prison guards are among the nations's unskilled service proletariat, more hired help, some of whom may be only part-time. Offering low pay and few fringe benefits, prison entrepreneurs will be able to recruit guards only from the margins of the labour market. Although civil service correctional workers could hardly be said to evoke the 'majesty of the law', private guards are likely to command even less respect in these circumstances. The example of private security companies hired to patrol New York City's homeless shelters suggests some of the problems of authority that are likely to appear in private gaols and prisons that hire on the cheap.

To patrol shelters, city officials hired security guards 'who are poorly educated, poorly trained, unstable or themselves homeless' (Nix, 1986). Arguments and fights between guards and clients are common, recently resulting in the arrest of two private security guards charged, in separate incidents, with stabbing two homeless men to death. Suzanne Trazoff, a spokesperson for the New York

City Human Resources Administration, observed: 'There isn't enough difference between guards and clients', and guards are desperate to prove their strength over prisoners. 'That's a classic institutional pathology, because they are typically indistinguishable by education, training, or temperament from most residents', observes Robert M. Hayes, counsel for the Coalition for the Homeless (Nix, 1986). Complicating shelter conditions are overcrowding, staff shortages, and overworked, ill-equipped security staff.[11] Guards are engaged in a daily physical and mental tug-of-war with clients 'who pit their remaining dignity against authority they consider condescending and, sometimes, abusive' (Iverem, 1987: 29). Poor screening by private security firms nationwide has sometimes resulted in the hiring of convicted criminals and those with serious alcohol and drug problems.[12]

In institutions with guards who are in an especially uncertain position of authority, as one might expect in private prisons, accountability can be enhanced with the presence of social welfare personnel — teachers, social workers, and psychologists — who could serve as informal monitors; yet these are costly items and not likely to be of high priority in profit-conscious organizations.[13] If accountability is to be maintained, special systems of monitoring contract compliance will be essential, and particular attention must be given to clearly defining contractor roles and responsibilities.[14] This has yet to be done. Tolchin (1985c) reports that at the CCA gaol facility in Tennessee, corrections officers acknowledge that 'government oversight is sometimes spotty. Only one county official serves as "liaison" at the Chattanooga gaol, and he was absent the day a visitor made a tour'. In a Criminal Justice Institute study of juvenile and adult corrections agencies run by the private sector (Camp and Camp, 1984), the two most common problems mentioned by respondents were monitoring the performance of providers, followed closely by poor quality of service. Much of the savings accrued from private contracting could be offset by the special costs of creating a regulatory bureaucracy (Wecht, 1987: 835). And one must ask questions about the probable effectiveness, whatever the cost, of penal oversight mechanisms in light of how much the conservative political agenda has already blurred the ideological and ecological boundaries separating the private from the public realms. Is it likely that prison monitoring bodies would be more effective than other government regulatory agencies, such as those that oversee the nuclear power industry, occupational safety conditions, or the airline industry? Would penal regulation be free from the conflict of interests, intense lobbying, and the bias of industry-trained agency personnel that characterize the State's regulation of other private industries?[15]

Political and ideological issues

Neoconservatives dismiss the notion that 'public services should be organized for service, not for profit' as merely a 'sentimental objection' (Poole, 1983: 117). Privatization advocates claim that by eliminating 'multiple interests' in order to focus exclusively on market forces, criminal justice is advanced. The 'new source of supply' thereby created, Logan and Rausch (1985: 303) argue, would open the bottleneck of prison sentencing. Capitalist suppliers would possess 'flexibility' to meet the changing demands of criminal justice market: 'At least at the margins, then, the prison system must be able to expand and contract as the shifting demands of justice require' (Logan and Rausch, 1985: 114). As it is, say critics, the tail is wagging the dog: 'prison flow should respond to crime rates, which are largely beyond state control' (Logan and Rausch, 1985: 114); this new flexibility would support the objectives of the 'just deserts' model of justice. But, Bowditch and Everett (1987: 9) point out, evidence suggests that just the opposite may be the case: 'prison populations have historically expanded to fill available space'; this is because political and economic factors influence arrest rates, decisions to prosecute, and sentencing severity. The development of private prisons adds new pressure: Private contractors 'can lobby in ways that a public agency cannot lobby', observes Mark Cunniff (Tolchin, 1985g); these include 'political action committees, honorariums, weekends in the country, dinners and other inducements to legislators' that are denied public servants.

In pointing to the purported superiority of profit-and-loss incentives over those that motivate 'budget-based organizations', Logan and Rausch (1985: 312) claim that the latter are defective because they 'depend for support on their ability to appeal to a broad constituency'. The authors continue their critique: 'They must be all things to all people and alienate no one. This compromises their effectiveness because they cannot make the hard, controversial choices necessary to concentrate efforts successfully'. For example, advocates of private corrections tout the entrepreneur's ability to circumvent such 'complicating factors' as voter approval on bond issues and regulations concerning public hearings and legislative policy review. This kind of arrogance was involved in the rationalization of the Iran–Contra operation. In a newspaper interview with Senator Daniel Patrick Moynihan of New York on the 'US "privatized" foreign policy of Iran', the Senator observed: 'They believe that since Government doesn't understand the dangers, it's necessary to circumvent the Government'.

The result, the critics say, was a 'parallel government' with its own treasury, air force, envoys, communications network and chain of command, accountable to neither State Department nor Congress. (Tolchin, 1987a: A10)

The ramifications of that operation are extensive, another Senator observed: the foreign policy mechanism was privatized much the same way as other programmes have been privatized by the Reagan Administration.[16] The privatization of corrections must be understood as part of a larger political agenda also, a development which includes 'deinstitutionalization' and 'deregulation'. Often associated with 'neoconservatives', whose objective is not a smaller, less intrusive state, but a 'reconstructed' state and civil society (Miliband and Panitch, 1987: 5), privatization is an effort to 'depoliticize' the economy and society (O'Connor, 1986: 234). Critics of private corrections argue that, quite apart from legal or administrative issues involved in privatization, the preoccupation with fiscal efficiency deflects attention from political issues and further removes corrections from democratic control.

Summary and conclusion

America's system of prisons and gaols is in a crisis of overpopulation, the result of a decade-long hard line in criminal sentencing and a recent flood of drug-related convictions. This combines with an unwillingness on the part of taxpayers to finance adequate new prison construction. Unless there is a major change in policy, the future looks even more grim; in New York City, for instance, police reports (Roberts, 1987) indicate an upsurge in crime: 'young men are committing crime longer than expected', and 'their young successors are committing more crimes, more serious ones and sooner'. The city's crack epidemic is largely responsible for the doubling since 1983 of New York State's prison population; 70 per cent of the 50 000 in state prisons have been sentenced for drug law violations. And at the Federal level, 13 000 convictions for drug law violations in 1986 represented a 134 per cent increase over the number of such convictions in 1980 (BJS, 1988: 1). These changes in crime trends are, unfortunately, concurrent with Federal and state sentencing reform, the efforts of which, most observers agree, will mean increased prison commitments and longer time served by individuals, and the recent Supreme Court ruling in favour of 'preventive detention', which promises to add thousands more. The private solution appeals to many politicians and correctional officials, especially in states like Texas (*Business Week*, 1987: 33) which are experiencing fiscal crises.

In the course of our chapter, we have seen that many of the administrative and legal issues involved in privatization raise serious questions as to whether going private really is cheaper; there are no reliable studies on comparative cost-effectiveness. But, whatever the savings, critics argue that there are more important questions of accountability involved in privatization. One thing seems certain: if only for reasons of legal liability, special mechanisms for governmental oversight will be necessary. But what are the prospects that these regulatory bodies will be impartial, especially in cases which might involve deliberate challenges to private 'authority'?

There is a potent symbolic issue in penal privatization: an action so daring as entrusting penal power to profit-makers says something about what the State thinks of prisoners politically. In his critique of the efficiency claim made by penal entrepreneurs, Michael E. Smith, executive director of the Vera Institute, observes: 'Justice is not a service, it's a condition, an idea. It's not like garbage collection. Inmates are not garbage' (Tolchin, 1985g). As long as prisoners are unorganized they can be handled like any ordinary service. John Mack, a writer who served in Sing Sing, comments:

Fewer than a handful of inmates have any radical political consciousness. There are few, if any, racial religious groups or right-wing racist cliques. The vast majority are what Saul Bellow refers to as the mindless 'super-fluous population', the 'doomed people' who have been 'written off'. And the administration seems to know how to handle them. (Mack, 1984: 224)

The kinds of controls private guards exercise, however, involve contradictions that could prompt prisoners to new thinking. And there is an entrepreneurial prospect on the horizon that could add class conflict to the other tensions: the introduction of private industrial contracting of convict labour power.

Putting convicts to work would hold a dual attraction to penal entrepreneurs: convict idleness would be reduced, thereby eliminating a major factor in prison violence and general disruption among long-term prisoners, and, secondly, a profitable industrial operation would give the company a direct competitive advantage. Under the guise of 'vocational training', prisoner labour power could be exploited as an additional source of profit. But what about charges of labour exploitation or unfair business competition? What would be the difference between private prisons today, and the convict lease system of the postbellum South? To avoid such parallels, profiting from some version of the Free Venture programme would seem prudent. Proponents of Free Venture industry argue that penal industry can be meaningful in a correctional sense only if it simulates as much as possible conditions on the outside. According to Schaller (1981), prison industry should reinforce work norms through 'realistic' jobs performed in a 'normalized' prison work environment, with a wage scale that is competitive with the free world (Auerbach et al., 1979; Hawkins, 1983; Funke, 1983).

The introduction to a penal setting of a 'satisfying' labour system, including 'fair' wages, with sick leave benefits and 'vacations' as proposed by Auerbach et al. (1979: 22–3) could be expected to meet considerable resistance by prison staffs, however. The assignment of 'guard-workers' to discipline a class of 'prisoner-employees' who are working under 'normalized' conditions would produce an unusually strained industrial relations situation because 'normalization' flies in the face of the 'less eligibility' principle, the chief advocates of whom are prison guards (Rutherford, 1984). The condition of prisoners, according to Jeremy Bentham (1843), 'ought not be made more eligible than that of the poorest class of citizens in a state of innocence and liberty'. Guards possessing few skills and lacking personal autonomy at work are not likely to be very concerned with producing a 'meaningful' work experience for prisoners. Maguire et al. (1985) report studies that indicate the ways in which systems of accountability are bypassed in practice, and one could expect that guards would work to undermine 'business-like' industrial operations which threaten to render their wards 'more eligible' than they.

Regardless of whether or not private prisons invest in convict labour power, or merely provide more prison space economically, preoccupation with efficiency deflects attention from more important issues. In his criticism of private prisons, David Rothenberg, Executive Director of the Fortune Society, remarks:

> We must remind ourselves that the goal in the criminal-justice system is not to have efficient or profitable prisons, but rather to have less crime. Efficient prisons, without addressing the real issues of crime, would be one more irrelevancy in criminal justice. (Rothenberg, 1985)

At best an irrelevancy at worst prison privatization will subvert justice by circumventing accountability; expanding and prolonging confinement for profit interests; busting public employee unions; exploiting convict labour; and, worst of all, temporarily helping the public avoid facing the consequences of imprisonment as a first line of social defence. Arguments over efficiency conceal a conservative political agenda. Whilst the Sisyphean struggle to find adequate cell space for an ever-expanding penal population continues, badly needed alternatives to incarceration are being neglected. In California, for instance, more than one in three young men was arrested at least once from 1974 through 1985, foreshadowing years of overcrowding that promises to overwhelm the state's current $3.2 billion programme to build new prisons. A recently released study (Bishop, 1987) suggests that the state faces a prison population of 'nearly 100 000 by 1991 in a system that would have a capacity for 55 000'. This grim prospect has led enlightened officials to see the futility of current policies, not only in California but also in New York, which faces a similar problem.[17] New York City Correction Commissioner Richard J. Koehler, in a newspaper article on the city's violent and overcrowded gaols, suggested that perhaps a better way to spend money might be to provide better social and economic opportunities for youths:

> After spending my life in the city, including 20 years in police, I say what the hell good is jail? It costs too much and we get almost nothing for it, except they don't do a crime while they're in the box. And that's all we get. (Martin, 1987)

Notes

The author wishes to thank Anne E. Rowland for her patient editorial work.

1 An unusual turn of events saw the Correction Commissioner of Tennessee fined and nearly jailed for contempt of court (*New York Times*, 5 December 1985) for not explaining why an inmate spent two and a half weeks too many behind bars. The inmate's conviction was overturned, but he could not be readmitted to the state prison from county jail because of overcrowding, and the county refused to release him because he was a state inmate.

2 The State of Texas, for instance, has been threatened by a Federal judge with an $800 000-a-day fine until it alleviates prison overcrowding (*Business Week*, 20 April 1987: 33).

3 Other financial deals include a $300 million prison leaseback plan put together by E. F. Hutton for the State of California, and a $65 million gaol leaseback for the City of Philadelphia (Tolchin, 1985b: 14).

4 For a recent bibliography focused on the private financing and operation of correctional facilities, see Immarigeon, 1987. Two works which do consider the politics of privatization are Ericson et al., 1987, focused on Canada, and Ryan and Ward, 1989, which critiques privatization policy proposals in Britain, especially the notions advanced by the Adam Smith Institute. For a report on current developments in private-sector prison industries in the USA, with an annotated bibliography, see Auerbach et al. (1988).

5 For instance, Travis Snelling, former budget director of Virginia's Department of Corrections, is a vice-president of CCA; Behavioral Systems Southwest is co-owned by Ted Nissan, a former California parole officer, and Buckingham Security of Lewisburg, Pennsylvania is run by Charles Fenton, a former chief warden at three Federal prisons, along with his brother Joseph, a Pennsylvania businessman.

6 In New York, for instance, a state with the second largest prison population, the Correction Officers Union is quite strong, and members frequently picket prison sites and the state capitol to pressure the legislature for increased budget support for more guards and better security (see, for example, 'Adirondack guards picketing to protest budget', *Press Republican*, 21 March 1987). And state politicians keep an ear to correctional workers as voters, especially in rural regions of Midwestern and Northeastern states, where correctional workers and their relatives constitute a formidable constituency. The diminution of democratic controls under privatization will be discussed later in this chapter.

7 See Wecht (1987) for an excellent examination of the Constitutional implications of delegating correctional authority to private parties. The author concludes that 'privatization will require not only strict contractual standards, but, more import-

antly, greater judicial willingness to review prison practices and to guarantee the rights of prisoners' (1987: 815). He observes that this may undermine the private nature of these prisons and eliminate their economic advantage.

8 This conceptual distinction is raised by Clifford D. Shearing and Philip Stenning, editors of *Private Policing* (1987). The authors, however, employ it as a basis of *distinction* between private police/security and private imprisonment.

9 Following Galbraith (1983:4–8), we distinguish between authority and power, and between *instruments* of power, which can be condign, compensatory or conditional, and their *source*. The term 'condign', which in normal usage is an adjective to punishment, is used by Galbraith to mean something close to 'coercive' power as defined by Dennis H. Wrong (1979). See also Sennett (1980: 18–19). According to Galbraith, the term 'coercive' 'less specifically implies the instrument to which the individual (or group) surrenders, that to which brings submission' (1983: 5); 'condign power wins submission by inflicting or threatening appropriately adverse consequences'. This is the sense in which we employ the term 'coercive'.

10 As appears to be the case in the example of the Volunteers of America's (VOA) county facility in Roseville, Minnesota, which is the nation's first privately operated women's gaol. VOA operates in the tradition of social welfare providers, and attempts to operate with authority based on 'persuasion' and 'inducement' (Wrong, 1979: 32–4, 44–9). In stark contrast to CCA's technocratic approach to power, Roseville emphasizes direct staff interaction, informality and inmate responsibility, creating an atmosphere in which 'security and treatment are the same', according to its director (Shipp, 1985: 29; Gustafson, 1984): 'the first thing VOA did was turn off the television surveillance cameras. . . . that stuff is truly contrary to our purpose' (Gustafson, 1984). The 35-inmate facility is in its fifth year of operation, a period without a single lawsuit.

11 Contracting poorly trained security personnel could prove far more costly than public policing, as suggested by a $50 million negligence suit filed recently against New York City and the Globe Security Systems Company on behalf of a woman who was attacked in a women's shelter (*New York Times*, 27 August 1987).

12 The consequences of which can bring harm to the rich and powerful as well as to the homeless, as was the case in the murder of Iris Stiff, a Houston socialite and managing director of the Alley Theater. She was robbed and strangled in her downtown office by an employee of Security Guard Services, Inc., who was found to have been a convicted felon, imprisoned for, among other things, killing his three-year-old son. The original suspect was another security guard at the building, also an ex-convict, who had served 40 months in an Ohio prison (Reavis, 1982).

13 Personnel costs account for almost 80 per cent of total prison operating costs (Hornblum, 1986: 54). And one cannot be too confident of management's concern for safeguarding prisoners' rights, if Charles Fenton of Buckingham Security is an example. As warden of Lewisburg Federal penitentiary he was among a group of prison officials who were found by a Federal jury in 1980 to have 'inflicted cruel and unusual punishment on two inmates', who testified to having been 'beaten with ax handles while they were handcuffed and shackled after arriving by bus from Atlanta' (Tolchin, 1985a). Buckingham Security has a proposal to 'build a $20 million, 715-cell maximum security penitentiary north of Pittsburgh. It is intended to house child molesters, those in protective custody and others who need protection from the prison population, and it is expected to draw prisoners from several states' (Tolchin, 1985a).

14 Contracting for services diffuses responsibility; those inquiring about penal conditions can more easily be given the run-around, as in the case of a Houston, Texas, minister who, trying to get a library and English lessons introduced at a CCA alien detention centre, got pushed back and forth between CCA and the INS: ' "whenever we have a problem, I.N.S. tells us to go to C.C.A., and C.C.A. tells us to go to I.N.S.," Father Flores said' (Tolchin, 1985c).

15 A recent example of which concerns the Nuclear Regulatory Commission, whose officials have been assailed by members of Congress as biased, improperly favouring the nuclear power industry (Tolchin, 1987b: A1; see also Wald, 1987).

16 And the Reagan administration appointed a commission to study ways in which more government functions — including the Federal penal system — can be turned over to private business (Brinkley, 1987).

17 In June 1988, the New York State prison system was operating at 114 per cent of its legally defined capacity. Gaols in New York City were at 106 per cent — overflowing with more than 16 000 inmates awaiting court dispositions or serving less than one year for misdemeanour offences. City officials have resorted to some unusual measures in their effort to reduce overcrowding at Rikers Island, the main penal compound; these include the creation of two gaols 350 miles north, on the Canadian border, and — in a move reminiscent of the eighteenth-century English hulks — the reconditioning as floating prisons of a city ferryboat and two British troop barges used in the Falkland Islands (Uhlig, 1987), as well as the construction in 1989 of two more prison barges.

References

Adamson, Christopher R. (1983) 'Punishment after Slavery: Southern State Penal Systems, 1865–1890'. *Social Problems*, 30 (5): 555–69.

Applebome, Peter (1987a) 'Texas, in Emergency, to Free 185 from Crowded Prisons', *New York Times*, 17 August: 11.

Applebome, Peter (1987b) '1,000 New Inmates a Week Jam too few Cells', *New York Times*, 1 March: E 5.

Auerbach, Barbara, Lawson, R. H., Luftig, J. T., Ney, B., Shaller, J., Sexton, G. and Smith, P. (1979) *A Guide to Effective Prison Industries, Volume 1, Creating Free Venture Prison Industries: Program Considerations*. Philadelphia: American Foundation, Inc.

Auerbach, B. J., Sexton, G. E., Farrow, F. C. and Lawson, R. H. (1988) 'Work in American Prisons: The Private Sector Gets Involved', *Issues and Practices*. Washington: National Institute of Justice.

Barnes, Harry Elmer (1972) *The Repression of Crime: Studies in Historical Penology.* Montclair, NJ: Patterson Smith. p. 279–80. (First published 1926.)

Bean, Ed (1986) 'Private Jail Firms Betting they Have Best Idea', *Wall Street Journal*, 30 August.

Becker, C. and Stanley, D. (1985) 'The Downside of Private Prisons', *The Nation*, 15 June: 728–30.

Belkin, Lisa (1989) 'Rise of Private Prisons: How Much of a Bargain?', *New York Times*, 27 March.

Benidt, Bruce (1985) 'Prisoner-run Program Gives Inmates Education and Hope', *Minneapolis Star and Tribune*, 16 June: 1A.

Bentham, Jeremy (1843) *Works*.

Bishop Katherine (1987) 'California Studies Data on Prisons', *New York Times*, 7 April.

Bowditch, Christine and Everett, Ronald S. (1987) 'Private Prisons: Problems within the Solution', *Justice Quarterly*, 3 (2).

Brinkley, Joel (1987) 'Reagan Appoints Privatization Unit', *New York Times*, 8 September.

Bureau of Justice Statistics (1985) *Bulletin*, 'Prisoners in 1984', April.

Bureau of Justice Statistics (1986) *Bulletin*, 'State and Federal Prisoners, 1925–85', October.

Bureau of Justice Statistics (1988), *Special Report*, 'Drug Law Violators, 1980–86', June.

Bureau of Justice Statistics (1989), 'BJS Data Report, 1988', April.

Business Week (1984) 'Convict Labour has the Unions Worried', 16 April: 51.

Business Week (1987) 'Jails could be Texas' Next Ten-gallon Business', 20 April: 33.

Camp, Camille G. and Camp, George, M. (1984) 'Private Sector Involvement in Prison Services and Operation', Criminal Justice Institute for the National Institute of Corrections, Washington, DC (February).

Cannon, Amanda W. (1986) 'Private Sector Management Contracting in Prisons', Unpublished Paper, Committee on Corrections, Probation, and Parole, Senate, State of Florida.

Cohen, Stanley (1985) *Visions of Social Control: Crime, Classification*. Polity Press.

DeWitt, Charles B. (1986) 'Ohio's New Approach to Prison and Jail Financing', *Construction Bulletin*, National Institute of Justice.

Ericson, R. V., McMahon, M. W. and Evans D. G. (1987), 'Punishing for Profit: Reflections on the Revival of Privatization in Corrections', *Canadian Journal of Criminology*, 29 (4): 355–87.

Fixler, P. E., Jr. (1984) 'Behind Bars we Find an Enterprise Zone', *Wall Street Journal*, Nov. 29: 34.

Franklin, Ben A. (1987) 'Nuclear Officials Assailed As Biased', *New York Times*, 22 April: A-1.

Funke, Gail S. (1983) 'National Conference on Prison Industries: Discussions and Recommendations', National Center for Innovation in Corrections, George Washington University (June).

Galbraith, John Kenneth (1983) *The Anatomy of Power*. Boston: Houghton Mifflin Company.

Gargan, Edward, A. (1983) 'The Nation's Prisoners Join the Labor Force', *New York Times*, 28 August.

Gustafson, Paul (1984) 'Women's Jail is First Run by Private Concern', *Minneapolis Star and Tribune*, 20 November: 1-B.

Hawkins, Gordon (1983) 'Prison Labor and Prison Industries', in M. Tonry and N. Morris (eds), *Crime and Justice: An Annual Review of Research*, vol. 5: 85–127. Chicago: University of Chicago Press.

Hindus, Michael S. (1980) *Prison and Plantation: Crime, Justice and Authority in Massachusetts and South Carolina 1767–1878*. Chapel Hill: Univ. of North Carolina Press.

HMSO (1988) *Private Sector Involvement in the Remand System*. Cm 434. HMSO.

Hornblum, Allen (1986) 'The Privatization of America', *Bell Atlantic Quarterly*, III (4): 47–55

Howard, John (1777) *The State of the Prisons in England and Wales*. Warrington.

Hurst, John (1983) 'Operating Prisons for Profit Goal of Entrepreneur Building here', *Los Angeles Times — Washington Post News Service*, 29 December.

Immarigeon, Russ (1987) 'Privatizing Adult Imprisonment in the U.S.: A Bibliography', *Criminal Justice Abstracts*, 19 (1): 123–39.

Iverem, Esther (1987) 'Tension Lives at Big Shelter near Bowery', *New York Times*, 28 March: 29.

Krajick, K. (1984) 'Prisons for Profit: The Private Alternatives', *State Legislatures* (April): 9–14.

Kuttner, Robert (1986) 'The Private Market Can't Always Solve Public Problems', *The Privatization Review*, Spring.

Logan, Charles H. and Rausch, Sharla P. (1985) 'Punish and Profit: The Emergence of Private Enterprise Prisons', *Justice Quarterly*, 2 (3): 303–18.

McConville, S. (1987) 'Aid from Industry? Private Corrections and Prison Crowding', in S. Gottfredson and S. McConville (eds), *America's Correctional Crisis*. New York: Greenwood Press. pp. 221–42.

Mack, John (1984) 'Writing Off the Doomed', in Michael A. Kroll, 'Prisons for Profit', *The Progressive* (September): 18–22.

Maguire, M., Vagg, J. and Morgan, R. (1985) *Accountability and Prisons: Opening up a Closed World*. London and New York: Tavistock.

Martin, Douglas (1987) 'Violence Grows in Crowded New York Jails', *New York Times*, 15 April.

Miliband, Ralph and Panitch, Leo (1987) 'Socialists and the "New Conservatism"' *Monthly Review*, 38 (January): 1–16.

Mullen, Joan (1985) 'Corrections and the Private Sector', *Research in Brief*, Washington: National Institute of Justice, March.

New York Times (1985) 'Breaking up Government's Monopoly on Prison Cells', 3 March.

New York Times (1985) 'Plan by Tennessee Governor is Aimed at Prison Crowding', 18 September.

New York Times (1985) 'Jail Crisis almost Jails Chief of Tennessee Prison System', 5 December.

New York Times (1987) 'Texas Prison System Closes', 17 August.

New York Times (1987) 'Ex-Shelter Resident Sues over Attack', 27 August.

New York Times (1987) 'Reagan Sets 2% Raise for Federal Employees', 30 August.

New York Times (1989) 'U.S. Inmate Count was up 7.4% in 1988', 24 April.

Nix, Crystal (1986) 'City Criticized for Way it Selects Shelter Guards', *New York Times*, 1 November

O'Connor, James (1986) *Accumulation Crisis*. New York: Basil Blackwell.

Poole, Robert, W., Jr. (1983) 'Objections to Privatization', *Policy Review*, 24: 105–19.

Reavis, Dick, J. (1982) 'Scarecrow Cops', *Texas Monthly* (May).

Reske, H. J. (1985) 'Burger wants Bench Vacancies Filled', *Plattsburgh Press Republican*, 30 December: 77.

Robbins, Ira P. (1985) 'Statement of Ira P. Robbins Before the Subcommittee on Courts, Civil Liberties and the Administration of Justice of the House Committee on the Judiciary Concerning *Privatization of Corrections*', 13 November 1985.

Roberts, Sam (1987) 'Things to Come: As Society Rots, Crime Will Rise', *New York Times*, 5 April.

Rothenberg, David (1985) 'Not Profitable Prisons, but Less Crime', 'Letters', *New York Times*, 13 February.

Rutherford, Andrew (1984) *Prisons and the Process of Justice*. London: Heinemann.

Ryan, M. and Ward, T. (1989) *Privatization and the Penal System: The American Experience and the Debate in Britain*. London: Open University Press.

Savas, E. S. (1982) *Privatizing the Public Sector: How to Shrink Government*. Chatham, NJ: Chatham House Publishers, Inc.

Sennett, Richard (1980) *Authority*. New York: Alfred A. Knopf.

Sexton, George E., Farrow, F. C. and Auerbach, B. J. (1985), 'The Private Sector and Prison Industries', *Research in Brief*, National Institute of Justice (August).

Schaller, Jack (1981) 'Normalizing the Prison Work Environment', in Fogel, D. and Joel, Hudson (eds), *Justice as Fairness: Perspectives on the Justice Model*. Cincinnati: Anderson.

Shearing, Clifford D. and Stenning, Philip (eds) (1987) *Private Policing*. Newberry Park, CA: Sage Publications.

Shipp, E. R. (1985) 'Group that Aids Ex-Convicts Tries Hand at Running Prison', *New York Times*, 17 February.

Stancill, Nancy (1984) 'Ruling Clouds INS Plan for Private Jails', *Houston Chronicle*, 8 May.

Stewart, James, K. (1985) Interview on 'Breaking up Government's Monopoly on Prison Cells', *New York Times*, 3 March.

Tai, Wendy S. (1984) 'Control Data among Firms Bidding for Prison Role', *Minneapolis Star and Tribune*, 20 November: 1-B.

Tolchin, Martin (1985a) 'As Privately Owned Prisons Increase, so do their Critics', *New York Times*, 17 February.

Tolchin, Martin (1985b) 'Companies Aid in Easing Crowded Jails', *New York Times*, 17 February.

Tolchin, Martin (1985c) 'Jails Run by Private Concern Force it to Face Questions of Accountability', *New York Times*, 19 February.

Tolchin, Martin (1985d) 'Governors Cautious in Endorsing the Private Operation of Prisons', *New York Times*, 2 March.

Tolchin, Martin (1985e) 'Privately Operated Prison in Tennessee Reports $200,000 in Cost Overruns', *New York Times*, 21 May.

Tolchin, Martin (1985f) 'Private Concern Makes Offer to Run Tennessee's Prisons', *New York Times*, 13 September.

Tolchin, Martin (1985g) 'Experts Forsee Adverse Effects from Private Control of Prisons', *New York Times*, 17 September.

Tolchin, Martin (1985h) 'Prospects of Privately Run Prisons Divides Pennsylvania Legislators', *New York Times*, 15 December.

Tolchin, Martin (1986) 'Bar Group Urges Halt in Use of Privately Run Jails', *New York Times*, 12 February.

Tolchin, Martin (1987a) 'Critics say U.S. "Privatized" Foreign Policy on Iran', *New York Times*, 20 January.

Tolchin, Martin (1987b) 'Nuclear Officials Assailed as Biased', *New York Times*, 22 April: A-1.

Uhlig, Mark A. (1987) 'Troop Barge Proposed as Floating Prison', *New York Times*, 5 June.

Wald, Matthew, L. (1987) 'Retiring U.S. Official Assails Nuclear Plant Safety', *New York Times*, 7 June.

Wecht, D. N. (1987) 'Breaking the Code of Deference: Judicial Review of Private Prisons', *The Yale Law Journal*, 96: 815–37.

Weiss, Robert P. (1987a) 'Humanitarianism, Labour Exploitation, or Social Control? A Critical Survey of Theory and Research on the Origin and Development of Prisons', *Social History*, 12 (3): 331–50.

Weiss, Robert P. (1987b) 'The Reappearance of "The Ideal Factory": The Entrepreneur and Social Control in the Contemporary Prison', in John Lowman, R. J. Menzies and T. S. Palys (eds), *Transcarceration: Essays in the Sociology of Social Control*. Aldershot: Gower Publishing Company.

Wrong, Dennis H. (1979) *Power: Its Forms, Bases and Uses*. New York: Harper & Row Publishers.

3 PRIVATIZATION AND PENAL POLITICS

The current debate about privatizing prisons in Britain raises important issues. These range from the essentially practical, such as whether the introduction of private capital can help to reduce prison overcrowding, as its advocates claim, to ethical considerations about the morality of making corporate profits from the unfortunate social necessity of inflicting pain. The debate also raises a series of questions about the proper relationship between the State, the private sector and the penal system as a whole which progressive groups in Britain find difficult to answer. Their dilemma stems partly from their premise — so popular in Britain and the USA in the 1970s and 1980s — that the infliction of pain should not be the sole preserve of the State and its professionally qualified employees, but should be returned to the community by such measures as half-way houses and juvenile diversion programmes. The idea that some of these decentralized initiatives might be run by profit-making organizations rarely surfaced as the problem it has since become.

In this chapter Mick Ryan and Tony Ward look again at the British penal apparatus as a whole, including the contribution made by the voluntary sector; they consider what the proper role of the State might be; they indicate more precisely what is meant by 'privatization', and the extent to which private interests might contribute towards the evolution of a progressive penal politics that best reflects the diversity of interests the criminal justice system should serve.

The authors examine the politics of privatization and challenge the assertion that privatization can insulate the penal system from political pressures. Rather, they argue, it may well signal a re-politicization of the penal sphere and may encourage the development of new issues and concerns.

There are significant differences in the way in which the privatization debate is constructed in different countries, and it will inevitably be shaped by each particular social and cultural climate. In developing a radical response to the proposed privatization in the penal system, the authors resist the temptation to offer a blanket rejection of privatization. Instead, they explore the political space that could be opened up if privatization continues to be pursued. In so doing, they emphasize that the balance of political forces will be crucial in determining both the extent and impact of privatization.

Privatization and Penal Politics

Mick Ryan and Tony Ward

Some ideological contours

The suggestion that prisons might be privatized should not entirely surprise us. During the last decade or so ideas about the role of the State have changed significantly in several leading Western countries. In the USA, for example, at both federal and state levels there has been a call to reduce public expenditure wherever possible by hiving off public functions to the private sector. In this drive to 'roll back the State', the federal state itself has taken a leading part, and President Reagan's Task Force on Private Sector Initiatives was specifically intended to involve the private sector more directly in the delivery of hitherto public services (Mullen et al., 1985: 1). This federal initiative has been well received by the private sector, and entrepreneurs continue to come forward with their own schemes to diminish 'big government' and augment their corporate profits.

Despite significant differences in governmental structure, it is easy to see the parallels between the British and the American experience. Through a series of Stock Exchange flotations of those public utilities previously owned and managed by the State, Mrs Thatcher has transferred a whole range of industries and services back to the private sector. Stringent controls on expenditure have also been introduced, and a number of Conservative-controlled local authorities have been encouraged to privatize public services such as the collection and disposal of domestic waste. Even Regional Health Authorities — they run Britain's socialized medical services — have been forced to introduce private tendering for hospital cleaning.

What all this suggests is that on both sides of the Atlantic privatization has come to occupy a central place on the political agenda of the Right. So much so, perhaps, that it would not be unreasonable to believe that privatizing prisons is nothing out of the ordinary, but rather just one more step along a clearly discernible continuum. In our view, however, it would be unwise to interpret the suggestion that prisons should be privatized quite so narrowly, since at a crucial ideological level the idea is far fron being 'nothing out of the ordinary'.

Let us put it this way. Since the coming of industrial capitalism the State has intervened more and more in the social and economic domain, and nowhere has this intervention been more obvious than in the State's increasing control over criminal justice. By the early decades of the twentieth century the State was already well on its way to achieving virtual control from beginning to end. Through its growing power over the police it influenced the process of prosecution; it appointed those who passed judgement and increasingly directly controlled those who delivered punishment, whether in institutions or the community. This extension of the State's authority over criminal justice, its now near-monopoly of this space, is taken to be one of the settled features of Western industrial democracies. It is precisely this which makes privatizing punishment so audacious. It strikes at the very heart of the State's authority and sends out the message — the crucial message — that nothing is sacred. To put this point more directly, if the State can be rolled back even here, then limiting its authority still further in other spaces is surely possible.

To argue that this helps to explain why privatizing prisons is so popular with the political Right is not to deny that there are some on the Right — including prominent backbench Conservatives like Ivor Stanbrook — who are far less enthusiastic about privatization than others, and with good reason; nor to deny that the advocates of privatization have shown a clear preference for conducting their case in practical rather than ideological terms — as a solution to prison overcrowding, for example (see Home Office, 1988a). However, it does perhaps help to explain why those advocates of privatization are so determined to press on even if it means ignoring some of their own more dubious assumptions, and sweeping aside what hard evidence there is, a good deal of which is surely against them. They hear, it seems, only what they want to hear; or more appropriately in this case, perhaps, see only what they want to see.

The response of the Left and most penal reform groups in Britain to the suggestion that prisons might be privatized was at first a curious mixture of outright disbelief and thinly disguised moral outrage. This was later translated into, or perhaps more accurately, combined with, a more considered approach and the search for evidence from here and abroad to demonstrate that the idea of prisons for profit was an unlikely proposition and, moreover, was largely irrelevant as a solution to the crisis of prison overcrowding. While we admit to feeling a certain moral outrage ourselves, and at the same time agree with many of the objections raised by the Left and the penal lobby, we also feel that their response was not as sharply focused as it might have been. At times it was frankly ahistorical and it failed to make crucial distinctions, such as that between the allocation and delivery of punishment but, perhaps most obviously, that it failed more often than not to extend the privatization debate to the soft end of the penal

system where some forms of private involvement contain oppositional potential which the Left would be wise to exploit and defend.
Before we can return to these distinctions, however, it is necessary to
offer a more detailed assessment of the debate in Britain as it has
developed so far.

The advocates of privatization and their critics

Support for the idea of private prisons in Britain originally came from
three main sources: the Adam Smith Institute, a pressure-group
espousing a free-market philosophy; the Conservative majority of
the House of Commons Select Committee on Home Affairs; and
individuals such as McConville and Hall Williams (1985) of the SDP,
and Lord Windlesham (1987), chairperson of the Parole Board, who
proposed a limited degree of privatization, especially of remand
facilities. Ranged against them were the Labour members of the
Home Affairs Select Committee; the Prison Officers Association
(POA), which is affiliated to the Trades Union Congress; and groups
campaigning for prison reform such as the Howard League, the
National Association for the Care and Resettlement of Offenders
(NACRO), the Prison Reform Trust and the Labour Campaign for
Criminal Justice.

A fundamental premise on which all the advocates of privatization,
except McConville and Hall Williams (1985), agree, is that the prison
crisis is caused by a lack of prison space. Peter Young expresses this
point simply in *The Prison Cell*, a report prepared for the Adam
Smith Institute: 'Not enough new prisons are built because the
Government — and electors — have higher spending priorities such
as more hospitals and better education' (Young, 1987: 1). This is a
strange interpretation of the spending priorities of the present British
government. As Rutherford (1986: 90) points out, 'over the six-year
period up to 1984/5, spending on the English prison system rose by
30%, compared with 14% on health and social services and 1% on
education'. The notion that the prisons were starved of resources
under earlier governments is equally a myth, as King and Morgan
(1980) have shown. It is true that when, as in some US states, electors
are asked directly, through bond issues or referenda, to support
capital investment in prisons, they are often reluctant to do so (see,
for example, Jacobs and Berkowitz, 1983) and this has been an
important factor behind American privatization initiatives (Weiss,
this volume); but there has been no counterpart to this experience in
the British context.

More fundamentally, Young makes no attempt to justify his assertion that not enough prisons are being built. Nowhere, either in *The Prison Cell* or in the more theoretical *Omega Report* (ASI, 1984) on justice policy, do the Adam Smith Institute's researchers confront the arguments of those, like Rutherford, who maintain that Britain has more than enough prisons but puts too many people in them. This is not because they subscribe to a crude 'law and order' ideology. On the contrary, much of the *Omega Report* is spent debunking the idea that the State, by providing more police or more prisons, can offer any simple solution to crime. The report acknowledges that 'if punishment systems are to be reformed and applied effectively' it is essential to 'clear our thinking' about the purposes of sentencing. The report's contribution to this worthy enterprise, however, comprises merely a few banal remarks on deterrence, rehabilitation, etc., followed by the observation (ASI, 1984: 53) that 'The right balance of motivating principles is, of course, a matter of ethical judgement upon which the economist cannot decide'. (Economists, as we all know, are incapable of ethical judgement!) The proposal, which in 1984 seemed novel and even 'loony', for private management of prisons, lends an air of radicalism to a report that is otherwise very short of fresh thinking.

The Home Affairs Committee, in its inquiry into 'The State and Use of Prisons' of which its report on privatization is a by-product, did have to confront the arguments about prison building, since they were put squarely before it by the Prison Reform Trust. The Committee unanimously endorsed the government's prison building programme, the most ambitious since the 1840s, on the ground that changes in sentencing policy were 'a long term solution', but the 'prison service has to find accommodation immediately' (House of Commons, 1987a: para. 15). But even on the most favourable assumptions about privatization, commissioning and building new prisons takes several years, whereas measures, such as executive release, that could be taken to reduce the prison population would have an immediate effect and provide a breathing-space for sentencing reform.

All the Home Affairs Committee majority's arguments in favour of privatization (which they insist is not privatization but 'contract provision') rest on the claim that it will provide quicker and better buildings. Astonishingly, the report offers no argument whatever in favour of its proposal to contract the *running* of prisons to private companies, as distinct from hiring firms to build prisons, or possibly leasing the buildings from them as proposed by McConville and Hall Williams (1985: 41). The Committee's entire case for this fairly major innovation is contained in the question-begging proposition that 'the state should be the sole provider of a service only when no-one exists who can provide the service at less cost or can provide a better service' (para. 9).

The Adam Smith Institute does advance a theoretical case for privatizing the running of prisons, which is an extension of its argument about prison building — namely that electorates and elected governments cannot be trusted to take economically rational decisions about penal policy:

> Overcrowding and cell-sharing are the by-product of a system influenced by political considerations and subject to political forces that allow capital investment to suffer and which reduce flexibility to change.... Any realistic solution is likely to involve greater capitalization, or more effective use of manpower, wider uses of technological innovation, and new alternatives to imprisonment, perhaps based in turn on technological improvements.... This is unlikely to occur within the context of the present, policitally-managed system, and some more radical solution is therefore attractive. (ASI, 1984: 52)

Distrust of the democratic process, as Roy Hattersley (1987) reminds us, is characteristic of the libertarian Right. In any case, it is absurd to suppose that fundamental questions about the penal system can somehow be 'taken out of politics'. If the government awards a contract to a private company under which the company can fire prison officers or fit probationers with electronic bracelets, that is just as much a political decision as if the government did these things itself. As Stephen Shaw of the Prison Reform Trust points out in a response to the *Omega Report*, 'Most costs are politically determined: how many prisoners do we want; how much overcrowding; how much security; how much work, education and training?' (Shaw, 1985). The State, as the sole customer and regulator of the prison business, would inevitably retain ultimate responsibility for these decisions. The idea that privatization would entail removing key decisions from the political process also underlies the Howard League's (1987) critique of the concept in its Memorandum to the Home Affairs Committee:

> Removing a person's liberty is the most severe sanction available to the justice system. Such an action must be a matter of public policy, answerable to Parliament. If society wants prisoners to return as full members of the community then it must take responsibility for them... The state cannot abdicate the responsibility and burden of care for those people who have offended against society... People are imprisoned in the name of the Sovereign and this cannot be delegated to someone else.

These arguments, which are very similar to those of Thomas (1987) and NACRO (1988), blur the crucial distinction, to which we pointed earlier, between the *allocation* and *delivery* of punishment; and the League's vague references to 'society', 'the state', 'the Sovereign' and 'responsibility' confuse the issue still further. The State is an ensemble of different agencies, some of which — not least the Prison Department of the Home Office — enjoy a large measure of autonomy; and 'responsibility' can take many different forms. To say that because the Prison Department is 'answerable to Parliament' — in the sense that the Home Secretary can be asked questions about it — 'society' is somehow 'responsible' for what it does, is at best a constitutional fiction; while the notion that 'the Sovereign' (usually taken to be the Queen in Parliament) can run prisons without delegating this duty to anyone seems to leave reality behind completely. If we look at the specific mechanisms by which the government elected bodies or the courts may exercise responsibility for prisons — civil liability for the mistreatment of prisoners; the promulgation and enforcement of standards; the role, if any, of local authorities — it is clear that there is no *necessary* connection between any of these forms of accountability and public ownership. It would be quite possible (though politically unrealistic because of the cost involved) to devise legislation under which persons were privatized and simultaneously became much *more* accountable to Parliament, local government and/or the courts. Whether prisons are run by government employees, and whether those who run them are effectively answerable to democratic institutions, are quite different questions.

Both the Howard League and the POA draw an analogy between current proposals and the 'finely-tuned system of extortion' (POA, 1987: para. 4) operated by eighteenth-century gaolers. There is no serious prospect, however, that the government will 'abdicate responsibility' to anything like the extent that a return to eighteenth-century practices would entail. Eighteenth-century gaolers derived most of their income from their prisoners, not from the State; and because the State had little fiscal interest in the prisons, and 'squalor carceris' was considered inevitable or even desirable, there was no serious attempt (except by a few reforming magistrates) to regulate or inspect prison conditions (McConville, 1981). What is now being proposed is a system under which private organizations are paid by the government to run prisons, and are subject to some form of inspection to ensure that they meet their contractual and statutory obligations. There is a much more recent precedent for this kind of arrangement: the management of reformatory and industrial schools from 1854 to 1933, and of the majority of approved schools from 1933 to 1969. These institutions were not prisons and they were run by charities, not for profit; but the reformatories and approved schools, at least, were unmistakably penal institutions where offenders were deprived of their liberty pursuant to the sentence of a court. It is difficult, therefore, to maintain that the committal of convicted offenders to privately run institutions breaks any long-standing constitutional principle.

This brings us to another important weakness in the Howard League's 'abdication of responsibility' argument. Since what is denounced is the diminution in the role of the State, it makes no difference whether the State 'abdicates' in favour of a profit-making or a voluntary body. Nor is it clear why the argument should apply only to prisons, and not to the administration of non-custodial sentences, which also involve substantial deprivation of liberty. In their oral evidence to the Home Affairs Committee, however, the Howard League's representatives were at pains to stress that, while they had 'sounded a note of caution about going down the commercial privatization route', they also saw 'considerable opportunities for breaking . . . the Home Office monopoly' by greater involvement of voluntary organizations (House of Commons, 1987b: Q. 262). In a Supplementary Memorandum on provisions for young people, the League specifically argued for supervision schemes to be contracted from non-profit agencies: 'Greater diversity and innovation is likely to result when a variety of agencies are involved as is demonstrated by the experience of Massachusetts and Utah' (ibid.: 95). The League does not seem to have clearly thought out the distinctions of principle between different kinds of privatization.

Arguments against the profit motive
The strongest points made by the opponents of privatization are those which relate specifically, or at least primarily, to the profit motive. There are four main arguments of this type, none of which has been adequately answered by the advocates of privatization.

(1) In the words of the POA:

> The moves towards privatization can only exacerbate the already serious situation in our prisons where financial considerations take precedence in the decision-making process, often to the detriment of humanitarianism and considerations affecting the safety of staff. Privatization and its attendant profit making motivation cannot take account of population chemistry . . . (ibid.: 101)

As the Adam Smith Institute documents make clear, a more commercial approach to questions of staffing, free from 'political fears about strikes or unemployment' (Young, 1987: 4) is precisely what privatization is intended to achieve. The danger is that this will produce prisons, like some of those described by the POA (1987), run with the maximum of technology and the minimum of human contact. The report prepared for the Home Office by the management consultants Deloitte, Haskins & Sells (1989) confirms that the potential contractors they spoke to aim to reduce staff–prisoner ratios by relying on new technologies and prison designs.

(2) Principles of natural justice could be infringed if the existing disciplinary powers of prison governors were transferred to private companies who might have a vested interest in their application. For example, the company might earn extra fees if the prisoner lost remission. This objection could be countered by transferring many of the governor's powers to independent tribunals, but this would go against the aims of privatization which are to reduce personnel and simplify procedures. A similar conflict of interests could arise where reports by prison staff influence a prisoner's chances of parole (Pennsylvania General Assembly, 1985: 30) — though not under the Adam Smith Institute's proposals since they would abolish the parole system. Neither of these points applies in the same way, or with the same force, in the case of remand prisons or bail hostels, which is why a recent government discussion document (Home Office, 1988a) suggests that privatization might best get started in just these areas.

(3) Far from reducing undesirable political pressures on the penal system as the Adam Smith Institute claims, privatization would increase them, creating a powerful lobby with a vested interest in a high prison population. According to one Louisiana Sheriff, prison contractors already 'have salesmen tell you what a great bunch of guys you are, and how they'd love to contribute to your campaign' quoted by Tolchin, 1985; see also Weiss, this volume).

(4) Finally, there is the ethical point that is unacceptable to engage for profit in the deliberate infliction of suffering. Young's analogy with grocers, who 'make profit by catering for human hunger' (Young, 1987: 34) is absurd; the real analogy is with people who make a profit by deliberately starving others. A more apposite parallel, perhaps, is with mercenaries: whatever moral qualms one might have about the calling of a soldier (especially if one doubts the justice of the war), it is generally felt that there is something especially repugnant about killing people on a commercial basis. The same surely applies to the business of punishment.

It could be said in response to these arguments that they all apply to State and non-profit agencies as well. Financial considerations, as the POA recognizes, already play a large part in prison management; the impartiality of governors in disciplinary proceedings is questionable, to say the least; State agencies (such as the police: Reiner, 1985) and non-profit organizations can constitute powerful political lobbies; and as the Home Affairs Committee points out, prison officers and other state employees gain financially from their work. The point is not, however, that there is any great virtue in the existing system, but that privatization would exacerbate some of its worst features.

To those who take the view, and there are many, that just about everyone involved in delivering punishment makes money out of it, we would make the following additional points. It is, of course, true that there are many people who make a living from the penal system: social workers, prison warders, probation officers and so on. It is true, as well, that their financial interests can affect policy-making: for example, one reason for the POA's resistance to any relaxation of prison censorship has been that it would mean less work for their members. However, to equate these wage earners with those who wish to exploit the penal system for corporate gain is quite simply wrong for a number of reasons. Most fundamentally, perhaps, it fails to make the obvious distinction between those who sell their labour and those who own and control capital. But more than just that, it fails to acknowledge the fact that many of those who engage in the distasteful business of inflicting pain do so partly in order to mitigate the full force of what they see as an unfortunate social necessity. In other words, most are involved because they care about the people in their charge, and caring is high on their list of priorities. Now it may well be that some of the groups we have mentioned care more than others, that perhaps some of them hardly care at all, but many of them do. To equate their contribution with that of venture capitalists whose first priority is to make a 'fast buck' seems to us to be highly misleading.

Private prisons and the State in the USA and Britain

Young (1987: 38) dismisses the objections raised by critics of prisons for profit as 'theoretical speculation'. By contrast, his own report claims to provide 'hard conclusions based on the facts of what actually has happened' in the USA: namely that private prisons both save money and result in 'a dramatic improvement in conditions for prisoners'. The Home Affairs Committee also relies heavily on the American experience, and although the government's green paper on private remand centres is more cautious in this respect, it claims that the Americans have overcome some of the key problems posed by private prisons, particularly that of monitoring (Home Office, 1988a: para. 22).

We have discussed the distortion of the American experience in these reports at some length elsewhere (Ryan and Ward, 1989: chapters 2–3), but it bears repeating that our view that there is insufficient evidence to support any 'hard conclusions' about the success or failure of privatization is shared by every major report published by a federally funded agency or state government in the USA, including those which favour further privatization (Commonwealth of Massachusetts, 1987; President's Commission on Privatization, 1988). The main point we wish to make here, however, is that a comparison between the British privatization debate and events in the USA confirms that claims for the greater accountability or efficiency of the public or private sector have to be judged in relation to the specific legal, constitutional and administrative frameworks within which they operate.

Whereas British prisons are financed and administered entirely by central government, American prisons and gaols are divided between federal, state and county authorities; and the headway which the private sector has made at the county and, to a lesser extent, state levels is largely attributable to the difficulties of funding and management which state and local governments have encountered. In this context there is some sense in the view that privatization can insulate the penal system from political pressures. It can circumvent the requirement for voter approval to raise money for new prisons through bond issues, or avoid debt limitations that may have been approved by the electorate, and it can take county gaols out of the hands of the elected sheriffs. For the same reasons, criticisms of privatization for eroding democratic accountability may be more pertinent in the USA than in Britain.

Arguments about the inefficiency of public sector institutions similarly need to be looked at in their administrative and financial context. Local gaol administrators in the USA, as Robert Weiss (this volume) points out, often lack necessary expertise in delivering specialized prison services; and the fragmentation of the system does not make for cost-effectiveness. The time needed for public sector agencies to raise the necessary capital contributes to delays in prison construction, and at least partly explains why private companies can sometimes do the job faster (Robbins, 1988: 144–5). Thus even if the evidence for the relative efficiency of the US private sector were as clear cut as some British advocates of privatization would have us believe, great caution would be needed in applying these results to Britain where the same considerations do not apply.

As the green paper acknowledges (para. 17), it is also important to take account of the differing constitutional and legal backgrounds of the two systems. This is not a simple matter, since in both countries the legal ramifications of prison privatization are largely untested; but comparison is made a great deal easier by the publication of an impressive study of the relevant US law commisioned by the American Bar Association (Robbins, 1988).

The most obvious difference between the two legal systems is that the USA has a written constitution and Britain has not. When American civil libertarians question the constitutionality of delegating governmental responsibility for prisons to private entities (ACLU, 1986) they are raising a genuinely difficult legal issue. Under both federal and state constitutions, according to Robbins (1988: 11), 'the question is an extremely close one, and it would not be surprising if a court were to rule against constitutionality'. In Britain it is questionable whether private prisons could be introduced under the existing law, but a simple act of parliament would put their legality beyond challenge, whatever issues of constitutional principle they might be thought to raise.

Even if private incarceration *per se* is not unconstitutional, it appears from Robbins's analysis that the US courts are likely to severely circumscribe the powers of prison proprietors to make their own rules and adjudicate alleged infringements of them (Robbins, 1988: 63–5). It is unclear as yet what disciplinary powers will be conferred on British contractors,[1] but the scope for contesting their decisions in the courts will be much more limited (see Fitzgerald, 1985; Treverton-Jones, 1989).

The US constitution also affords prisoners certain protections, such as that against 'cruel and unusual punishment'. Because the operation of a prison, even if it is contracted out to a private body, legally constitutes 'state action', both the private contractor and the contracting authority can be held liable for any infringement of an inmate's constitutional or legal rights. This was made clear by the 1984 case of *Medina* v. *O'Neill*, after an inmate in a privately run immigration detention centre was shot and killed by a guard untrained in the proper use of firearms (Robbins, 1988: 72–119). British prisoners have fewer legal rights, and even where they are able to sue the private contractor, there is no indication in the green paper that the government intends to accept any liability for the contractor's wrongdoing.

In addition to these constitutional points, there is a vital difference between British and US contract law. In the USA, a contract can, expressly or by implication, confer rights on 'third party beneficiaries', and it appears that prisoners or even members of the public could take advantage of this doctrine to sue private prison operators which break their contracts with governments (ibid.: 141–9). In English law, no one who is not a party to a contract has any right to sue if it is broken. The 'clear and enforceable standards' which the Home Office (1988a: para. 69) promises to include in contracts for the running of remand centres will be enforceable only by the Home Office itself.

What all this suggests is that, unless the British government lays down more stringent legislative safeguards than it has so far indicated, private prison inmates in Britain may be in an even more vulnerable position than their American counterparts. What it does not suggest is that American law provides a solution to all the problems of prison privatization. On the contrary, even the most rigorous safeguards are likely to founder on the realities of prison life. For example, Robbins (1988: 65) suggests that 'the only input that a private-prison company constitutionally might have concerning whether a prisoner had violated a disciplinary rule is that of a complaining witness before a judicial officer'. But the company's position cannot be equated with that of a private citizen complaining, say, that her house has been burgled, because (like the police) the company can adopt a policy either of relentlessly enforcing every rule, or of turning a 'blind eye' to minor violations, and its choice of policy could be influenced by its vested interests. Similarly, the system of monitoring favoured both by Robbins and by the green paper, by which a public official would be stationed permanently in the private institution, may look tough in theory, but the most carefully drafted contract will not stop this official being co-opted into the culture of the institution in which he or she will spend so much time. The suggestion that the American experience affords a proven solution to the problems of monitoring (Home Office, 1988a: para. 23) is quite unfounded, as Robert Weiss's contribution to this volume shows.

The Left: negotiating private space

It should be clear from the above assessment that in the main we agree with those on the Left and in the penal lobby who oppose privatizing prisons. However, we do not agree with what appears to be a consistent premise in their arguments, namely that there is somehow a fixed and unalterable relationship between the State and the penal system. Attachment to such a premise is not only ahistorical, it also carries with it the danger of ignoring the complexities of the penal system in any given period. The historical reality, if we can take this point first, is that the relationship between the State and the penal system changes over time, particularly when it comes to the delivery of punishment rather than just its judicial allocation through the courts. So, to take an obvious example, the prisons came under State control sometime — depending on how one defines 'State' and 'control' — between 1815 and 1877, whereas previously they were farmed out to private interests. The simple fact that we have come to accept this close relationship between the State and the prison is no guarantee that it will, or should, continue, even if on the face of it such a relationship does seem to be one of the more settled features of

Western industrial democracies. Arguments for it have always to be made, and as we have already seen, in present circumstances the evidence in support of such arguments — say on the great virtue of public accountability — is not so easy to marshal as the Left has traditionally believed. This perhaps helps to explain why the Left's initial sense of moral outrage quickly turned into something more considered, even if it is *still* unwilling to take as seriously as it should the attack on its usually unstated premise about the fixed relationship between the State and the prison.

However, while this relationship is the main concern of the present debate over privatization, we would like to stress the obvious point that the modern penal system is a very complex one which stretches from prisons at one end through juvenile training centres to super-vision in the community (Garland, 1985). Furthermore, while it is true that the State has continued to extend its control over the soft end of the system, say by taking over the organization and manage-ment of probation, the delivery of punishment in this part of the system has often been a joint enterprise between the State and private interests. This involvement of the private sector, whether it be in the provision of half-way houses, or the organization and management of entire community projects, has not been the object of *blanket* criticism from the Left. Indeed, in recent years what might loosely be called the New Left has often lent its active support to such intervention. The argument is reasonably straightforward.

There is an anxiety, a very real anxiety, that the formal penal apparatus is growing in size and complexity and in the process is spreading out into the community (Cohen, 1985). While it is true, as Garland (1985) reminds us, that this spillover began much earlier, the pace of community surveillance is seen to be quickening. There are now demonstrably far more probation officers, far more social workers, than ever before. It is partly in an attempt to blunt the impact of this expansion that many of the Left have deliberately set out to involve themselves in community projects which, however kindly they might be described, are still about delivering punishment. However, the fact that they are privately managed as opposed to being firmly locked into the formal State apparatus is seen to give project workers a great deal of autonomy. From this space they hope to generate opposition, to produce an environment which transforms the 'offender' from being a passive recipient of the State's power to punish into someone who is positive and critical. This is not meant to imply anything necessarily grand, some sort of overarching political sensibility, but something which is perhaps far more limited and personal — say, making clients aware of their legal or welfare rights, or making black people and women aware that their place in the penal system is often partly the outcome of wider institutional processes which work against them, and which they should fight.

We would stress, however, that while we endorse the radical potential of such a strategy, it is not our intention to deny that some State functionaries also negotiate successfully for radical space, since our experience is that they do. Nor do we wish to imply that all privately managed projects carry the same radical potential, since clearly they do not. Indeed, what some private interests get up to is, as we shall see, a real cause for concern. What we would argue, however, is that within the existing penal apparatus the Left's still modest experience of operating such a strategy suggests that it is a meaningful way of conducting political opposition, even if its wider transforming potential in association with other forms of client-led alternative politics — 'let's forget the formal apparatus of bourgeois democracy' was the seventies slogan — has turned out to be disappointing. (For more on the New Left and its strategy see Ryan and Ward, 1986.)

At this stage it is also important to contrast the radical strategy outlined above with the ethos of much of what is loosely termed the voluntary sector. Many agencies in this sector are indeed involved either directly or indirectly in delivering punishment, and sometimes work cheek by jowl with radical initiatives, but their appeal is fundamentally different, articulated more in terms of forcing those in their charge who have problems with the law to 'face up to their obligations', with little if any regard to the social and political context of crime and criminalization. This approach takes on board the process of normalization, quite uncritically, and the fact that voluntary rather than State agencies are at work is largely, if not wholly, irrelevant.

We say 'not wholly' irrelevant because we are aware that blurring the boundary between the formal and informal apparatus of penality carries a real expansionary potential (Cohen, 1985: 56–67). This was already in evidence in the Victorian period, when the charitable reformatory and industrial schools enabled tens of thousands of children to be processed through the courts as 'vagrants' or 'truants'. More recently this potential has been increasingly exploited in the proliferation of non-custodial measures such as intermediate treatment, and quasi-judicial processes of mediation or diversion, which are needed to cope with the ever increasing number of people being processed by the police. As Davis (1987) observes in a short but perceptive article on privatization:

> By tradition such disposals would have been firmly based within the court system and most often run by Social Services or the Probation Service. In Criminal Justice Limited they have become firmly lodged with the 'voluntary' . . . sector.

> When, for instance, the National Association for the Care and Resettlement of Offenders began negotiating with government to provide employment projects for ex-offenders they could not have envisaged (could they?) that they would become a multi-million pound, Manpower Services Commission, organization. Similarly, the Rainer Foundation could not have imagined that they would, in a few short years, rival budgets of large social services departments . . .

Funding groups like these offers the government a way out of a dilemma: how to expand the 'soft end' of the apparatus of social control without pouring money into the 'nanny state' of social workers and probation officers that it is ideologically committed to 'rolling back'. It has not been difficult to find voluntary groups who, in their laudable desire to keep people out of custody, are prepared to work closely and quite uncritically with State agencies, promoting improved 'delinquency management', helping 'delinquents' to improve their 'self image', to stand up to 'peer pressure' and so on. The spectacular expansion of the organizations mentioned by Davis contrasts with the hard-pressed probation service (NAPO, 1985) whose unwillingness to get tough has recently led the Conservative government to threaten to bypass it in favour of more compliant voluntary and/or commercial agencies (Home Office, 1988b).

It might be argued in defence of voluntary organizations like the Rainer Foundation that their hands are tied, that to be too critical would simply jeopardize their funding. There is undoubtedly something in this view, but frankly even in its own terms such a defence is inclined to portray the State as some sort of ever-watchful, all-pervading monolithic power which it clearly is not, at least not yet. In practice, it has always been possible to accept State funding and then use it discreetly in a radical way. Consider, for example, the Newham Alternatives Project. Started by Radical Alternatives to Prison in the early 1970s, the project was intended to take advantage of the then recently introduced deferred sentence. The idea of this sentence was that a local magistrate or a judge could defer passing sentence on a convicted offender if he or she thought that a change of circumstances, say the offer of employment, might encourage the offender to settle down and keep within the law in the future. The Newham Alternatives Project was to be that positive change of circumstances, a centre offering a range of support activities from literacy classes to help with making welfare claims (Dronfield, 1980). Whether or not the Project ever quite lived up to its very radical pretensions is a question which has been dealt with elsewhere; what really concerns us here is that it did manage to attract financial support, sometimes in kind — premises for example — from both the local and the central State as well as from voluntary bodies (Ryan, 1978: ch. 5). True, satisfying the Home Office was never easy given the radical nature of the project, and there was opposition from local magistrates and, interestingly, from the probation service too. But the project did manage, for a period at least, to withstand these pressures, and is a useful example of how really quite radical initiatives can operate from within and around the formal penal system.

We would suggest that it was the potential for similar forms of radical intervention which helped to sustain the Left's interest in the so-called Massachusetts experiment, and not just the fact that it was a bold attempt to find a range of alternatives to custody. Briefly, when Jerry Miller was first appointed to run the Massachusetts Division for Youth Services he set out to reform the institutional system and to put an end to the abuses which had been reported. He soon found, however, that his reform initiatives were being frustrated by those staff who actually ran the system, and so he decided to close down most of the institutions more-or-less overnight, providing instead a range of alternatives, starting with university accommodation and then moving on to community homes and fostering units run by community or voluntary agencies. While it is true that there is now some scepticism about what some of these alternatives really amounted to, and that from the point of view of the Left in Britain their radical potential has yet to be exploited, fragmenting the delivery of punishment in this way at least provides space for private, non-State agencies to organize and oppose, and this is surely something that the Left should continue to exploit. We accept, of course, that such fragmentation is likely further to blur the distinction between the formal and the informal apparatus of penality, and we are all too well aware that this might facilitate an extension of the State's power to punish; but such anxieties should not deter us from intervening critically where we can.

The Massachusetts experiment involved non-profit-making agencies. Even from a non-radical point of view, we are convinced that this is likely to secure the offenders' best interests, and for much the same reasons as we put forward earlier against the idea of prisons for profit. It is therefore with some anxiety that we learn from the National Institute of Justice in the USA that interstate companies have made 'significant gains' in this market (Mullen et al., 1985).

This is not to deny that, just as voluntary bodies can sometimes behave very much like State agencies, so they can also act in much the same way as profit-making corporations. The Eckerd Foundation, which runs the 'Youth Development Centre' in Florida referred to earlier, seems to be a case in point, especially as regards its employment practices (Levinson, 1985). Many of the US corporations in the corrections industry in fact originated as non-profit-making bodies, and adopted a more commercial structure as a response to the harsher fiscal climate of recent years (Taft, 1983). It is a common phenomenon that 'organizational maintenance', a preoccupation with financial survival, comes to take precedence over an organization's original idealistic goals (Kramer, 1981; McMahon and Ericson, 1984: 120–7). To avoid this fate a non-profit project needs clearly defined goals and values — whether radical or otherwise — which can guide its decisions and sustain the commitment of its workers, even if this means following Stan Cohen's (1980) difficult advice that they 'should know when to self-destruct and move (like a guerilla army)' into some other part of the system'.

Conclusion: critical criminology with its hands up

It is easy to see why some radicals believe that the current debate about punishment for profit is diversionary. In the first place, it offers no real solution to the present penal crisis; in the second, and arguably far more important, the extension of non-State agencies represents an unwelcome extension of social control, and whether it is done for profit or not is perhaps largely irrelevant. It should be clear from what we have already written that we are not entirely unsympathetic to this position. However, it does seem to us to be far too pure, and for the following reasons.

To begin with, while we share the view put forward by others in this volume that privatization at the hard end of the system will probably not be extensive, it will none the less have some impact on those who are in prison, and on those who guard them. We have tried, alongside others, to evaluate what this might amount to, and to decide whether or not we think it desirable. We do not believe that it is right to brush aside (or marginalize) these essentially practical concerns, as some criminologists have sought to do, in pursuit of some wider concern about 'widening the net', or whatever.

This brings us to a second concern, namely the more-or-less defeatist view with which some criminologists have reacted to the extension of control at the soft end of the penal system in the context of privatization.[2] Let us reiterate at once that we are all too keenly aware of the sinister potential at work here. However, what we have tried to do in the face of this extension of social control is to articulate how space might (and can) be found to limit its penetration. While we have accepted that many voluntary agencies have been penetrated — some of them willingly — by the State, so blurring the boundary between the formal and the informal apparatus of penality, it is both demonstrably wrong and defeatist to give the impression that this is true of all such agencies; and what is more to the point, the very blurring which some critical criminologists are so worried about can, by virtue of the uncertain status it confers on many projects, actually help radical agencies to survive and stay in business, even if only for a limited period.

We do not want to overstate the radical potential of such opposition. On the other hand, to assume that just about all private involvement at the soft end of the penal system can be looked upon as an uncritical extension of the State's awesome power to punish is surely for critical criminology to come out of its corner with its hands up and, in our view, its eyes shut. Surely one lesson post-structuralism has taught us is that the State is far more leaky than many on the Left had previously assumed, and that even the *official* apparatus of penalty is not monolithic: it is pervasive and spreading, but also porous and susceptible to penetration.[3] On the basis of this analysis, and even if Ericson et al. (1987) are right that the State is bent on the 'publicization' of the private or voluntary sector, critical criminology should still come out fighting; there is still space to be negotiated.

We are well aware that most of the behaviour defined as 'crime' is undesirable, that it must somehow be regulated, but we are equally aware that most of the people selected for processing as 'criminals' are themselves the victims of manifold social injustice. If, as socialists, we are going to intervene in the day-to-day politics of crime control, and there are good reasons why we should, then we need to develop responses which take account of both these points. We are not proposing a strategy of crude duplicity, of perpetrating sabotage under the guise of cooperation, but rather an attempt to move towards a more pluralistic form of penality of the kind hinted at by Garland:

> a progressive penal politics would begin to conceive of a penal object that is neither the 'responsible individual' of the free-market system nor the 'irresponsible client' of the Welfare State. It would try to envisage means whereby punisher and punished are not always the state and the individual, and whereby the penal relationship is not one of the unquestionable ascendancy (either through knowledge or power). (Garland, 1985: 262–3)

Precisely because of their ambiguous relationship with the State, private, non-profit-making projects at the soft end of the penal continuum provide a site where such an ambiguous, ambivalent and tentative politics might begin to take shape.

It is less easy to detect even a glimmer of radical potential in privatization at the hard end of the continuum. However, the *debate* about privatizing prisons, rather than being merely diversionary, may have the merit of forcing the Left, and more specifically the British Labour Party, to confront key issues that they have hitherto neglected: the accountability, or lack of it, of the prison system; the justification, or lack of it, for the prison building programme; and the position of prison officers as workers. On the first point, it is necessary to face the uncomfortable fact that private prisons might, in theory, be *more* accountable than their Home Office counterparts. At least, one presumes, CCA (Great Britain) Ltd would not appoint the members of Boards of Visitors, the Inspectorate of Prisons would not be a company department, and the inspectors would not be seconded company executives. This is not to say that private prisons would in reality be subject to effective scrutiny — the American experience suggests they would not — but rather that, as in other fields, the privatization lobby may unwittingly do the cause of greater democracy a good turn by exposing the State system as the unaccountable bureaucracy it is.

Turning, finally, to the position of prison officers, there are signs that the threat of privatization is helping to bring about a *rapprochement* between the POA on the one hand and the penal lobby and the Labour movement on the other.[4] Though any alliance will no doubt be a cautious one on both sides, the POA's unmistakable shift to the left, its support for reducing the prison population, and its dislike of being used as scapegoat by a union-bashing government, all point to another fissure in the supposed monolith of the State which the Left would be foolish not to exploit.

Notes

1 There is a marked difference on this point between the Home Office (1988a) and Deloitte, Haskins & Sells (1989), with the latter taking the view that all disciplinary powers should remain in public hands. Their proposals for accomplishing this, however, are problematic to say the least.

2 We believe that the otherwise excellent and perceptive analysis by Ericson et al. (1987) exemplifies this defeatism. For further discussion of their views and of the role of the voluntary sector in Britain, see Ryan and Ward, 1989: ch. 5.

3 We take this to be the implication of Foucault's (1977) work on the prison, in the light of his later elaboration of his theory of power and resistance (Foucault, 1984: 82–8). For a critique of more pessimistic interpretations of Foucault's work, see Matthews (1987).

4 For example, at the 1987 Labour Party Conference the POA addressed a fringe meeting organized by the Labour Campaign for Criminal Justice on the theme 'Prisons — Civilized or Privatized?'

References

ACLU (1986) Resolution passed by the Steering Committee of the National Prison Project. Washington DC: American Civil Liberties Union.

ASI (1984) *Omega Report; Justice Policy*. London: ASI Research.

Cohen, Stan (1980) 'Introduction', in Dronfield (1980).

Commonwealth of Massachusetts (1987) *Prisons for Profit*. Boston: Legislative Research Council.

Davis, Martin (1987) 'Criminal Justice Limited', *Criminal Justice*, 5 (2). London: Howard League.

Day, Patricia and Klein, Rudolf (1987) 'The Business of Welfare', *New Society*, 80: 11–14.

Deloitte, Haskins & Sells (1989) *Report on the Practicality of Private Sector Involvement in the Remand System*. London: Deloitte, Haskins & Sells.

Dronfield, Liz (1980) *Outside Chance: The Story of the Newham Alternatives Project*. London: Radical Alternatives to Prison.

Ericson, Richard V., McMahon, Meave W. and Evans, Donald G. (1987) 'Punishing for Profit: Reflections on the Revival of Privatization in Corrections', *Canadian Journal of Criminology*, 29 (4): 355–87.

Fitzgerald, Edward (1985) 'Prison Discipline and the Courts', in Mike Maguire, John Vagg and Rod Morgan (eds), *Accountability and Prisons*. London: Tavistock.

Foucault, Michel (1977) *Discipline and Punish: The Birth of the Prison*. London: Allen Lane.

Foucault, Michel (1984) *The History of Sexuality: An Introduction*. Harmondsworth: Penguin.

Garland, David (1985) *Punishment and Welfare*. Aldershot: Gower.

Hattersley, Roy (1987) *Choose Freedom*. Harmondsworth: Penguin.

Home Office (1988a) *Private Sector Involvement in the Remand System*. London: HMSO.

Home Office (1988b) *Punishment, Custody and the Community*. London: HMSO.

House of Commons (1987a) *Third Report from the Home Affairs Committee: The State and Use of Prisons*, 1986/87 HC 35-I. London: HMSO.

House of Commons (1987b) *Third Report from the Home Affairs Committee: Minutes of Evidence*, 1986/87 HC 35-II. London: HMSO.

House of Commons (1987c) *Fourth Report from the Home Affairs Committee: Contract Provisions of Prisons*, 1986/87 HC 291. London: HMSO.

Howard League (1987) 'Memorandum submitted by the Howard League', in House of Commons (1987b).

Immaregeon, Russ (1987) 'Prison Bailout', *Dollars and Sense*, 128: 19–21.

Jacobs, James B. and Berkowitz, Laura (1983) 'Reflections on the Defeat of New York State's Prison Bond', in James B. Jacobs, *New Perspectives on Prisons and Imprisonment*. Ithaca and London: Cornell University Press.

King, Roy D. and Morgan, Rod (1980) *The Future of the Prison System*. Farnborough: Gower.

Kramer, R. M. (1981) *Voluntary Agencies in the Welfare State*. Berkeley: University of California Press.

Levinson, R. B. (1985) *Private Operation of a Correctional Institution*. Washington, DC: National Institute of Corrections.

McConville, Sean (1981) *A History of English Prison Administration*, vol. I. London: Routledge & Kegan Paul.

McConville, Sean and Hall Williams, Eryl (1985) *Crime and Punishment: A Radical Rethink*. London: Tawney Society.

McMahon, Maeve W. and Ericson, Richard V. (1984) *Policing Reform: A Study of the Reform Process and Police Institution in Toronto*. Toronto: Centre of Criminology.

Matthews, Roger (1987) 'Decarceration and Social Control: Fantasies and Realities', in J. Lowman, R. J. Menzies and T. S. Palys (eds), *Transcarceration: Essays in the Sociology of Social Control*. Aldershot: Gower.

Mullen, J. et al. (1985) *The Privatization of Corrections*. Washington DC: National Institute of Justice.

NACRO (1988) *News Release*, 28 November. London: NACRO.

NAPO (1985) *Criminal Justice: an Alternative Strategy*. London: National Association of Probation Officers.

National Institute of Justice (1985) *The Privatization of Corrections*. Washington DC: National Institute of Justice.

Pennsylvania General Assembly (1985) *Report on a Study of Issues Related to the Potential Operation of Private Prisons in Pennsylvania*. Harrisburg: Legislative Budget and Finance Committee.

POA (1987) 'Memorandum Submitted by the Prison Officers Association', in House of Commons (1987b).

President's Commission of Privatizaton (1988) *Privatization: Toward More Effective Government*. Washington DC: US Government.

Reiner, Robert (1985) *The Politics of the Police*. Brighton: Wheatsheaf.

Robbins, Ira (1988) *The Legal Dimensions of Private Incarceration*. Washington DC: American Bar Association.

Rose, Gordon (1967) *Schools for Young Offenders*. London: Tavistock.

Rutherford, Andrew (1986) *Prisons and the Process of Justice*. Oxford University Press.

Ryan, Mick (1978) *The Acceptable Pressure Group: A Case Study of the Howad League and Radical Alternatives to Prison*. Farnborough: Saxon House.

Ryan, Mick and Ward, Tony (1986) 'Law and Order: Left Realism against the Rest', *Abolitionist*, 22: 29–33. London: RAP.

Ryan, Mick and Ward, Tony (1989) *Privatization and the Penal System: The American Experience and the Debate in Britain*. Milton Keynes: Open University Press.

Shaw, Stephen (1985) 'Private Prisons: Profit Behind Bars', *SOVA News* (Spring). London: Society of Voluntary Associates.

Taft, Philip B. (1983) 'Survival of the Fittest', *Corrections Magazine* (Feb.): 36–43.

Thomas, J. E. (1987) 'Dangers for Prisoners when the State Stops Guarding the Guards', *Independent*, 28 July.

Tolchin, Martin (1985) 'Experts Foresee Adverse Effects from Private Control of Prisons', *New York Times*, 17 September.

Treverton-Jones, G. D. (1989) *Imprisonment: The Legal Status and Rights of Prisoners*. London: Sweet & Maxwell.

Windlesham, Lord (1987) 'Inappropriate Prisoners', *Times*, 7 July.

Young, Peter (1987) *The Prison Cell*. London: ASI Research.

4 RECONSTRUCTING POLICING

The impact that the private sector has had upon policing has been appropriately described as something of a 'quiet revolution' (Stenning and Shearing, 1980). The relatively slight attention that has been paid to this issue is surprising since its development raises some fundamental questions both about the effects of the modern division of labour between 'public' and 'private' policing in contemporary society, and about the processes of social control and the state in general (Spitzer and Scull, 1977; South, 1984).

The shift towards private policing has a number of significant effects. It changes both the style and object of policing. The massive growth of private policing, which now outnumbers public policing in Britain, America and Canada, has deeply affected the nature of crime control methods, the styles of policing and the relations between the police and the public.

The predominance of private policing has increased the emphasis upon proactive rather than reactive forms of intervention; this means that the general aim is increasingly to anticipate and deflect crime rather than attempt to clear it up after the event. It also encourages a shift of focus away from prosecution towards a preoccupation with recovering stolen property. The responsibilities of private security police are to their immediate employers rather than the general public, and accountability is therefore direct and particularistic.

The relation between the private and public police is necessarily ambiguous. On the one hand private police can serve to extend and reinforce the activities of the public police while on the other hand their presence can be seen as a competitive force straining the legitimacy of the public police. The tensions are endemic, and as private policing agencies take on more and more functions there are renewed calls for stricter control over the operations of private companies (South, 1988).

The call for more adequate regulation of the activities of the private security sector needs to be taken seriously — not least because of the way that policing in society is changing and the role that private arrangements are playing in such a change. Public confidence in the police is volatile and there is evidence that, in the UK at least, it has recently suffered a decline. At the same time, advocates of privatization welcome the claims made for the cost-effectiveness and innovative potential of private security services. We clearly need, therefore, to examine more closely the relationship between private security and the public police. Nigel South's chapter begins to do this by drawing upon both available literature and original research to distinguish four 'models' that throw light upon different aspects of the complex relationship between these two bodies and how this relationship may develop in the future. These models represent various possible 'views' on this relationship and are described as based upon elements of 'compromise', 'complementarity', 'competition' and 'circumvention'. According to one's perspective the models will have differing degrees of validity, but they offer an important starting point for assessment of the impact of private security on policing and related activities.

The chapter concludes that there is clearly now a significant amount of powerful opinion and precedents set to encourage the further privatization of elements of the criminal justice system. Lest the seriousness of such developments should be under-emphasized and the negative consequences go unexplored, democratic societies need to pay more attention to the changing interface between private security and the public police and to put in place more effective mechanisms for ensuring the accountability and regulation of both.

Reconstructing Policing: Differentiation and Contradiction in Post-War Private and Public Policing

Nigel South

In this chapter I am principally concerned with a discussion of developments in private security and public policing in the post-war period, up to the early 1980s. At some points I shall clearly be writing specifically about the UK, at other times about the USA and Canada, but in drawing out what I see as some prevailing or developing trends and themes I will be quite consciously generalizing about aspects of the changing contemporary division of policing labour and consequent implications for the 'reconstruction' of policing and the administration of public and private justice.

I shall first offer a summarizing outline of the post-war state of public policing interpreted as a context for the take-off of growth of the private security sector (see South, 1984), especially with regard to crime prevention. The issue of crime prevention is taken further in a brief discussion of the different parties, public and private, who, in recent decades, have come to engage in new forums concerned about losses resulting from crime — commerce, insurance, private security, the police and others. I then present an overview of the relations which have been developed between private security and public policing. This section, which forms the core of the chapter, draws out four models for the interpretation of these complex relations: *compromise*; *complement*; *competition*; and *circumvention*. The chapter elucidates these four 'partial truth' perspectives as a means of illuminating the contradictions and imbalances in the public police/private security sector relationship. I also seek to put on the agenda the potential for the corruption of justice (see South, 1983) and how different priorities for public and private 'policing' can simultaneously shift, whilst also expanding, the selection and 'processing' of formally and informally recognized 'offenders'.[1] The chapter concludes with a brief discussion of possible future trends and proposals that may herald the further privatization of some policing, crime prevention and other criminal justice services.

Changes in post-war policing in Britain; policy, establishment and practice and the growth of the private security sector

The state of the police in the post-war years of the 1940s and 1950s[2] provide some of the context in which private security found its preconditions for serious take-off. The diverse nature and sources of problems facing the police in these years reflected social and economic change, not least increased geographic mobility. 'Localized' crime might still be seen as either a familiar or threatening dimension of 'community' life, and the expectations of local people and the police force were that such matters could and should be dealt with by local 'beat' officers (see Scraton, 1982: 46). But the development of what has been called 'project crime' (see McIntosh, 1971, 1975) meant that the professional criminals involved might be dispersed geographically, did not cling to easily penetrated or identifiable networks, were organized in their communications and in the disposal of their gains, and, importantly, were mobile across local and even national boundaries. Perhaps few achieved such comprehensive organization and sophistication, but the elements of the pattern meant that the police had to respond in some way, developing inter-force cooperation, mobility, new strategies for information-gathering and surveillance, while at the same time coping with 'new' social problems related to housing redevelopment, post-war social dislocation, the rise in traffic-related offences and the relative decline in police staffing (Scraton, 1982: 46). A police service that was seen by the sympathetic as suffering from poor pay and poor working conditions, with a declining establishment of officers, was also seen by both critics and senior police spokespersons as 'losing the war against crime; ... the constant reminder, both in the media and in the statistics, that crime was "out of control", underpinned [an] atmosphere of crisis' (Scraton, 1982: 46).

Private security emerged[3] out of this 'atmosphere of crisis' making strong claims to be able to help with the control of crime through its emphasis on and orientation to *prevention*. Whilst still a small-scale commercial development, even in the late 1950s in Britain (though not in North America — and with a boom around the corner in the 1960s), there is still some irony in their acceptance on these terms. As Shearing et al. point out:

> The modern public police were established in the early 19th C. in England in large measure because there was widespread dissatisfaction with the post-crime, apprehension-oriented approach of the private security initiatives in force at the time (Radzinowicz, 1956b). Yet today, it is this very complaint that is frequently laid at the feet of the public police ... and it is as a preventive before-the-fact rather than after-the-fact force that private

security defines itself and contrasts itself to the public police. It is thus ironically, under the very banner on which the public police once marched that contract security is now selling itself as an alternative to the public police. (1980: 184)

This alternative now offers a wide range of services, having considerably and consistently expanded throughout Western industrial societies in the post-war period. Uniformed guards, patrol and armoured vans, alarm systems and surveillance technology proliferate. Less visible dimensions of the private security sector embrace the activities of private investigation and information collection services, whilst other agencies market their expertise in providing bodyguards, anti-terrorist consultants and mercenaries (South, 1988). The selling of such services, perhaps most politically 'acceptable' at the level of basic functions ancillary to those of the public police, is attractive to customers for a variety of reasons and has gone almost wholly unopposed by successive UK governments. In the 1980s the idea of the private provision of some (but not all) policing and security services has appealed to some New Right commentators concerned with criminal justice on the basis that such private services provide a yardstick by which to measure the efficiency of public police delivery of services, they 'ensure that new methods are explored' and they can be cheap (see Adam Smith Institute, 1984: 23).

Thus the reasons for any success enjoyed by the private security sector in laying claim to the preventive approach are not *simply* the result of any real (or merely perceived) failure or inadequacy of the public police. There are other factors that must be examined in attempting to explain the kind of commensalism that has developed between private security and the public police. One suggestive point of view on the rescuscitation of old-style private initiatives alongside the 'new police' is offered by McClintock:

> The return in recent years to forms of private initiative can be dismissed as a retrograde step only on the basis of the ideal of policing that existed at the beginning of this century, or in terms of policital philosophy. The present system of crime prevention and law enforcement based partly on civil policing and partly on private security firms may be seen as the result of our ideology of a mixed economy, rather than of any inherent weakness in civil policing in our advanced industrial society. The criminologist is interested in the distribution of responsibilities between the civil police and private security firms and the extent to which their sharing works out successfully in practice through physical protection of property, with financial protection afforded through state compensation or private insurance. Little is known about the way these systems interlock. (1976: 22)

Despite the fact that over ten years after McClintock's statement there is still little known about such interlocking relationships, successive governments have seemed remarkably casual about their development. This is not to suggest that sinister conspiracies have been allowed to flourish, merely that open access to information has not been encouraged either.

It is sometimes suggested that if the private security business had not existed then the police would have had to invent it, for they are 'constitutionally' proscribed from performing wide-ranging commercial crime prevention services on private property (although, of course, the powers under which they can gain access to private property for a variety of reasons are by no means limited and have undergone some extension in recent years.[4] Any such commercial provision would in any case be militated against by other pressures stemming from personnel shortages and public expenditure limitations. In the post-war period, recognition of such problems has actually sought a solution in narrowing the functions and responsibilities of the police in certain directions and concentrating them in others — for example, their role in the maintenance of public order. First evident in the Oaksey Report of 1949 and made more explicit in the recommendations of the 1962 Royal Commission, public policy was redirected, remoulding the parameters of police responsibility. In what may be construed as a 'deal' offered by the Commission, the police received additional funding in return for shedding certain duties (such as cash-transit escorts), generally tightening up fragmented and overstretched resources and giving priority to actual law-enforcement duties. New opportunities in the field of policing for hire were readily perceived by many (Mart, 1975).[5] No new controls were instituted (or even on the agenda), concerning those who might step in to fill vacant positions in the fight against crime. It is clear by this point, the early 1960s, that whatever certain individual police officers or politicians, let alone the public, might think, government policy-makers and their advisers had conceded, recognized and to some degree begun to welcome, the private security sector as a part of the country's overall crime prevention resources.

At this level, this acceptance is best contextualized within the slow embracing of the crime prevention concept in post-war British policing practice and training.[6] Again related to alarm about a new rise in crime, crime prevention exhibitions and campaigns were seen as a way of changing public and commercial attitudes to what they could do for themselves (cf. Bennett and Wright, 1984: 20). The first exhibition was held in Sussex in 1943, but it was not until 1950 that the first national campaign was launched, followed in 1956 by the Cornish Report which set out the basis for crime prevention development. In 1963 the Home Office Crime Prevention Unit at Stafford was opened in order to provide for training of officers and the development of new techniques. Specialized crime prevention officers were appointed in new crime prevention departments within each local force (ibid.; Draper, 1978: 155; Kerr, 1979a: 123).

Naturally, a variety of interested parties, including the major private security companies and the insurance industry, sought more than merely informal and occasional liaison over such developments and in 1967 formal channels of cooperation and communication aiming to 'enable representatives of commerce and industry to discuss problems of crime prevention and to make recommendations' (Dring, 1976: 66) were institutionalized with the setting up of the Standing Committee on Crime Prevention by the Home Secretary. From the start, membership of the Committee included representatives of the British Security Industry Association (the trade association for the major and medium-scale private security companies). The other bodies represented were the Association of Chief Police Officers, the Metropolitan Police, the Scottish police, the Confederation of British Industry, the National Chamber of Trade, the British Insurance Association, Lloyds, the Association of British Chambers of Commerce, and the Trades Union Congress. The Committee has since been replaced by the Standing Conference of Crime Prevention which has considerably broadened its representative membership and adopted an annual 'Working Group' programme, producing reports on a variety of relevant subjects.

The 'Pressure on police resources allows private security to prosper' arguments

At this point, the arguments concerning the pressures on the strength of the police 'establishment' (staffing levels, recruitment and loss) should be noted.

Throughout the 1960s and 1970s the mainstream private security companies in Britain expanded rapidly, and smaller companies also joined the market in increasingly competitive style (see MATSA, 1983). At the same time, the public police service was changing significantly in terms of its organization, priorities and the selection and direction of its resources. Given such developments, representatives of private security interests, of the commercial and industrial worlds and of the police themselves began to put forward more clearly the argument that there was an acceptable need for recourse to basic private security services by the 'public' because the police were under pressure. The range of explanatory motifs adopted is familiar: the growth of social problems related to rising crime, youthful unrest, racial tension, trade union militancy and so on. The key underlying argument, however, was that the police were understaffed and under-resourced and, hence, having taken on board a host of other priorities, could no longer offer the same high profile in the provision of basic patrol and crime prevention services.

If one accepts this redirection of policing priorities and resources, then, clearly, this argument is not without foundation — even discounting the filling of authorized establishment levels in most forces since the 1979 Conservative government. What is interesting and disturbing about it is not that it is absolutely wrong — in its partial view of the commensalism that has developed between the police and private security it is correct, at least as far as it goes. But the worrying matter is that it reflects such an apparently untroubled collusive, or at least agreed, view of the basis on which it is necessary to accede to fundamental changes in the contemporary organization of policing functions and responsibilities in society — what Stenning and Shearing (1980) have called a 'quiet revolution in policing'.

In 1964 the police establishment in England and Wales numbered 80 390. In 1974 it was 102 086. In other words, in the decade of what was the period of most rapid initial growth of the private security sector (as opposed to the late 1970s and early 1980s relative consolidation and rapid increase of profits (Raw, 1983)) the public police establishment actually saw a significantly large increase in recruitment. In 1974 the recruitment figure of 7545 was higher than for any year since 1957. Against this, of course, must be set the high wastage figures which offset recruitment gains. In various years the former have considerably undermined the latter. However, net recruitment figures rarely seem to have justified the dismay and demands for more and more money and resources with which politicians and senior police officers frequently greet them.

Whatever interpretation of the figures one might wish to adopt, by the late 1960s and early 1970s, the view was widely accepted in commercial and industrial circles, as well as by many in the police and Government, that the police were understaffed and under pressure and, furthermore, that the use of private security services did not reflect simply selfish concern for personal or asset protection, but rather amounted to good citizenship in taking pressure off the hard-pressed police. Certainly, whereas in the past many Chief Constables and other senior police officers had been suspicious of private security, and at times openly antagonistic, by the early 1970s this reaction was definitely muted in at least some quarters (see Bowden, 1978: 248).

What did continue to worry many senior officers at this time was that, while pressures on their limited resources might indeed result in prioritization in their work which allowed space for private security to prosper, at the same time private security remained parasitic upon the state in so far as it relied (and still relies) upon the police to provide a 'comprehensive back-up service' (to use the private security companies' description of their own services). Both the conservatism and the commercial reasoning of the private security business meant that they were as worried as the police planners about less than full establishment recruitment levels, however much they owed to stepping into the shoes of an absent police presence.[7]

In a slightly different version of the resources argument, and in some disagreement with the attitudes of senior police officers, police 'on the ground', as represented by the Police Federation, have been consistently worried by the growth and functions of the private security sector. Some of the ire which the Police Federation felt about the apparent assumption of police powers by private security and even the appropriation of the police image through the wearing of similarly styled uniforms, emerged around the revelation in 1961 that a number (small but still unclear) of private security personnel had been authorized by the Metropolitan Police Commissioner to carry firearms. Kerr outlines the Federation response:

> In 1961, in answer to a Parliamentary question, it was revealed that the Metropolitan Commissioner had 'issued firearm certificates to thirty-three persons permitting them to carry firearms belonging to their employers when escorting consignments of bullion or banknotes. Certificates have been issued to responsible persons in four firms enabling them to hold firearms and ammunition for these purposes.'
>
> Shortly afterwards the Police Federation announced that it intended to ask the Home Secretary to end the carrying of firearms by bank guards and other persons similarly employed on security duties. The Federation, it said, 'is anxious to stop any measures which may provoke criminals to carry firearms and thereby put at risk the lives of innocent members of the public and members of the police forces. The police are not and do not wish to be armed.'
>
> The Federation went further. 'The Federation is of the view that under no circumstances should security guards wear uniform hardly distinguishable from those worn by the regular police, or security firms be permitted to operate *unless the local Chief Officer of Police or some other appropriate authority is satisfied with the credentials of the directors or proprietors and with their methods of operation.'* (Kerr, 1979b: 123; emphasis in original)

Officially, the practice of allowing security guards to carry firearms ended in 1966 (although unconfirmed reports of companies retaining firearms have persisted over the years and it certainly seems unlikely that those agencies that claim a specialist expertise in bodyguard and anti-terrorist protection are successfully selling their expensive services without being able to demonstrate to clients that they have access to firearms, legitimately or not). Certainly nothing happened between the early 1960s and the end of the decade to change the general view of the Police Federation on this issue. In 1970 the Chair of the Federation, Inspector Reg Gale, was reported as saying:

> It should not be necessary for any company to do some of the things they are doing now; some of the duties are a police function. I'm not suggesting we want to do a nightwatchman's job, wandering around testing door locks. I'm not suggesting that we want to do the pay side that some of the larger firms do. But I have felt that the guarding of large sums of money or bullion is a police job and we can undertake it. (Gale, 1970)

However, given the conditions which stimulated the growth of private security services — not least the perceived limitations on police resources — it would not have been unreasonable to query in 1970, as now, whether the police actually *could* have taken on these expanding demands. Others in the force, especially in urban areas, were undoubtedly sceptical (see Draper, 1978: 161).

I shall turn next to a more detailed focus on relations between the police and private security. But first, having sketched the modification of views on private security held by senior police staff and noted the consistency in the 1960s to early 1970s of the more negative perspective of the lower ranks, we should briefly note the profile generally adopted by private security in its relations with the police as these became more cordial throughout the 1970s and into the 1980s. This is succinctly summarized by Shearing and Stenning, and it is interesting that although they are writing principally with reference to Canada, their comments are accurately applicable to private security in Britain.

> The view most frequently cited in the trade literature, and the one which appears to receive the widest support from within the private security community, is that both private security and the public police are committed to similar general objectives and that private security makes its contribution to these objectives by complementing the public police. Given that a passive non-threatening face is one which private security executives often assume to avoid provoking a negative response from the public police, it is not surprising that advocates of this view tend to minimize the extent to which the interests and activities of private security and the public police conflict. (1981: 219)

It should, however, be noted that in the context of the late 1980s, with the privatization of public services being actively pursued by the present government, representatives of the police and other services (such as probation) have registered deeper misgivings about the expansion and lack of control over the private security sector (ACPO, 1988; South, 1989).

Relations between private security and the police in practice and law: compromise, complement, competition and circumvention

Compromise

Perhaps one real test of the true extent of cooperative compromise between the police and private security is the extent to which mutual trust extends to 'mutual consumption of each others services' (Shearing and Stenning, 1981: 224). For Shearing and Stenning there seems to be ample evidence in Canada of private security utilizing police services and also of the public police using private security specialists for various services. This is a pragmatic recognition of a changing division of policing labour (South, 1984) wherein different resources are directed in different directions. Yet the implications are not simply that the market and the public sector are developing new conduits of service delivery, but also that the style and accountability of 'policing' are changing. For example, while there may be an expectation and in many cases a legal requirement that the police should be called in to deal with a discovered offence, *in practice* the discretionary powers and facilities of private security can blur this understanding and hence some 'offenders' never come to the attention of the police or formal criminal justice system.

None the less, it is the case that private security do need and do want to have recourse to public law enforcement. The most obvious area where this is a matter of operational necessity for them is in responding to alarm calls. In the opposite direction, it has been the case in the USA and Canada for many years that, as Shearing and Stenning observe,

> Public police ... also rely to some extent on private security for some services and will sometimes seek the cooperation of private security personnel in complex or technically difficult investigations (e.g. commercial fraud cases or cases involving highly technical equipment such as computers, polygraphs, etc.). (1981: 225)

A hint of this apparently very North American type of activity occurring in the UK is given in a front page story carried by the *Sunday Times* on 10 February 1980, reporting Army officers in Northern Ireland buying their own personal telephone tapping equipment:

> A Sunday Times investigation shows that the officers are among a rapidly expanding number of clients using private security firms to tap telephones.

It must be said, however, that evidence of British police employment of private security at this level is either sketchily journalistic or anecdotal. None the less, the mutual cross-over of advice, research and development expertise, and of personnel (from the police to private security), keeps the issue of police utilization of private security services high on the agenda of trends to watch for.

Compromise by no means necessarily implies equality, and in the relationship between private security and the police (viewed from this perspective), power undoubtedly lies with the latter. In general, however, this power has not been directed negatively towards or against private security. Rather it has, with logical regard for the benefits of the division of policing labour, been directed towards insistence on more efficient cooperation as part of any compromise about recognition and responsibility. The best illustrative case is that of the effectiveness of burglar alarm installation, monitoring and response. Previous security practice — and theory — has been to sell alarms as much on the basis of their noise attracting immediate response (from intruders as well as police or private security and neighbours or passers-by) as on their visible siting being a deterrent (more sophisticated sales strategies argue that because burglars may disable visible alarm systems there should also be hidden back-up systems). The real problem, however, is that there are so many false alarms. As far as the police are concerned, the alarm side of private security may be valuable but it has suffered (and still suffers) from a very bad case of 'the technology that cried wolf too often'. The response of the police to this issue is of interest because it reflects the spirit of willingness to compromise with private security, in so far as demands for corrective action have not been directed simply and solely at private security companies but also at commercial users of alarm systems in a way that brings private security directly and intrinsically into the operational police response to crime.

Senior police officers and planners are conscious of the demands made by insurers for alarm and protection systems as deterrent and discovery mechanisms, based on the assumption that even if intruders are not put off by the visibility of alarms they may at least be sufficiently disconcerted by them actually going off to leave the premises before they have done whatever they were going to do. However, this working assumption of the past few decades can no longer realistically fit with policing priorities. Time-delays between alarms activating calls to the police and the actual bell or siren being activated to warn intruders has been one suggested development (Burden, 1980: 118). Alternatively, and increasingly, commercial alarm monitoring centres are becoming the 'sifting and sieving' system for deciding the genuine character of alarm alerts, calling in the police on a direct line to police operations rooms *only* where the alarm seems likely to be genuine (ibid.: 120–1). The criteria on which such judgements might be made are presumably open to negotiation in policy and practice between the public and private sectors, but such a development also carries two other implications. First, that private security plays an even larger role in the changing direction of public and private policing resources and the selection of offence categories which merit the disposal of public policing resoures. Second, such developments indicate the *strategic* acceptance of private security into the division of policing labour *by* the public police services, albeit one with a very clear hierarchy in which the police utilization of private security as a sifting mechanism for alarm calls is double-edged, placing the latter in a service role which they accept anyway, yet also placing upon them traditional responsibilities of the public police to respond to reports of crime.

These developments should not, however, be allowed to suggest that private security has been wholly and unequivocally accepted by the police, even at these 'helpful' levels of alarm checking and response. There remains a great deal of ambivalence about the relationship (see Draper, 1978: 166). In particular, the issue of 'effective' vetting of private security personnel continues to be disputatious (ACPO, 1988). The large, medium, and some small, security organizations have repeatedly claimed for many years that their employee checking and vetting procedures are highly effective and thorough. Many have hinted, and some said on record, that they have had access to Criminal Records Office information in carrying out their checks. This is of course encouraging to their clients but causes some considerable concern among unimpressed police officers who point out that such access would be not only improper but illegal (Draper, 1978: 166). Representative of the majority police view may be the position noted by Shearing and Stenning (1981: 221) of a British Detective Inspector commenting on private security involvement in 'investigative work'. According to this officer, such a practice was 'fraught with danger', concluding that 'private security should be restricted to the defensive and passive stance which their preventive role implied' (ibid.; cf. French, 1979: 29).

On the other hand, there are *some* suggestions in the UK, and certainly elsewhere, that the services of the private security sector have been used by the public police for more than just the utility offered by their preventative and monitoring security services. Indeed, the quasi-formal use of the private security sector by the public police in fairly sensitive roles (whether as 'passive' sources of information or in 'active' supplementary investigative roles) should not be entirely surprising. In their research in Canada, Shearing et al. came across hints of this but also found the matter difficult to fully establish and document. Thus they observe:

Before we leave our consideration of private security clients, one final observation should be made. Three of the agency executives interviewed (two dual agency and one private investigation agency) reported that the public police were among their most important clients. This finding raises an aspect of the relationship between the public police and private security that has been neglected in the literature, namely the public police as clients of private security. Unfortunately our findings did not provide information on the nature of the services provided to the public police, other than the implicit suggestion that they are of an 'investigative' nature (Shearing et al., 1980: 102)

Complement

Close to the idea of a compromise emerging in practice between private security and the police but identifiable as a different viewpoint, is the notion of complementarity. In this vision the relationship is not so much one of interpenetration, but rather one in which both police and private security go about their business side by side. Each is aware of its boundaries and limitations and knows what it is doing within them. According to this kind of view, the trade-offs found in the compromise relationship are rendered unnecessary by some honourable recognition of mutual complementarity. As with the 'ways of seeing' the relationship which I call competition and circumvention, these are not *simply* viewpoints: they do, of course, also reflect partial realities within the wider anomalous relationship between the private security sector, other private interventions in the criminal justice and other 'social' services, and the State.

Central to the complementarity view is the contention that there is a need for private security because of (a) limitations on police powers with regard to routine access to private property, and (b) the way that the police have not been able to keep pace with certain consequences of long-term economic change. Hence while the *compromise* account sees private security as commercially developing as they negotiate entry into certain 'policing' activities, the complement view sees their existence and resurgence (see South, 1987) as almost historically and economically inevitable. As one senior British police officer has pointed out,

> the legislation created to deal with nuisances such as obstruction, obscene language, noisy conduct and the like, to be found, for example, in the Highway Acts, the Town Police Clauses Acts and the local bye-laws, does not extend to 'private' places, and should a patrolling police officer come upon this sort of conduct in the 'private' areas of high density developments or enclosed shopping centres for example, there is generally nothing he or she can do about it. In consequence, even if we had the necessary manpower, which generally we do not, we do not normally deploy patrolling officers in 'private' areas where they can only operate as 'scarecrows'. (Knights, 1979: 2)

Police powers, operational practice and the expectations of the occupational culture have probably changed considerably since Knights was writing at the turn of the decade, although even then he acknowledged that 'times have changed' and that the expansion of housing estates, shopping complexes and so on had led 'most police forces to accept that they have a responsibility for patrolling some parts' of these areas. Nevertheless, he added, the police are quite willing, if not eager, to look to the owners of private property 'to seek their own salvation' (1979: 3).

Other accounts from within the police service have also emphasized broad economic and historical factors in explaining the postwar growth of private security. For example, John Alderson, former Chief Constable of Devon and Cornwall, has suggested two main reasons for such growth:

> '[First] the massive expansion of industry generally and consumer goods stored and available and bullion on the move vulnerable to theft. I think the second reason is the police have not been able to keep pace with this massive growth. I think without private security at all we would have much more crime than we do at the moment. I would imagine myself, that although private security has always, in our history, been a very important part of prevention of crime, it's probably more important today than ever it has been before.'
> *Interviewer:* 'So the private security firms are filling a vacuum left by the proper police?'
> *Alderson:* 'Not so much a vacuum — but this massive growth, you could argue that it's created a vacuum. The police have grown too you see. The police force has doubled in size over the last twenty years — in spite of this, the normal police could never keep pace with the guarding and escorting of goods, warehouses, bullion and the like.'

Some commentators, both independently and from within the police service, have argued that if there is a commercial market for the provision of policing services then the police should be in, raising revenue and standards of service. In the context of a broader argument for the privatization of a variety of public services, Seldon (1977: 108) has put forward the case that the police 'could render a wider range of services than is commonly supposed' and envisions them alongside private security in a competitive market. However, the complementarity view is sceptical of such a position, suggesting that it does not realistically take into account the complexity of the relationship between organizational size, clients and services (cf. Carter, 1974; Smith, 1979). To be fully competitive, this argument runs, a security organisation should be able to cater for the 'total coverage' needs of national and international companies. For the police to attempt to organize such a service would, according to Peter Smith of Securicor, 'raise questions of administrative complication' over arranging reciprocal trading agreements between local police forces and also the 'possible difficulty of rivalries between local forces' (Smith, 1979: 28). Doubt is also cast upon the ability of the police forces to market themselves commercially as a service to be privately paid for, especially given their traditional status as publicly funded, and the established need for sales representation to convert reluctant managements to a new state of security consciousness. Further, expending such effort and then employing police officers with a higher standard of training, education and pay than commercial security staff would, it is argued, be inefficient, uneconomic and, if cheaper private security firms were still in operation, generally uncompetitive. Thus private security is seen as already geared to the market-place in a way which it would be difficult and inappropriate for the police to emulate. The latter have their own areas of work and responsibilities to the general public and, according to this line of argument, commercial security would not and does not seek to encroach upon or challenge these. Complementarity is a happy basis upon which to continue and to those who subscribe to it (in part or whole) it is a view with the comforting virtue of being seen as in line with the movements of the times.

A neglected aspect of the complementary relationship emerges out of the law relating to civil claims for damages, and interestingly recalls some of the spirit of criticisms of the eighteenth-century use of the militia to provide protection for mercantile interests in, for example, local disputes. Although 'traditional' public confidence in the police must have been seriously damaged over the past decade or so by cases of corruption, deaths of those held in custody (see Scraton and Chadwyck, 1987), and the tactics employed in policing local communities and in industrial disputes, none the less the complementarity view commentators are probably right to observe that were the police also to be carrying out private security-type roles then the likelihood of their being held liable to civil claims for damages would rise considerably (see Smith, 1979).[8] Whatever position might be taken on the desirability of such a development, the implication that it could profoundly reshape police–public relationships — and not necessarily for the better — is unavoidable. The commercial space that private security occupies in the modern division of policing labour (see South, 1984) is economically and politically functional to the state and to its organization of civil policing provision is a very real sense — and not simply in a crudely theoretical way.

Complementarity of approach and function also follows from the changes of direction that the police have undergone since originally conceived as a preventive force. According to their General Instructions of 1829, their success was to be gauged by the 'absence of crime' and not by the 'detection and punishment of the offender after he has succeeded in committing the crime' (Radzinowicz, 1968: 163; Shearing and Stenning, 1981, 216). Despite attempts to 'get back to the community' through, for example, beat patrols and neighbourhood watch schemes, the police are undoubtedly still tied to a reactive mode of policing 'which measures effectiveness primarily in terms of detection and punishment' (Shearing and Stenning, 1981: 216; Manning, 1980: 226). *In contrast*, as Shearing and Stenning point out, private security companies that specialize in guard, patrol, alarm and surveillance services 'are not only committed to prevention but have selected foot patrol as their practical means of surveillance' (1981: 217). The attraction of such 'selection' might lie in large part in the fact that it is cheap, but transport mobility, radio communication and electronic surveillance supplement the basic routine patrols.

The real significance of this private organization of prevention and surveillance, however, lies in the question of whom is defined as the 'legitimate subjects of security interest' (ibid.). Shearing and Stenning contend that 'Peel's dream' of a preventive police force is slowly developing as the shape of modern policing changes. But public policing is contributing less to the realization of this goal than private security (ibid.). Now, whilst analytically this proposition contains some degree of truth, it is also a slightly romantic vision of the fulfilment of 'Peel's dream'. More dangerously it detracts from the significance of the other observations made by these authors in their discussion of private security's extension of surveillance beyond 'traditional "problem populations"' (ibid.). Private security is indeed preventive of crime — but of that criminal activity which is directed at their *employers* rather than the general public which Peel's police were supposed to serve.

In an earlier study (1980), Shearing et al. emphasize the corollary of this dichotomization of 'who is served' by reference to the relevance of the criminal law to private security and public police:

> because private security persons seldom operate explicitly within a legal context, the criminal law, in contrast to civil law, is much less relevant to private security than it is to the public police who are much more likely to invoke the criminal law as a method of order maintenance. (1980: 250)

For these authors this point is also fundamentally related to the tendency for private security to be primarily concerned with prevention as opposed to public police preoccupation with detection. Indeed, they suggest, for private security 'detection is often regarded as no more than a means of identifying weaknesses in existing loss prevention strategies' (ibid.). These points suggest one highly significant characteristic of private security's relationships to law, but also raise a slight difficulty with the line of argument developed by

Shearing and Stenning in subsequent comments on the demarcation between private and public agencies' involvement in detection and investigative work. To take private security's relationship to law, what should be emphasized is its operation in the realm of private justice; its use of, and use as, a mechanism for ensuring discretion. The relevance of civil law as opposed to criminal law allows a greater degree of and control over the discretionary potential of law and prosecution. With regard to the involvement of private security in investigative work, Shearing and Stenning have subsequently clearly acknowledged that this is not a clear-cut matter but have astutely argued that the issue is pivotal to the viability of the 'complementarity' view.

Whilst stronger in North America and in some other parts of Europe than in the UK, conflict has certainly emerged around the involvement of private security in investigative undertakings. Such conflict seriously strains the credibility of the complementarity argument. For Shearing and Stenning (1981: 221–2), the 'tenacious' adherence of private security executives to such a view — despite their evident awareness of their industry's encroachment into what is supposedly the territory of the public police — suggests that 'its utility arises from the political function it serves in avoiding police hostility and police resistance to the growth of private security and not from its theoretical value'. Other commentators have sought to 'accommodate' such overlap between public police and private security by suggesting that the latter is merely 'supplementing' the former (Kakalik and Wildhorn, 1971: 18). However, as Shearing and Stenning comment, 'this analysis identifies private security forces as playing a subsidiary role and is, like the associated notion of complementarity, politically useful from the point of view of both these security forces' (1981: 222). It is not difficult to discern some apparent validity in the complementarity viewpoint, but Shearing and Stenning are of course quite correct in demystifying its explanatory attractions and pointing out that it serves a 'political function'. However, it is not merely useful to the private security sector or police, but also to the State — not simply in explaining its acceptance of private security, but also its direct employment of it.

In the UK the utility of invoking a version of the complementarity view can be illustrated by reference to the controversy that has bubbled over the past two decades about the employment of private security to 'guard and escort immigrants' (*Observer*, 27 March 1983) at the major London airports of Heathrow and Gatwick. Introduced in 1971, the services of Securicor in providing guards for 'suspected illegal immigrants' has been a recurrent issue of civil rights debate — and little governmental response. (The passing of the contract in 1988 to Group Four was not accompanied by any statement on the matter.) The issue surfaced again in 1983 when the Commission for Racial Equality began to examine it as part of a wider investigation into immigration procedures. At this time (March 1983), around 50 guards were employed at a cost estimated by the Home Office at £250000 per year (*Observer*, ibid.). The responses of the Home Office to criticisms of this practice present a complementarity view which stresses that private security is not part of the State's own resources — yet they are trusted because the State employs them for other tasks and further, their employment in this particular task is justifiable, indeed desirable, precisely because they are not State employees and hence are not seen as 'oppressive' as the use of the police might be viewed in such circumstances. As the *Observer* report notes,

> Ironically, the Home Office says that it is precisely because Securicor is also used by the Government to escort cash and valuables that no special legislation or arrangements are needed to enable the firm to escort people . . .
> Securicor was brought in because the Home Office considered that the use of the police to control people who were not criminals would be to oppressive and because it was felt that immigration officers, who are civil servants, could not be asked to perform such tasks. (*Observer*, 27 March 1983: 3)

Thus this 'commercial support' version of the complementarity view of private security allows the Home Office to respect the sensibilities of trade-union-organized civil servants and also minimize the kind of criticism that might follow from the 'oppressive' use of the public police in such a role. The complementarity view does indeed, as Shearing and Stenning suggest, serve a 'political function' and, for those at the heart of politics, it is 'politically useful'.

Competition
In this chapter and elsewhere (South, 1983, 1984, 1988) I have emphasized the obvious importance of the private interest that employs and directs private security activities — and the implications of this in terms of resorting to discretion in the realm of private justice. At the same time, however, it is worth noting that it is not simply the *presence* of the private interests of clients in connection with private security that distinguishes the latter from the public police. The distinction can also be made on the basis of the *absence* of specific clients to whom the public police must feel accountable or by whom they can be operationally directed. This is not to say that the police operationalization of its own priorities and discretion necessarily reflects an egalitarian spirit and undetectable lack of bias or prejudice (see Scraton, 1985), or that evidence of their actions in

industrial disputes is not disturbing (see Police Monitoring and Research Group, 1987a; Scraton and Thomas, 1985), or that the ground has not been well laid by many for serious consideration of various proposals for an effective system of police accountability (see Police Monitoring and Research Group, 1987b; Lea and Young, 1984; Kinsey et al, 1986). Rather the distinction is popularly made because the police are held to work for 'the public interest'.

In an important sense, as Reiss and Bordua argue, the police are their own 'clients':

> The police in a sense are a service without clients. The police service the public as a collectivity rather than distributively. Enforcement must be initiated where there is no victim and/or complainant. Given the lack of guidelines either from the public as client or from a specific victim or complainant as client, the police can become, in effect, their own clients. We take this to be one of the fundamental features in the oft mentioned tendency of the police to develop a supermoralistic perspective and to see themselves as engaged in a 'private' war on crime. (1967: 30)

This observation is of further interest here in that it also begins to suggest that we should consider distinctions within what might be seen as a spectrum of 'vigilantism', which would include moralistic *police* vigilantism, self-serving, retributive *public* vigilantism, and *privately* organized and paid-for vigilantism (among other possible models).

The distinction between the public interest to which the public police are held to be committed and the considerably more parochial interests to whom private security answer, is drawn in a crude but vivid image by Davies, an advisor to the Ontario Police Commission, in offering the following headed-notepaper designs for the public police and for private security:

> The necessity of private police forces is dictated by the needs of individuals and corporations who can afford this deluxe service. I wonder if the mastheads of the two forces should be different. Would the masthead of the public police force be that of people and would the masthead of the private police force be that of money? I would think so. (Davies, 1974: 44)

This view sees the fundamental distinction between the police and private security as resting on the question of who pays them and therefore whose interests they evidently serve.[9] This is a view which would predict some friction between the two parties, especially where direct overlap or blurring of services occurs (cf. Draper, 1978: 163). Certainly some in the police service have seemed almost resentful of the very existence of private security as a competitive presence. As Sir Robert Mark put it, they 'seem to offer an indefinable belittlement of the police function' (Mark, 1977).[10] Others, of course, acknowledge a version of the complementarity view sympathetic to those who wish to privately purchase security services to supplement those offered by the police (cf. Draper, 1978: 162). Whichever view is favoured, consideration of the desirability or otherwise of regulation of private security and/or privatization of some police services frequently follows.

Whilst various forms of licensing and regulation arrangements covering private security exist in many countries, these are generally of a tokenistic nature. In the UK, despite calls from Members of Parliament, civil liberties and low pay groups, as well as a substantial voice within the private security industry itself, successive governments have favoured what they call self-regulation. This effectively means no regulation (cf. Home Office, 1979; South, 1985: 188–97; 1988). Senior police officers in North America and the UK have expressed concern over this lack of effective accountability (a position which may seem ironic to some) — but commonly they also express reservations about any system of licensing that may seem to bestow *police* powers or authority upon private security.

Of course, if private competition from without is unnerving to some in the police, the prospect of privatization of services *within* the police force is even more disturbing. Whilst generally accepting the benefits of some civilianization of police support duties, forces in both North America and the UK are predictably wary about any initiatives which may threaten their staffing establishment. In the UK, a 1986 Department of Environment circular on *Competition in the Provision of Local Authority Services* elicited highly principled and slightly defensive responses from members of the Association of Chief Police Officers, raising among other issues the matters of security vetting, the need for operational flexibility and for managerial certainty in the direction of staff. The police are as conscious as any other 'local government service' that privatization is now far more than a matter for political argument — it is political and economic reality (cf. South, 1989).

It is highly unlikely that the wholesale privatization of the police service would ever be contemplated by any currently recognizable government. However, advocacy of 'healthy', 'true' competition between police and private security in the provision of such services as property guarding would not be at all surprising from some quarters (see Adam Smith Institute, 1984). Market forces, efficiency and other cost–benefit criteria would presumably be held to be the principal determinants of who earned the competitive 'edge'.

Certainly, such arguments would not necessarily have to see private security as disadvantaged in relation to the strength and breadth of those legal powers which the police hold. In the UK, the USA, Canada and other countries with similar legal systems, private security enjoy a *routine* access to the property which they are paid to protect that is formally denied to the public police. Similarly, despite laws guaranteeing the individual's right to go about unmolested and protected from undue or unlawful interference or restraint, in practice private security can be very effective in negotiating the consent of individuals to be stopped and searched. This can occur in public places such as department stores where embarrassment and the intimidation of a formal approach by someone in apparent authority elicits compliance or may even be a condition of employment that requires employees to be willing to submit to a search. As Shearing et al. have argued on the basis of their research,

> whatever the reason, it is clear that private security persons are often able to obtain consent for what they wish to do with relative ease. This diminishes the practical impact of the differences in legal powers between the public police and private security. Indeed, it could be argued that the private security persons probably find themselves in as good a position as most police officers as they are able to 'persuade' people to consent to their interference. (1980: 43)

The effective operation — and legitimation — of private justice systems is, after all, based on those same hegemonic notions of 'active consent and participation' upon which the organization of the labour process and market relations are based (cf. Scraton and South, 1981: 58–9; 1984; Burawoy, 1979: 27; De Sousa Santos, 1985: 318).

Perhaps the key point about the competition perspective is that, as Shearing and Stenning (1981: 222) argue, it disputes those distinctions drawn between the public police and private security on 'the basis of either the nature of their activities or on the public or private nature of the property where these activities occur' and, instead, 'directs attention to the context of control in which private and public security forces operate'. In other words, the *privatization* of security means exactly that, and the benefits accrue to those owners and controllers of private or valued property who can pay for such a service. The security of people and of information also become commodified within this relationship between the buyers and sellers of private security.

Of the compromise, complement and competition viewpoints, this last is the most adequate (albeit still partial), because it moves from the sphere of limited and parochial interests to begin to consider (within a conflict as opposed to consensus model of society) the specificity of those interests that private security serves and puts on the agenda questions of civil liberties, equality of access to fundamental services like protection from crime, and the accountability of private 'policing' agencies.

Circumvention

The viewpoints of compromise, complement and even competition all presuppose that, to a greater or lesser extent, private security activities at least tend to accord with the 'public interest'. Even the 'conflict' tendency within the competition viewpoint does not wholly break with this presupposition in identifying the tailoring of private security activity to fit the demands of specific property-owning employers. It may be a distinction of subtlety, but another partial-truth perspective can be put forward in which emphasis is placed upon the ways in which private security is much more routinely involved in the circumvention of public rules of law and of coopera-tive expectations which the public police may have (see South, 1983).

This view rests most crucially upon the full utilization of private security's powers of discretion. This pivot is noted by Shearing and Stenning when they observe that,

> even when a private security organization is committed to a mode of policing in which investigation, apprehension and prosecution are domi-nant strategies, it will often be found that the bases for such an organiza-tion's exercise of discretion within this mode are markedly different from those of the public police. In particular, the exercise of discretion by such private security personnel will often be far more influenced by their perceptions of the interests of their immediate employer than by any generalized conception of the public interest. (1981: 210)

In cases of shoplifting, theft, fraud and less-definable 'offences', such as industrial espionage, a privatized form of plea-bargaining underlies the private justice system which responds before the matter needs to reach the formal legal system. Indeed, such matters need never reach a court of law. In the case of much commercial crime, deterrence may be a principled policy to emphasize but it can also be easily outweighed by the attraction of restitution of the lost property and the quiet drawing of the veil of discretion over any potentially embarrassing circumstances such as breach of security, managerial incompetence, and so on. Thus the offer of not pressing charges or calling in the police, even where there are the strongest legal and moral obligations, can be a strong bargaining tool. In any such successful bargain, the formal legal process is circumvented, the party represented by private security is satisfied by restitution and informal application of sanctions, the offender is free without public blemish (although they may now be a part of some private justice records system), and only the principle of law suffers. A relationship of sorts still exists here with the public police and the formal legal system because if the bargain fails then these become the next set of resources that the private system may, or can at least threaten to, turn to. The former become a manipulable threat to offenders and a legitimate and cheap way of dealing with offences where necessary.

Finally the very laws and rules that govern access to information held by the police are circumvented. This occurs not only in the checking of criminal records and other personal background of private security employees — a boast made by major, respectable companies as well as the less scrupulous — but also in credit-reference, investigation and personal-protection work. This routinely occurs on a mundane level, but in the case of internationally orientated investigation agencies it can also involve private information-gathering, tapping official sources beyond frontiers. Circumvention of this kind may involve degrees of cooperation with public policing and other official agencies, but it is necessarily covert and almost invariably based on corruption — at the very least of public trust (see South, 1983).

Conclusion

In this chapter I have shown that the privatization of various aspects of policing and other regulatory activities in society (cf., for example, Henry, 1983, 1987) has been a developing reality in the post-war period on a broad and substantial scale. It is not a product of recent governmental and market preoccupation with privatization of services. Nor can it be simplistically interpreted as an example of 'creeping capitalism' eroding the provision of public services. It may have some effect in this direction in some areas of police service deployment of resources, but the public police are evidently not withering away as a result of market force competition. As I have illustrated, there are different ways of looking at what is a complex relationship between public and private sectors. But where does this lead us once we have acknowledged the significance of the development, presence and activities of the private sector?

First, in foreseeable future circumstances it is unlikely, to say the least, that the private security sector is going to go away. It has been a buoyant and 'recession resistant' industry in most major Western economies since, at least, the 1960s and all indications suggest that it will continue to grow, albeit with certain areas of operation contracting while others expand (see South, 1988: 29–33). So, second, should there be concern about such growth, and third, if so — what might be done?

Private security agencies are involved in a very wide range of activities. At one level, it would seem difficult to argue that if the public police cannot or will not patrol certain areas that suffer from high crime rates or fear of crime, then whilst the rich can afford to pay for a private service the poor should be left to bolt their doors. Councils might well wish to develop 'user-friendly' security packages involving home security devices and patrols. This is, however, one of many levels where the issue of regulation and accountability must be raised, for any payment of public money to organizations in the business of policing for profit must receive a good and accountable service. At other levels, though, quite apart from the politics of acceding to privatization by buying private services that ought to be publicly provided, the political dimensions of many of the activities that private security agencies undertake are cause for concern. Services that are explicitly anti-Trade Union, that involve the infringement of civil liberties by covert spying and information gathering, and that involve the preparation of reports, creation of files and passing of judgements which the subjects are unaware of (see Bunyan, 1976; Bowden, 1978), are clearly something that demands legislative control. Similarly, any continuing trends to build upon the discretionary potential of private security a yet more elaborate system of private justice that can channel the offences of the office suite away from the criminal justice system, whilst minor offences on the urban streets are even more heavily targeted by legislation and by the public police, must be monitored and fought. There is also an international dimension to private security in the form of information-gathering and selling, and a growing trade in the provision of bodyguards and mercenaries. In terms of law, justice or morality, these are not commercial enterprises which can be ignored.

Nationally and internationally, as private security has grown alongside the expansion of 'mass private property' now open to the public although owned by corporate enterprise (Shearing and Stenning, 1983), 'a degree of sovereignty [has switched] from state to capital, which is an authority far less subject to regulation and scrutiny' (Cohen, 1985: 136). The privatization of policing which has occurred thus far in Britain has not, it should be remembered, been encouraged (until 1979) by a strong ethos favouring such trends. However, in the present climate the urgency of arguing for strict, publicly administered regulation and accountability is stronger than ever.

The New Right is serious in its proposals and well argued in its case for the privatization of a whole range of policing and criminal justice elements. The Adam Smith Institute *Omega Report* suggested that 'local police authorities might ... contract out certain minor areas of police activity, such as inviting tenders for traffic control' (1984: 31). 'Wheel clamping' in London has already been contracted out to private companies. Increased use of private security patrols to 'supplement police services' and to enable 'a variety of new methods to be assessed one against the other' is another suggestion (ibid.: 31), while the report also observes that 'crime detection itself is an activity where an increased measure of reliance on private investigation agencies could bring technical and operational improvements (ibid.). Any moves in this last direction would almost certainly see opposition from an unusual alliance of the police service and civil liberties bodies. But these *are* issues which are on the debating table of the Right and they should be taken seriously as the recommendation of the Conservative members of the House of Commons Home Affairs Select Committee (1987) which urges 'the Government to allow private companies to build and run jails on an experimental basis' (*London Daily News*, 1987: 10).

Given this influential opinion, it is perhaps instructive to note that while the Adam Smith Institute 'Omega' report also made the case for privately contracted prison services, it added that this development 'would require government (or independent) monitoring to ensure that agreed standards are kept to' and suggested that 'this would not really pose any great problem' (1984: 66). Some acknowledgement of a requirement for the monitoring of such developments may seem, at least, mildly comforting. However, the notion that truly effective *regulatory* monitoring would 'not really pose any great problem' hardly conveys a sense of serious commitment to the exercise. The fact is that, unless the intention is to opt for the all too familiar model of a 'watchdog without teeth', then the development and administration of an effective mechanism would actually pose quite considerable problems. Such a recognition is the realistic foundation for a system to ensure regulation and accountability. With regard to both private security and private prisons a compromise on 'agreed standards' dictated by considerations of commercial feasibility must not be allowed to degenerate into tokenistic 'minimum standards'.

The further privatization of criminal justice system services — and the private appropriation of their symbolic affinity with the provision of *public* services by the State — must be challenged and resisted on grounds of tradition and legitimacy, legality and accountability, and ethics and morality. It is necessary to argue pragmatically against the market forces position and defend the public provision and administration of criminal justice and social services. If we are beginning to open up the spaces in which to formulate how a democratic socialist society might organize its own forms of social justice and 'policing', then we must take seriously issues of individual human rights and public service organization and delivery (see Pierson, 1986). Uncomfortable tensions can sometimes exist between the two, but it is only right that these be honestly recognized and addressed. Certainly there is no historical inevitability about the superseding of publicly directed and accountable policing or prisons by private enterprise. In the case of the existing privatization of 'policing' services and the continued growth of the private security sector, the time has never been more urgent than now to introduce a system which *ensures* the public regulation and accountability of private arrangements for policing and security.

Notes

My debt in this chapter to the work of Clifford Shearing, Philip Stenning and their colleagues at the Center of Criminology, University of Toronto, will be more than evident to all those familiar with their prolific output on this subject. My grateful thanks go to them and to Robert Weiss at the State University of New York at Plattsburgh, NY, for generously sharing ideas and for their supportive interest. This chapter is drawn from work conducted for a slightly different project (South, 1988), to which too many people have contributed to acknowledge here, but the exploration of the specific relationships discussed in this chapter has benefited from the interest and support of Sue Harris, Gerry Mars, Roger Matthews, Phil Scraton, Ann Singleton and Jock Young. Thanks also to Alison Inman for a refreshing legal view. Naturally, all those mentioned would probably be among the first to disclaim any responsibility for how this chapter has turned out.

1 The adequacy of holding to these traditional dichotomies of 'public' and 'private' is provocatively and suggestively questioned by De Sousa Santos (1985). Albeit not without some subsequent criticism, Cohen (1979) has also addressed what he described as the blurring of the public and the private. His discussion is broadened in Cohen, 1985: 134–6. I have addressed this issue in relation to attempting to analytically define or 'place' the private security sector within a continuum of social control forms in South, 1984, 1988.
2 I draw here on the work of Phil Scraton. Scraton (1985) offers a particularly accessible and useful survey of developments in post-war policing.
3 Although historically, of course, this was the *re*emergence of forms of private policing that have a clear lineage predating the establishment of the 'new' police with the creation of the London Metropolitan Police in 1829 (see South, 1987).
4 Police powers of search and detention have also been enhanced by, for example, provisions of the Prevention of Terrorism Act, 1974 and subsequent amendments; and by the Police and Criminal Evidence Act, 1984, implemented in January 1986.
5 In Britain it is in a sense surprising how long it took for the issue of police protection of commercial private premises, goods or payrolls to become a component of debates about the efficiency of public policing. As early as 1909, the pioneering American writer on police management, Leonard F. Fuld, had argued most strongly that the police should not have to take on 'extraneous duties', including assisting 'private corporations to protect their money' (Fuld, 1909; More, 1979: 186).
6 But for a broader picture, see South, 1984.
7 In the late 1970s some academic commentators took up the essentials of this argument about under-resourced police and the growth of demand for 'social control' leading to resort to private alternatives, and went beyond a Galbraithian analysis of 'private affluence thriving upon public squalor' to directly relate the

expansion of private security to the 'fiscal crisis of the state' (see Spitzer and Scull, 1977; for one critique of this analysis see South, 1984). This analysis is not wholly wrong; it is simply limited. Part of it, however, offers significant arguments about the problems of police budgeting. Thus:

> It is well known that productivity in labour-intensive organizations rises considerably slower than in their capital intensive counter-parts, with the result that greater levels of expenditure on police budgets are required simply to maintain the same level of service in real terms (cf. Gough, 1975). When this fact is considered in connection with the recent growth of unionisation in policing [in the USA, or stronger expression of claims from the Police Federation in Britain] and other public services, we may better understand why public police are hard put to provide the kind of sophisticated and expensive services that modern corporations require. (Spitzer and Scull, 1977: 25)

Among others, Shearing and Stenning have argued that the implication of this type of explanation

> is that private security would not exist today if the growth of the public police had not been limited.... Certainly the fiscal restraints that have affected public police budgets are real enough and this most assuredly has had some influence on the growth of private security. However, the limited focus on this and 'other proximate causes' (Carson and Young, 1976) of modern private security, in the absence of a historically grounded analysis of the structural changes at work, results in both an inadequate explanation of the development of private security and a distorted picture of the historical nature of the relationship between private and public security forces. (1981: 226–7)

8 It should be emphasized that civil claims for damages against the public police have anyway been rising significantly in Britain in the past five to six years: 'a reasonable estimate would be a fourfold increase in this period' (Franklin, 1987: 1184). 'Litigation mindedness', the availability of legal aid, increased experience of the legal profession over this issue and media interest are among factors which may have contributed to this development. Provisions of the Police and Criminal Evidence Act, 1984, may 'increase the number of such actions' (ibid.).

9 Although some recent developments in the USA, where free enterprise is being seen as offering *Strategies for Supplementing the Police Budget*, begin to challenge any 'fundamental' basis to such a distinction in a serious way. Proposals in a document with the above title, produced by the US National Institute of Justice, suggest charging for some services, soliciting contributions from private sources and making use of assets seized from illegal operations. The report does acknowledge that 'charging a fee for essential police services may hurt those who need the services most: the people in the poorer neighbourhoods'. Mansfield, 1985: 2225; Stellwagen and Wylie, 1985).

10 Although this sentiment did not prevent Sir Robert, like many other police officers, from joining the ranks of a private security firm upon retirement — in this case as a director (Penrose, 1987).

References

ACPO (Association of Chief Police Officers)/North Wales Police (1988) *A Review of the Private Security Industry*, unpublished report, North Wales Police.

Adam Smith Institute (1984) *The Omega File: Justice Police*. London: Adam Smith Institute.

Alderson, J. (1978) Interview transcript, *File on Four on Private Security*, London: BBC, Radio Four.

Bennett, T. and Wright, R. (1984) *Burglars on Burglary*. Aldershot: Gower Press.

Bowden, T. (1978) *Beyond the Limits of the Law*. Harmondsworth: Penguin.

Bunyan, T. (1976) *The History and Practice of the Political Police in Britain*. London: Quartet.

Burawoy, M. (1979) *Manufacturing Consent: Changes in the Labour Process Under Monopoly Capitalism*. Chicago: University of Chicago Press.

Burden, P. (1980) *The Burglary Business and You*. London: Macmillan.

Carson, W. and Young, P. (1976) 'Sociological Aspects of Major Property Crime', in Young (1976).

Carter, R. (1974) *Theft in the Market: An Economic Analysis of Costs and Incentives in Improving Prevention by Government and Private Police and Reducing Loss by Insurance*. London: Institute of Economic Affairs.

Cohen, S. (1979) 'The Punitive City', *Contemporary Crises*, 3 (4): 339–63.

Cohen, S. (1985) *Visions of Social Control*. Oxford: Polity Press.

Davies, F. (1974) 'Paper on Relations between Public Police and Private Security Forces', in Jeffries, F. (ed.), *Private Policing and Security in Canada: A Workshop*. Toronto: Center of Criminology, University of Toronto.

De Sousa Santos, B. (1985) 'On Modes of Production of Law and Social Power', *International Journal of the Sociology of Law*, 13: 299–336.

Department of the Environment (1986) *Competition in the Provision of Local Authority Services*. London: Department of the Environment.

Draper, H. (1978) *Private Police*. Harmondsworth: Penguin.

Dring, D. (1972) 'The Growth of Alarm Systems', in P. Wiles and F. McClintock (eds), *The Security Industry in the United Kingdom*. Cambridge: Institute of Criminology.

Dring, D. (1976) 'Agencies of Concern in Crime Prevention', in Young (1976).

Franklin, J. (1987) 'Why the Police are Sued', *Police Review*, 12 June: 1184–5.

French, J. (1979) 'Private Security Organisations: Threat or Benefit to Society?', *Police College Magazine*, 15 (2): 23–32.

Fuld, L. (1909) *Police Administration*. New York: G. P. Putnam.

Gale, R. (1970) 'News Report', *The Private Investigator*, August.

Gough, I. (1975) 'State Expenditure in Advanced Capitalism', *New Left Review*, 92.

Henry, S. (1983) *Private Justice: Towards Integrated Theorising in the Sociology of Law*. London: Routledge & Kegan Paul.

Henry, S. (1987) 'Disciplinary Pluralism: Four Models of Private Justice in the Workplace', *Sociological Review*, 35 (2): 279–319.

Home Office (1979) *The Private Security Industry: A Discussion Paper*. London: HMSO.

House of Commons Home Affairs Select Committee (1987) *Contract Provision of Prisons*. London: HMSO.

Kakalik, J. and Wildhorn, S. (1971) *Private Police in the United States: Findings and Recommendations*, vol. 1. (Rand Corporation Study for US Department of Justice. Washington, DC: Government Printing Office.

Kerr, M. (1979a) 'Confrontation or Cooperation?', *Police Review*, 26 January.

Kerr, M. (1979b) 'Who should Control the Security Industry?', *Police Review*, 2 February.

Kinsey, R., Lea, J. and Young, J. (1986) *Losing the Fight against Crime*. Oxford: Basil Blackwell.

Knights, P. (1979) 'Policing — Public or Private?' (Text of talk to ACPO/AMA/ACC Joint Summer Conference, Harrogate) in *Police*, 11 (11), July: 12, 14.

Lea, J. and Young, J. (1984) *What is to be Done about Law and Order?* Harmondsworth: Penguin.

London Daily News (1987) 'Private Prisons on Trial', 6 May: 10.

McClintock, F. (1976) 'Major Property Crime: Some Criminological Issues', in Young 1976: 18–23.

McIntosh, M. (1971) 'Changes in the Organisation of Thieving', in S. Cohen (ed.), *Images of Deviance*. Harmondsworth: Penguin.

McIntosh, M. (1975) *The Organisation of Crime*. London: Macmillan.

Manning, P (1980) *The Narcs Game*. Cambridge, Mass.: MIT Press.

Mansfield, C. (1985) 'When Crime Pays for Police', *Police Review*, 1 November: 2225.

Mark, R. (1977) in *Security Gazette*, July.

Mart, V. (1975) 'Private Police', *Police Journal*, 48 (2): 122–32.

MATSA (Managerial, Administrative, Technical and Supervisory Association) (1983) *Report on the Security Industry*. Esher: MATSA; see also Williams, D., George, B. and MacLennan, E. *Guarding against Low Pay*. London: Low Pay Unit. Pamphlet no. 29, 1984.

More, H. (1979) 'History of Police Management Thought', *Police Journal*, April: 181–96.

Oaksey, Lord (1949) *Police Conditions and Service*, 1 and 2, Cmd 7831, 7674. London: HMSO.

Observer (1983) 'Anger at Securicor Guard on Migrants', 27 March: 3.

Penrose, B. (1987) 'Police Chief is Set to Join Private Security Firm', *Sunday Times*, 14 June.

Pierson, C. (1986) *Marxist Theory and Democratic Politics*. Cambridge: Polity Press.

Police Monitoring and Research Group (1987a) *Policing Wapping: An Account of the Dispute 1986/7*. Briefing Paper 3. London: London Strategic Policy Unit.

Police Monitoring and Research Group (1987b) *Police Accountability and a New Strategic Authority for London*. Briefing Paper 2. London: London Strategic Policy Unit.

Radzinowicz, L. (1956a, 1956b, 1968) *A History of English Criminal Law and its Administration from 1750*, vols 2 (1956a), 3 (1956b) and 4 (1968).

Raw, C. (1983) 'Security Profits Cause Alarm', *Sunday Times Business News*, 31 July.

Reiss, A. and Bordua, D. (1967) 'Environment and Organization: A Perspective on the Police', in D. Bordua (ed.), *The Police: Six Sociological Essays*. New York: Wiley.

Royal Commission on the Police (1962) *Final Report*. Cmnd 1728. London: HMSO.

Scraton, P. (1982) *Policing Society; Policing Crime*. Issues in Crime and Society Course, Block 2, Part 6. Milton Keynes: Open University Press.

Scraton, P. (1985) *The State of the Police*. London: Pluto Press.

Scraton, P. and Chadwyck, K. (1987) *In the Arms of the Law: Deaths in Custody and Coroners' Inquests*. London: Pluto Press.

Scraton, P. and South, N. (1981) *Capitalist Discipline, Private Justice and the Hidden Economy*. Occasional Papers in Deviance and Social Policy, 2. Enfield: Middlesex Polytechnic.

Scraton, P. and South, N. (1984) 'The Ideological Construction of the Hidden Economy: Private Justice and Work-Related Crime', *Contemporary Crises*, 8: 1–18.

Scraton, P. and Thomas, P. (eds) (1985) *The State versus the People: Lessons from the Coal Dispute. Journal of Law and Society*, special issue, 12 (3). Oxford: Basil Blackwell.

Seldon, A. (1977) *Charge*. London: Temple Smith.

Shearing, C., Farnell, M. and Stenning, P. (1980) *Contract Security in Ontario*. Toronto: Center of Criminology, University of Toronto.

Shearing, C. and Stenning, P. (1981) 'Modern Private Security: Its Growth and Implications', in M. Tonry and N. Morris (eds), *Crime and Justice: An Annual Review of Research*, vol. 3. Chicago: University of Chicago Press, pp. 193–245.

Shearing, C. and Stenning, P. (1983) 'Private Security: Implications for Social Control', *Social Problems*, 30 (5): 493–506.

Smith, P. (1979) 'Who Watches the Watchdogs?', *Police*, 11 (10).

South, N. (1983) 'The Corruption of Commercial Justice: The Case of the Private Security Sector', in M. Clarke (ed.), *Corruption: Causes, Consequences and Control*. London: Frances Pinter, pp. 39–57.

South, N. (1984) 'Private Security, the Division of Policing Labour and the Commercial Compromise of the State', in S. Spitzer and A. Scull (eds), *Research in Law, Deviance and Social Control*, vol. 6. Greenwich, Conn.: JAI Press, pp 171–98.

South, N. (1985) 'Private Security and Social Control: The Private Security Sector in the United Kingdom, its Commercial Functions and Public Accountability'. PhD Thesis. London: Centre for Occupational and Community Research, Middlesex Polytechnic, Enfield.

South, N. (1987) 'Law, Profit and "Private Persons": Private and Public Policing in English History', in C. Shearing and P. Stenning (eds), *Private Policing* (Sage Criminal Justice Systems Annuals, vol. 23). Newbury Park: Sage, pp. 72–109.

South, N. (1988) *Policing for Profit: The Private Security Sector*. London: Sage Contemporary Criminology.

South, N. (1989) 'Criminal Justice Industries PLC? Some Notes on the Privatisation of Law Enforcement Related Services and the Issue of Accountability', in ISTD (ed.), *Punishment for Profit? The Proceedings of a Conference*. London: ISTD.

Spitzer, S. and Scull, A. (1977) 'Privatisation and Capitalist Development: The Case of the Private Police', *Social Problems*, 25 (1): 18–29.

Stellwagen, L. and Wylie, K. (1985) *Strategies for Supplementing the Police Budget*. Washington, DC: US Department of Justice, National Institute of Justice, Office of Development, Testing and Dissemination.

Stenning, P. and Shearing, C. (1980) 'The Quiet Revolution: The Nature, Development and General Legal Implications of Private Security in Canada', *Criminal Law Quarterly*, 22: 220–48.

Sunday Times (1980) 'Army Men Enlist the "Private" Tappers', 10 February.

Young, P. (ed.) (1976) *Major Property Crime in the United Kingdom: Some Aspects of Law Enforcement*. Edinburgh: School of Criminology and Forensic Studies, University of Edinburgh.

5 ELECTRONIC MONITORING AND HOUSE ARREST

The widespread development of surveillance mechanisms is a familiar component of contemporary society. Identity cards, fingerprinting, computers and video cameras, telephone bugs, are now regular features of modern disciplinary and regulatory systems. These new systems of electronic surveillance are distinguished from earlier forms of surveillance in that they are continuous, transcending distance and physical barriers. They are able to probe beneath the surface and watch without being watched. Most importantly, they are often able to engage certain populations in their own monitoring through 'self' control (Marx, 1985).

This movement towards mass surveillance took a significant turn in the 1960s when a series of experiments were initiated in which monitors were attached to or implanted in offenders in order that they could be continuously tracked by a central computer. These early electronic monitoring systems were used mainly on parolees and mental patients (Gable, 1986). The aim was to visually monitor 'controlees' twenty-four hours a day via a signal which was transmitted to a lighted map at the base station. Interestingly, under this 'primitive' method the controlee was not restricted to the home and could move freely in a prescribed area — usually about a square mile. Their use, however, raised much controversy during the 1960s, and fears about 'Big Brother', together with the practical problems of implementing these systems, brought them into disfavour.

The use of house arrest has a different history. It has been widely employed in relation to political 'detainees'. Historically, there has been extensive use of curfews and home confinement in relation to the maintenance of public order — particularly in periods of political turmoil. Using it, however, as a normal rather than as an exceptional control mechanism, and particularly as an alternative to incarceration, signals a new departure. As many critics have pointed out, it turns the home into a prison and blurs the boundaries between different spheres of social action. It generates a socially interchangeable milieu in which different agencies and institutions readily substitute for each other.

Using house arrest in combination with electronic monitoring presents a unique and novel combination of controls that promote new levels of intrusiveness while encouraging the decentralization of social control. The main justification for the adoption of this unique strategy is that it provides an alternative to prison which promises to save money while protecting the public. Against a background of increased overcrowding, combined with a general uncertainty about the effectiveness of existing alternatives, home confinement is seen to provide a sanction that is potentially more appropriate and less damaging than the existing range of custodial and non-custodial options.

A considerable investment has already been made in developing electronic monitoring equipment, and much of the hostility which was evident in the 1960s and 1970s has recently subsided. However, the use of home confinement is still an extremely controversial issue — particularly in Britain. Most of the leading criminal justice agencies are sceptical of its value, and the principal agency involved — the probation service — has formally disassociated itself from its adoption. Even so, the government remains undeterred, and an experimental scheme is underway in England and Wales and will be closely scrutinized.

In this chapter, Bonnie Berry and Roger Matthews examine the role and potential effectiveness of house arrest and electronic monitoring in order to determine how they might most usefully be employed. They also examine whether or not these techniques will together or independently save money, or are likely to have any significant effect on such problems as prison overcrowding.

Electronic Monitoring and House Arrest: Making the Right Connections

Bonnie Berry and Roger Matthews

Are we entering a new era in the history of punishment — an era in which the prison will be increasingly replaced by new forms of surveillance and containment? Existing forms of punishment have been neatly divided between 'inclusive' community-based responses and 'exclusive' responses tied to imprisonment (Cohen, 1985). But the emerging forms of electronic monitoring and house arrest offer the possibility, their advocates claim, of creating a departure in the available modalities of punishment by offering a response based upon 'seclusion'.

The growing interest in this emerging approach to punishment has been fuelled by the spiralling penal crisis, a crisis which takes the visible and immediate form of problems of overcrowding but which is ultimately a crisis in the legitimacy of incarceration itself (Fitzgerald and Sim, 1979). Combined with this penal crisis is also a steadily deepening disillusionment in the field of community corrections. Much of the optimism which greeted the expansion of community-based corrections in the sixties and seventies has faded. The simplistic notion that the prison population could be reduced through the proliferation of community-based alternatives has been repeatedly discredited. Although the expansion of community alternatives has at times encouraged imaginative and constructive responses, there is little evidence that its expansion has served to reduce the size of the prison population. Rather, what we have seen is the simultaneous expansion of both the 'inclusive' and 'exclusive' options. This experience suggests that if this twin crisis is to be overcome it is not just a question of providing more of the same, but rather developing a substantially different approach than those which have been tried to date. Increasingly, a significant body of opinion is pinning its hopes on electronic monitoring and house arrest to overcome the present impasse (Austin and Krisberg, 1981; Matthews, 1987).

The initial development of electronic monitoring and house arrest has been largely attributed in some recent reports to the imagination of Judge Jack Love of New Mexico (who was apparently influenced by a Spiderman comic), and also to the energetic marketing and promotional work of certain manufacturers and entrepreneurs (Ackerman, 1986; Timko, 1986). Although these factors have certainly played some part in stimulating interest in this approach these are in themselves not sufficient conditions to explain the substantial level of interest that has arisen in the past few years. It is not only a question of explaining the recent origin of these ideas — which to be accurate were mainly developed in the sixties (Ingraham and Smith, 1972; Shapiro, 1972) — but also of explaining the nature of the response. There is no shortage of ostensibly good ideas. What needs to be explained is why certain ideas find attentive audiences at particular times and places.

It is against the background of the twin crisis in the contemporary forms of punishment that explanations need to be sought. The critical question is how electronic monitoring and house arrest relate to this crisis. It is on the basis of the particular claims that have been made on behalf of these emerging forms of punishment that interest has been created. These claims include the reduction of the prison population, reduced stigmatization, lower costs, and the provision of a form of punishment which both satisfies the public demand for intervention and protection while avoiding the debilitating effects of imprisonment. Although there has not been very much in the way of serious empirical evaluation of the use of these systems they are spreading rapidly in the USA. It has been estimated that there are currently 3000 to 4000 people subject to some form of house arrest and electronic monitoring, and these systems have been adopted in over thirty states (Ball et al., 1988).

The specific appeal of this approach to policymakers is not difficult to determine. Apart from the potential gains that have already been mentioned there are two central elements in this approach which have interested policymakers for some time. The first is the desire to impose different types of curfews — particularly on young offenders. These policies have, however, always suffered from the problems of effective enforcement. The second point of appeal centres on the perennial fascination that policymakers seem to have with any form of technology. The 'appliance of science' invariably carries connotations of comprehensiveness, speed and rigour. If this combination was not in itself irresistible enough, the implementation of electronic monitoring comes with the additional attraction that offenders can be encouraged to contribute to the cost of their own punishment by being invited in some cases to pay for the use of the necessary equipment.

There are a number of different types of electronic monitoring and surveillance devices from which to choose, but basically there are two main systems. The first involves the use of a tamper-resistant bracelet or anklet worn by the controlee and linked to a computer terminal. During the period of house arrest the controlee is telephoned and if the appropriate response is given it is assumed that he or she is at home. These systems can take either an 'active' or a 'passive' form. In the active version there is a continuous signal given out from the transmitter, while in the passive system the bracelet is inserted into the receiver and a signal is recorded. It is this type of system, where electronic monitoring has been used in conjunction with house arrest, that has predominated in the USA (Petersilia, 1986; Schmidt and Curtis, 1987).

The second type of monitoring device is different in that although it involves a bracelet or an anklet which emits a continuous signal, it does not require a home telephone and is therefore not tied to house arrest. This type of system involves a cell network that allows continuous monitoring of the movements of controlees and requires a more extensive and elaborate system of transmitters and receivers in order to relay the signal over a wide area. This form of electronic monitoring has remained largely undeveloped to date, despite strong support for this system from some quarters (Offenders Tag Association, 1988).

The initial attractiveness of the first type of monitoring device, linked directly to house arrest, undoubtedly lies in its potential ability to enforce curfews, but also in its offering a mode of punishment which has a great deal of flexibility, and which is potentially a great deal more versatile than some of the existing 'all or nothing' options. Thus:

> Home incarceration has a *good deal of fit* to a variety of circumstances in such a way that it can be employed alone or in concert with other programs, tailored to certain hours of the day, and perhaps even combined with incarceration in a traditional jail with home incarceration at weekends in certain cases. It also offers the possibility of practical use at various *stages* of the correctional process from pretrial detention through parole. (Ball and Lilly, 1988: 149; emphasis in original)

The flexibility of electronic monitoring and house arrest is impressive. It can be instigated by the offender or the court, it can operate in parallel or instead of existing sanctions, and it can be administered by a wide range of agencies — both public and private. But this flexibility can equally result in indiscriminate usage, which may lead it to be employed in ways that not only fail to reduce the level of incarceration but act to exacerbate the problems of punishment. Clearly, the manner in which electronic monitoring is employed and the point in the criminal justice system at which it is implemented will influence not only the effectiveness of the programme, but also the ethical and legal issues related to its use.

Much of the interest in these new forms of monitoring and surveillance has been centred on its ability to reduce the prison population. Given the flexibility of this form of punishment it has been suggested that it can be used at the pre-trial stage in order to reduce the remand population, at the sentencing stage in order to introduce more alternatives to custody, and also as a form of early release providing a viable form of home incarceration for certain categories of offenders. In order to evaluate the potential impact of electronic monitoring and house arrest on prison populations each of these options requires some investigation. The effectiveness of these new modes of punishment will vary considerably from country to country and state to state, but there may be some general implications that can be drawn from examining these options from a predominantly British vantage point.

Pre-trial release

The number of those incarcerated while awaiting trial in England and Wales has become a growing point of concern since the numbers involved have risen dramatically in recent years, and many of these remand prisoners are kept in the most dilapidated and overcrowded institutions in the prison system. There has been a virtual doubling of the remand population in England and Wales between 1978 and 1988 from 5613 (14 per cent of the prison population) to 10 512 (22 per cent of the prison population), while hundreds of prisoners are currently held in police cells because of the lack of accommodation in remand prisons (HMSO, 1988a).

Since remand prisoners are unconvicted and so technically innocent, it seems incongruous to incarcerate them, often for long periods, in these appalling conditions. And given that approximately one third of them are eventually not convicted the treatment they receive becomes even more indefensible. The familiar justifications for maintaining so many remand prisoners under such conditions are that incarceration is necessary in order to prevent defendants from interfering with or intimidating witnesses, or that defendants may otherwise fail to turn up for trial.

It is in relation to these considerations that home incarceration has been considered, as has the possibility of privatizing remand prisons (HMSO, 1988a, 1988b). The question is whether home confinement could provide an appropriate way of managing a significant percentage of the remand population while simultaneously providing the required levels of security. In its defence it is argued that not only could it reduce pressure on remand prisons but it would also allow defendants to continue working and to maintain family relations.

Although the prospect of reducing the size of the remand population is undoubtedly attractive, the potential for the use of electronic surveillance (ES) in this way appears limited, since

> The more suitable a person is for ES, the more suitable he/she would be likely to be for bail without ES, and people whose circumstances made it difficult for courts to grant them bail would present the same difficulties in relation to an ES condition (homelessness, unsuitable lifestyle, addictions). There would be the added problem that large numbers of defendants do not have a home telephone, and the remand period would be too short to make it practicable or justifiable to install one. (ACPO, 1988: 2)

Significantly, the growth of the remand population is due mainly to the steep rise in the length of time defendants await trial, combined with a steady increase in the number of persons appearing in court. The average length of time on remand for untried male prisoners has increased from 36 days in 1980 to 57 days in 1986 and for untried female prisoners it has increased from 25 days to 44 days over the same period (HMSO, 1987). There has in fact been an increase in the number of people granted bail and the major problem, as the Vera Institute recently indicated, is the length of time it takes to bring offenders to trial and the quality of information which is supplied to the courts (Stone, 1988).

Evidence from France appears to confirm this view. Attempts to reduce the remand population by extending the range of pre-trial supervision failed to reduce the remand population because 'they were not able to modify the main conditions of the process of imprisonment, especially delays in procedure and trial' (Faugeron, 1988: 6). In West Germany, where the remand population has declined substantially over the last few years, the reduction has mainly been a result of 'the increasing use of non-secure residential care for young offenders on remand rather than employing custodial institutions' (Graham, 1987).

These findings suggest that speeding up the process of bringing defendants to trial may be more effective in reducing the remand population than trying to create a series of compensatory measures which offer too little too late. These options are, however, not exclusive, and if it can be demonstrated that the availability of house arrest and electronic monitoring could encourage courts to increase the number of defendants receiving bail while maintaining reasonable safeguards then they may be of value at this stage of the process. If, on the other hand, such measures are adopted as a palliative or as a substitute for rationalizing the process by which defendants come to trial they could be a costly distraction.

The recent initiation in England and Wales of a number of pilot schemes for house arrest and electronic monitoring at the pre-trial stage of the process appears to be motivated by questions of expediency rather than being based upon any discernible theoretical or strategic rationale. These schemes, however, will be watched closely in order to determine their effectiveness and appropriateness. In the future, however — particularly if these pilot schemes are seen as unsuccessful — it is likely that, as in the USA, house arrest and electronic monitoring will be used predominantly as a sentencing option.

Sentencing

There is no shortage of alternatives to custody in Britain. In fact, it could be argued in relation to the growing disenchantment with community corrections, that the proliferation of alternatives which took place in the sixties and seventies — community service orders, diversion schemes, intermediate treatment, reparation and mediation schemes and the like — has already produced a surplus of these options. Their proliferation has resulted in an increasingly complex network of sentencing options that seem to have done little to reduce the level of prison overcrowding, but which has served to create a range of new and perplexing problems. To add electronic monitoring and house arrest to the existing array of dispositions could result in the creation of an alternative to the existing 'alternatives' rather than an alternative to custody.

Concern at simply adding new alternatives to existing 'alternatives' is particularly pertinent in the case of house arrest and electronic monitoring given its flexibility and adaptability. Since it can be used either as a sentence in itself or as an 'add on' to a variety of other sentencing options, it could too easily extend the armoury of the judiciary without making any significant impact on the level of incarceration (Corbett and Fersch, 1985).

Clearly, if house arrest and electronic monitoring are to have a positive impact upon sentencing practices and to serve to reduce the prison population, it must be shown that between them they can offer something uniquely different from the existing 'alternatives'. In short, they must be able to act as competing alternative sanctions for a significant percentage of the custodial population. Many of the existing alternatives were never really designed to be used in place of custody but rather tend to focus upon the 'soft' end of the continuum, such that there is in many countries a noticeable shortage of competing 'middle-range' sentencing options. As Elliott Currie has argued,

> The absence of credible sanctions short of incarceration is one of the most crucial limitations of contemporary criminal justice in America. On the

whole we either lock up offenders for unusually (and often unnecessarily) long periods or we do virtually nothing at all, oscillating between alienating harshness and sheer neglect. (Currie, 1985: 233)

One 'middle-range' sanction which has been developed in recent years is 'intensive' probation. Existing forms of probation were not widely seen as being rigorous enough, and probation lost much of its credibility as a sanction that could act effectively as a competing alterntive to custody. The growing use of intensive probation has been one of the main ways in which electronic monitoring and house arrest have been used in the USA. Interestingly, one of the early projects that was established in Kentucky and administered by the probation service involved house arrest *without* electronic monitoring. This approach, which has the benefit of direct contact between the probation service and the offender, also involved some community work and participation in reparation schemes. It did, however, have the distinct disadvantage of being very time-consuming. Under the pressure of increasing case loads — often combined with diminishing resources — the electronic monitoring devices appeared more viable (Lilly et al., 1987).

Seven out of ten convicted prisoners in the USA in 1982 were being dealt with in the community through either probation or parole, so the potential use of electronic monitoring appears significant — particularly in light of the increasingly diverse range of offenders being given probation (Petersilia, 1988). But the expansion of intensive probation based on some combination of house arrest and electronic monitoring within the British context may be fairly limited. In fact, it has been argued that these additional layers of punishment may well make little real difference and only involve unnecessary additional expense. For

If electronic monitoring is seen as an adjunct to a probation order or parole licence, it is worth noting that the vast majority of probationers and parolees in this country complete their period of supervision successfully without electronic monitoring, 85% of probation orders and 88% of community service orders are satisfactorily completed. Moreover they are applied to a much wider variety of offenders than the highly selected group considered suitable for electronic monitoring in the U.S.A., and last for much longer than periods of home confinement. It is, therefore, difficult to see what additional benefit electronic monitoring would offer in the supervision of offenders. (NACRO, 1988: 9)

Since the recurring justification given for electronically monitored house arrest is that it can provide a credible alternative sanction to imprisonment, it remains incumbent upon its advocates to demonstrate that it will be used in this way. That is, it needs to be shown that using house arrest and electronic monitoring, either to supplement existing forms of supervision or by itself, will encourage the judiciary to embrace this sanction rather than imprisonment. The evidence to date suggests that it is far from certain that all those who have been sentenced to house arrest with electronic monitoring would have, in reality, received a prison sentence.

Indicatively, in their report on the Kenton Country programme in Kentucky, Ball et al. pointed out that

> It is clear that home incarceration with electronic monitoring did provide a sentencing option for district court judges in Kenton County. However, the judges did not seem to use home incarceration as an alternative to jail, and the option had little effect as a jail depopulation objective. One judge thought of it as a 'prelude' to jail, another thought of it as 'not incarceration', while another thought of it as 'another' sentencing option. Thus far home incarceration has been used conservatively in Kenton County. It has not been seriously tested as an alternative to jail incarceration. (Ball et al., 1988: 85)

The major problem is ensuring that it is used in the vast majority of cases instead of imprisonment. If it is to be used for some other purpose then its advocates need to rapidly develop another rationale for its adoption. Judges, as we know from bitter experience, are extremely adept at rationalizing the use of punishments for purposes and populations for which they were never designed. For this reason it has been suggested on a number of occasions that it might be more appropriate to decide on the use of alternatives by an independent tribunal at the post-sentencing stage and before the offender enters prison (Ashworth, 1983; Skovron, 1988). Alternatively, it is a question of developing and enforcing more systematic sentencing practices across the board and specifying more precisely which sanctions are to be imposed upon which groups of offenders and under what conditions. Only in this way can the present haphazard and idiosyncratic system of sentencing be put on a more rational and realistic basis.

As in bail cases, the search for alternatives to relieve the pressure on the penal system has to be seen in relation to the conditions which have fostered the situation. One of the central conditions which has repeatedly been identified is the greater use of custodial sentences by the judiciary and the imposition of longer sentences (NACRO, 1988; Fitz-Maurice and Pease, 1982). Fitz-Maurice and Pease have estimated that a 15 per cent overall reduction in the length of prison sentences would be enough to remove the problem of overcrowding from British prisons. In the light of this figure it seems that it might be more appropriate to concentrate on devising ways of encouraging the judiciary to reduce the sentencing tariff, rather than develop more punitive 'alternatives' on the questionable basis that this is the best way of reducing overcrowding. Implementing a house arrest policy with or without electronic monitoring therefore needs to be accompanied by a revised and more rigorous sentencing policy if it is to have any real chance of achieving the desired effects. Implementing it without such reforms will almost certainly ensure that it will be used unsystematically and that its ability to reduce the prison population will be seriously impaired.

Early release

Employing electronic monitoring and house arrest in conjunction with early release policies is generally seen as a more certain method of reducing the prison population, since it is clearly directed only at the custodial population. But although this option raises some interesting possibilities, there is always a danger, as we have seen in the case of parole, that it can lead to the judiciary 'compensating' for the period of parole by extending the lengths of prison sentences.

In the wake of continuing overcrowding, early release has become a widely used tactic in many countries to reduce the penal population. Although it is clearly capable of reducing the level of overcrowding in the short term, its repeated usage can undermine the efficacy of the penal sanction in general. It also, by implication, questions the legitimacy of a sentencing policy that sends people to prison in ever-greater numbers in order that once they have been incarcerated they can summarily be released. This, in turn, suggests that it may be more expedient to devise the means for reducing the overall length of prison sentences. As James Austin has argued,

> When viewed as a long-term solution to prison crowding, early release is a poor substitute for a more permanent, rational and cost effective sentencing policy. It provides an excessive amount of discretion for correctional administrators, violates principles of equity and certainty in sentencing as assumed by the court, and increases the already low regard held for the criminal justice by the public. (Austin, 1986: 409)

In his evaluation of early release policies adopted in Illinois between 1980 and 1983 involving 21 000 inmates Austin found that although there was a net saving of approximately $1500 per release and that the policy effected a 10 per cent reduction in the projected increase in the prison population, there was evidence that this policy had jeopardized public safety and probably reduced the general deterrence function of prison.

It is precisely in relation to the problems of public safety and the maintenance of deterrence that support for house arrest and electronic monitoring is strongest. For if the savings of early release could be achieved without the attendant disadvantages then it becomes a much more acceptable policy.

Alternatively, it may be possible to substitute electronic monitoring and house arrest for intermittent sentences, as occurred in British Columbia (Ministry of Attorney General, 1987). In this case the targeted offenders were already spending five out of seven days out of prison in order to maintain their jobs and to continue to provide for their families. Most of those involved were reconvicted drink driving offenders serving a mandatory 14-day sentence, which translated into 25 days of house arrest. These offenders were selected on the basis that they did not endanger the public. In this programme although a few offenders were released from prison for five days a week the fact that they were selected on the basis that they were not a danger to public suggests that it is possibly the mandatory prison sentence which requires rethinking. House arrest in this instance merely serves to legitimate this sanction without actually realizing it.

Apart from early release policies electronic monitoring has been used in conjunction with work release programmes. In this context it is used with or without house arrest in order to facilitate engagement with work release programmes outside prison. For prisoners who otherwise would not be allowed to engage in outside work, the adoption of 'tagging' may provide enough security for the prisoner to take up employment without constant supervision.

Thus the use of electronic monitoring either in conjunction with or separately from house arrest can be used at various stages of the criminal justice process. Its usefulness will be determined as much by the specific context in which it is employed as by its general features. It needs therefore to be examined not only in relation to the particular country or state in each instance, but also in terms of the particular stage of the process at which it is used and in relation to the specific group of offenders on whom it is used.

In general, electronic monitoring and house arrest appear to evoke at least as many questions as potential answers. The very flexibility of these options carry their own dangers and it is clear that without a considered programme of implementation they are likely to add to the existing problems rather than resolve them. There is also the concern that the focus on these departures can be used either to compensate for poor practices or to prevent the development of more constructive penal policies. Most importantly, its adoption as a sentencing option calls for the reform of sentencing policies combined with a greater control of judicial and administrative discretion. Even if it is unable to do much to reduce the prison population, the use of electronic monitoring by itself may facilitate not only more work release programmes but it may also make weekend and conjugal visits more widely available to prisoners. If it is, however, to have any significant impact upon the current level of overcrowding then it will have to be seen as a form of punishment which is relevant for a large number of offenders. On whom, therefore, should this type of punishment be imposed?

On whom should it be used?

Part of the answer to this question is dependent upon which particular combination of house arrest and electronic monitoring is adopted. For as we have seen these two elements may be employed independently or in combination. However, it is apparent that they have to date largely been used in combination. This has affected the selection of the clientele. Any assessment of house arrest and electronic monitoring needs to consider its effectiveness with particular categories of defendants or offenders, for it may be more appropriate for some groups than others.

There are a number of restrictions that immediately come into play when deciding upon eligibility. The first and most obvious is that the 'controlee' needs a telephone, a known address and in some cases the finance to pay for the use of the equipment. Within most of the programmes initiated to date there have been a number of formal and informal restrictions on the type of offender who has been allowed to participate. Normally, violent offenders and those convicted of serious sexual offences are excluded. Additionally, some programmes preclude those convicted of serious property offences and those convicted of personal crimes are discouraged. In some cases those convicted of drug or related offences are not selected since house arrest might allow them to continue dealing in drugs from home. Also, because of the social and domestic problems which might arise from extended periods of home confinement, its use tends to be limited to a maximum of six months. And given that the emerging norm is that the equivalence of incarceration and house arrest is in the region of 1 to 3 then it means that only offenders serving very short prison sentences are considered suitable. Significantly, however, in countries like England and Wales the number of people serving three months or less has dropped dramatically from 3418 in 1980 to 2095 in 1986 (HMSO, 1987). In other European countries like Belgium prison sentences of six months are automatically moderated. In these cases the existing alternatives seem to be effective in reducing the number of short-term prisoners. The more enduring problem is finding ways of decreasing the number of middle- and long-term prisoners; and it is this population that will have to be considered if a substantial reduction in the average daily population in prisons is to be achieved.

In view of these conditions the range of application seems to be severely circumscribed in advance. Even among those who are generally supportive of the use of electronic monitoring and house arrest, there are reservations about the types of people on whom they might be used. Ball et al. (1988), for example, are cautious about its adoption and suggest that it is probably most relevant for juveniles and drunken drivers.

The interest in imposing curfews on troublesome youth is not new. The most recent attempt to impose a curfew or 'night restriction order' in England and Wales was contained in the Criminal Justice Act, 1982. John Pitts has argued that this approach is spurred by particular ideologies associated with juvenile delinquency. Thus:

> 'Night restriction' or the curfew forces parents to supervise their own children in their own homes. As such it reflects the abiding Conservative preoccupation with the idea that lawlessness is promoted by the abdication of responsibility for control and discipline by teachers and working-class parents. The curfew requires that the child or young person remain at home between 6 pm and 6 am for a period of three months. This effectively turns the home into a prison and parents into jailers. (Pitts, 1988: 54)

The bitter irony of this policy and ideology is that it is precisely the parents who have not exercised discipline in the past who would presumably be least equipped to enforce a policy of house arrest. This was one reason why house arrest for juveniles was always treated with ambivalence. But the introduction of electronic monitoring, it is suggested, may be able to provide a more effective form of house arrest by displacing the point of enforcement. Even so, the juvenile and young adult population represent possibly the most volatile and marginalized group within the community and are unlikely to be receptive to home confinement. As the number of juveniles in custody is falling the demand, in Britain at least, is likely to be minimal. There may be more interest in applying this sanction to the 17 to 21 age group, not because they constitute an appropriate population but because it would be politically expedient to focus upon this group which now constitutes one of the most serious problem populations within prisons. This group, however, is even less likely than juveniles to provide appropriate candidates for home confinement. Indeed, as the experience of Florida indicated, married and more mature offenders prove to be better at adjusting to the requirements of home confinement; while younger and less mature offenders experienced great difficulties in abiding by the conditions (Blomberg et al., 1987).

In relation to drunken drivers the case for home confinement is more persuasive. It is not surprising that this group has featured very prominently in the programmes implemented to date. According to the survey carried out by the National Institute for Justice, it was found that out of a total of 826 participants being monitored approximately one third were convicted of traffic-related offences (see Table 1). One of the reasons for selecting drunk drivers is the predisposition within existing programmes to select non-violent and more affluent offenders who are not seen as providing a threat to the general public — as long as they are not driving a car. Where there exist laws imposing short mandatory prison sentences on convicted drunk drivers, house arrest has been seen as an alternative way of dealing with this type of offender.

Table 1   *Sentence status compared to offence*

Offence	Sentenced	Pre-trial	Other and unknown	Total	Percentage
Major traffic	268	7	0	275	33.3
Drugs	109	10	0	119	14.4
Crimes *vs.* persons	40	6	1	47	5.7
Property offences	132	18	0	150	18.2
Sex offences	21	3	0	24	2.9
Frauds	28	0	0	28	3.4
Non-support	13	0	0	13	1.6
Probation violation	39	1	0	40	4.8
Multiple charges	73	3	0	76	9.2
Other	38	3	0	41	4.9
Unknown	8	0	5	13	1.6
Total	769	51	6	826	100.00

Source: Schmidt, 1987: 6.

However, for those with relatively spacious and comfortable homes spending thirty days on home confinement may be seen as a 'soft' option. It may be seen — particularly by those who remain in prison — as a way of privileging the better-off offenders (Peck, 1988). On the other hand, the availability of this option may encourage the processing of more white-collar offenders for whom a more suitable punishment is seen to be available. Either way, if it is used predominantly for these kinds of offenders its usage will make little impact upon the bulk of poorer offenders who constitute the vast majority of the custodial population. In fact, it would seem to be the case that the prevalent combination of house arrest and electronic monitoring is likely to be used where it is least needed, and that for the large majority of those incarcerated it is largely irrelevant.

This form of punishment also appears to be disproportionately applied to male offenders. This may be because house arrest may be seen as less suitable to women, who are in general already more restricted to the private and domestic realms (Siltanen and Stanworth, 1984). Indeed, it could be argued that many women are already subject to some degree of house arrest — either through patriarchal controls or through the fear of crime, or both (Jones et al., 1986; Santos, 1985).

It is possible that in the not too distant future there may be one group for whom some form of house arrest and electronic monitoring might be an appropriate sanction. This group involves the growing number of offenders who are known to be suffering from AIDS. The concentration within the prison of high risk groups — particularly intravenous drug users — could mean that the number of inmates who are seropositive could increase over the next few years to unmanagable levels. At present the response within prisons is to isolate those known to be infected with the AIDS virus, but as the numbers grow house arrest with electronic monitoring could become a possible alternative to incarceration for this group.

A recent survey in Europe found that more than 10 per cent of prisoners in the prisons investigated were seropositive (Harding, 1987). In some prisons the rates are much higher. In Spain, for example, it is estimated that almost half the inmates of Barcelona prison are seropositive. The spread of AIDS within prisons could well become the most serious problem facing prison authorities over the next decade. House arrest and electronic monitoring may provide a means not only of containing this population but also of providing some degree of surveillance and protection (Prison Reform Trust, 1988).

Alternatively, if we consider the forms of electronically monitored surveillance that are not linked to house arrest there are some interesting, but as yet undeveloped, possibilities which should be considered. One such possibility is the regulation of interpersonal violence through the development of a cell network system where offenders can move freely within a prescribed radius but give out a warning signal if they move outside that area. Like the forms of electronic monitoring linked to house arrest, this system has the advantage of allowing the offender to carry on working and in most respects lead a normal life. Such a system could be an effective way of keeping known offenders and victims apart, and may go some way to address the problem of interpersonal violence — particularly domestic violence. The technology is in principle available but has been neglected in favour of the systems linked to home confinement. This is partly because the manufacturers have to date seen the home telephone based system as more immediately marketable and profitable. A cell network system requires state initiative and coordination and also requires considerable initial capital outlay. Therefore the setting up of such a system would require not only the question of interpersonal violence to be taken seriously, but also the building of a political commitment to develop these new forms of technology. Technology is not neutral. Priorities cannot be set by commercial interests, or what is often euphemistically referred to as 'the market'; open public discussion is needed.

Thus the debate about electronic monitoring and house arrest is ultimately not purely technical but political. Implementation of programmes raises questions about crime and punishment that are of deep public interest, and also raises a number of general issues that require some consideration — most notably the problems of 'net widening', costs and effectiveness, as well as a number of legal and administrative and technical issues.

'Net widening'

Most commentators on this subject have expressed some concern over the possibilities of 'net widening' (Berry, 1986; Vaughn, 1987). But net widening is not, as many commentators seem to assume, necessarily an undesirable thing in itself. A great deal depends upon which types of offenders are being caught in the net. The preoccupation with net widening in the literature derives largely from a commitment to minimalism, and the view that the criminal justice system is essentially repressive and negative and that its expansion in any form is undesirable (see Matthews, 1988).

From this libertarian perspective surveillance in all its forms is seen as particularly sinister. Because it tends to be immediately associated with Orwellian images of 'Big Brother', it invariably attracts suspicion and condemnation (Marx, 1985). Consequently there is little consideration of the positive aspects of surveillance — in particular that it can be far *less* intrusive than other more informal control measures. Surveillance can be positive and supportive, and where it serves to reduce the incidence of crime — particularly violent crime — it can be a valuable regulatory mechanism.

However, the critical question regarding the expansion of the criminal justice 'net' is whether the intervention is effective and whether the clientele is appropriate. Net widening should only really become a concern if the intervention is unlikely to be effective or where it is certain to miss its target. Much of the genuine concern about net widening has arisen where attempts have been made to reduce the range or intensity of intervention and inadvertently other clientele have been hauled in. These less desirable forms of net widening either take the forms of 'skimming', 'trawling' or 'double tracking'.

The 'skimming' effect, which has been noted in relation to electronic monitoring and house arrest, occurs with the selection of a range of 'privileged' offenders or defendants who are invited/persuaded to embrace new forms of intervention which appear less onerous. By this process the existing forms of intervention are rationalized and maintained and the new agencies operate in conjunction with them. The establishment of this privileged option may encourage the processing of some types of offenders who arguably should not have been tangled up in the criminal justice system at all.

The 'trawling' effect operates to the extent that the range of agencies in the criminal justice system pick up the social debris, the misfits and the marginalized. These are holding agencies that serve to cater for those the central criminal justice agencies find it difficult to contain, including the mentally ill, the sick, the addicted and others who constitute a significant but often forgotten part of the criminal justice system. There is little evidence, to date, of electronic monitoring or house arrest being used in this way, but there are distinct possibilities that it could be in the not too distant future.

'Double tracking' refers to the process of setting up parallel but non-competing avenues of punishment through which offenders can be endlessly circulated. This is not so much net widening as the creation of different nets which increase the intensity and level of regulation (Austin and Krisberg, 1981). Where this occurs the new agencies or alternatives serve to divert offenders *into* rather than *out of* the criminal justice system. Alternatively, it can lead to a process of transcarceration, in which people instead of being decarcerated are shunted from one form of containment to another (see Lowman et al., 1987).

The experience over the last two decades or so is that the processes of skimming, trawling and double tracking can result from interventions that are initially justified on the basis of reducing costs and providing less intrusive alternatives. It is because of the very real possibilities of the unanticipated effects of particular forms of intervention that it is imperative that our analysis and policy is informed by a systematic view of the function of the criminal justice process. However, it should be emphasized that these processes are not invariably negative and that net widening, and indeed certain forms of surveillance, can be beneficial. The aim of the game is to make sure that the right fish end up in the right nets. The problem associated with restructuring the mechanisms of control have important consequences for the question of costs.

Costs

Making direct comparisons between the costs of house arrest and imprisonment is virtually impossible. Because of the skimming and double tracking effects associated with net widening the two forms of punishment are dealing with non-comparable populations and are supposedly aiming to achieve different results. There are also problems in trying to calculate exact costs of alternative programmes both in the short term and long term.

In the short term, if electronic monitoring equipment is used there will be a considerable outlay for the equipment. In the long term it is widely assumed that electronic monitoring will save money. This assumption, however, is normally based on the respective costs of incarceration versus home confinement. But the available evidence suggests that only three out of four of those given home confinement would actually have gone to prison. In the remaining quarter of cases the costs of electronic monitoring is probably added on to an existing probation or supervision order (Petersilia, 1988).

Even in cases where direct comparison of the cost of home confinement and incarceration appear ligitimate there are number of other considerations to take into account. Firstly, many of those given home confinement are 'low risk' offenders for whom the costs of incarceration would be below average. Secondly, the costs of incarceration remain roughly the same whether the prison is full or half-empty. For 85 per cent of the costs of incarceration are fixed costs, which can only be 'saved' if the institution, or some part of it, is closed down. Comparisons, therefore, of daily rates of incarceration per person are misleading, and the savings of removing a small number of people from prison are minimal.

On the positive side, in cases where home confinement allows offenders to keep their jobs and maintain their families the State may save money on welfare and family support. Also, where fees are collected from offenders the cost of the equipment and the supervision can be offset. In Florida, for example, it was reported that over $9 million was collected in fees from home detainees (Palm Beach County, 1987).

There has been at least one example of a pilot programme being closed down because it was considered to be too expensive (Petersilia, 1986). For the most part, however, the operators of home confinement claim substantial savings. But the figures do not always add up. Ball et al. (1988: 50), for example, claim that in the case of juveniles the daily cost of house arrest (without electronic monitoring) organized by the probation service works out at approximately one third of the cost of secure detention ($14.95 per day compared with \$45.57 per day respectively). However, given that the sentencing trade-off for home confinement versus imprisonment tends to be in the region of 3 to 1, then in these cases there appears to be no discernible saving. For significant savings to be made the cost of imprisonment would have to be at least five times the cost of home confinement, with or without electronic monitoring. This is because such costings would have to take into account the additional administrative costs for overseeing those agencies, and in a percentage of cases include the cost of locating, tracking and eventually reincarcerating those who break the conditions of curfew.

When considering the question of costs it is also important to bear in mind the opportunity of adopting policies like home confinement. For it may be the case that the other available sanctions for dealing with minor offenders — fines, community service, reparation etc. — are even less costly. It should also be remembered that one of the main rationales for incarceration was that in terms of punishment it offered certain economies of scale, and that providing a full network of facilities in the community and developing the necessary infrastructure would, as David Greenberg (1985) pointed out, almost certainly cost more than incarceration. It may well be, in fact, that home confinement is only economically viable if it involves an absolute minimum of contact with the detainee.

The question of costs is important but if it is to be a significant part of the justification for adopting home confinement then the calculations must be comprehensive and precise. The disparate use of home confinement to date, however, means that making such assessments is going to be an extremely difficult task. Whether costs at the end of the day are greater or less than those of imprisonment or other options has also to be balanced against the perceived effectiveness of the sanction.

Effectiveness

The immediate question that arises in relation to programme effectiveness is the level of security these systems afford. If home confinement and/or electronic monitoring are to be use in a significant number of cases then it will need to be demonstrated that they offer the public an adequate degree of protection. Correspondingly, if there is a high degree of 'failure' in terms of the controlee violating the conditions of home confinement then there are not only substantial costs involved in locating offenders, there is also potentially a great deal of time and effort involved in returning offenders to secure institutions, which may in some cases result in longer periods of detention than the original sentence.

Preliminary evaluations of the effectiveness of electronic monitoring and house arrest indicate that the 'failure' rate (that is the number of those who do not complete the programme) is in the region of 10 to 20 per cent. This is quite a significant level of failure, since most of the projects specifically select low-risk offenders; while those that currently administer these programmes have a vested interest in demonstrating significant levels of success.

Where home confinement is used for long periods there must be a very real possibility of creating a new range of personal and domestic problems. Extended periods of confinement could well lead to alcohol and drug dependency or heightened domestic conflict and violence. The pressure of placing the whole household under surveillance may in some cases produce explosive situations in which families may be torn apart even more frequently than occurs through imprisonment.

There is no doubt that wives, in particular, suffer from the incarceration of their husbands, both as a result of stigmatization and the reduction in family income (Smith, 1986). But home confinement, even if the income level is maintained, means that the other members of the household experience an erosion of privacy and can become both the enforcers and recipients of punishment.

Concerning those who successfully complete their period of home confinement there have been questions raised about the rehabilitative and deterrent value of this option. Since one of the primary justifications for house arrest is that it allows for the continuance of 'normal' family life and work relations, it can avoid the alienating effects of incarceration. Therefore, although it might not actually rehabilitate offenders — particularly given the short periods over which it is imposed — it at least avoids some of the debilitating effects of imprisonment. There are some, however, who claim that home confinement has an intrinsic rehabilitative value since 'normal' people learn conformity and discipline through work and associated responsibilities and that where home imprisonment or electronic monitoring make this possible, either by allowing continuance of employment or through work release programmes, these systems could have a positive rehabilitative value. In a context in which the committing of an offence is often identified as the outcome of a lack of responsibility by the offender, it seems paradoxical that the majority of formal sanctions that are mobilized serve to diminish responsibility further.

The notion that any form of intervention which lasts for a few months is going to make any profound difference to the motivation of individuals is probably unrealistic. But rather than think of rehabilitation exclusively as a form of individual transformation it should also be viewed as a social process. Ideally, we would want to develop forms of punishment which strengthened rather than severed the relation between the individual and the community. On this level, forms of punishment based on the principle of seclusion are likely to have little relevance (Cullen and Gilbert, 1982; Currie, 1985).

Importantly, despite the apparent decline of the rehabilitative ideal and the continued calls for stiffer penalties, there still appears to be a widespread public demand for rehabilitative programmes. Since it is unrealistic to segregate even the most serious offenders for more than a certain length of time, these offenders will have at some point to be accommodated within the general community, and it is not surprising that the general public have a strong interest in rehabilitation.

The rehabilitative value of house arrest and electronic monitoring, however, may be enhanced if they are applied separately. Where house arrest was linked to community service and face-to-face supervision as in Kentucky, it was seen as a more positive and constructive sanction. Similarly, where electronic monitoring is operated in a way that allows the development of normal social interaction without endangering the public or the potential victims, which could be possible with the cell net system, rehabilitation might become more of a reality.

Apart from the possible rehabilitative value of these measures concern has also been expressed over the potential deterrent effect. As with rehabilitation there is need to distinguish between forms of individual and social deterrence. Also, as with rehabilitation there is a need to reaffirm the value of deterrence and to move beyond the unfounded assertion that deterrence does not work. Most of our daily actions are profoundly shaped by deterrence. Even in cases where actions appear to be completely spontaneous and/or irrational they are invariably influenced by potential effects and outcomes (Wilson, 1983).

Thus the question that arises in relation to home confinement and electronic monitoring is what impact it is likely to have upon the propensity to commit crime. The difficulties of measuring these effects in any precise way have persuaded some researchers that the question itself is not particularly meaningful. As a result they have chosen to ignore, or at least play down, the role of deterrence. But some comparison has to be made about the propensity of offenders to recommit crimes, and it is important to gauge the impact on the relevant population of the general deterrent effects of home confinement.

As we have seen, one of the groups targeted for home confinement are drunken drivers who would otherwise receive short mandatory prison sentences. However, we cannot assume that home confinement is preferable to imprisonment in this type of case, where a short prison sentence is presumably being imposed precisely as a form of *special* deterrence.

The rehabilitative and deterrent effects of house arrest and electronic monitoring will also be deeply influenced by the agencies who administer the programmes and the clientele who are placed in them. But clearly, if these techniques are to gain public support and are to be seen as a viable option they will have to show their capacity to achieve these twin aims. Programmes will also have to overcome the various legal and administrative issues that currently surround their operation.

Legal and administrative issues

Although home confinement and electronic monitoring have only been available for a relatively short time, their use has already provoked an array of legal and administrative issues.

The legal issues which have repeatedly arisen have centred on questions of privacy, informed consent and equal protection. On all these counts there have been a number of test cases in the USA which have explored the legality of these forms of punishment. The overall result is that electronic monitoring has been deemed constitutional and its implementation has for the most part been upheld by the courts. Although there have been some attempts to lay down guidelines and safeguards for its use, it has generally been accepted as being less of an infringement of rights than the alternative available sanctions (Del Carmen and Vaughn, 1986).

Each country will have its own legal responses to the adoption of electronic monitoring. In Britain, which does not enjoy the kind of constitutional protection available in the USA there would be a need to develop legal safeguards and guidelines. In the present situation new legislation would need to be passed if electronic monitoring were to be adopted as a sentencing option for the courts. It would, however, be possible to implement electronic monitoring immediately for prisoners on remand. Pilot schemes have been introduced to use home confinement for some remand prisoners, and their operation will be closely observed. There is, however, some uncertainty over the most appropriate agencies to administer these programmes at present.

Just as it is the flexibility of electronic monitoring that forms part of the attractiveness of this option to policymakers, so it is the fact that it can be administered by a variety of agencies — both public and private — which makes it easy to operationalize, at least in principle. According to the National Institute of Justice Survey,

> These monitoring programs are run by a wide variety of types of organizations. About half (50.9%) are correctional agencies, either at the state or local level, including departments of corrections, parole boards and probation agencies. Almost a quarter (22.6%) are private monitoring service providers. The remainder are public agencies, including police departments, sheriffs and courts. (Schmidt, 1987: 8)

Whichever agency takes responsibility for organizing these programmes, they tend to supply some form of contract with controlees which sets out the conditions of participation and in some cases the implications for violations (Nelken, 1988). However, it is not always clear what level of violation is required to terminate involvement in such programmes, nor whether those who break the conditions of contract necessarily return to prison. Different agencies will employ different criteria and some will more readily than others refer the controlees to prison departments. Given the disparate nature of the agencies involved and their generally low levels of accountability there is an urgent need to establish clear guidelines if these systems are to operate.

Despite these legal and administrative ambiguities the development of electronic monitoring and house arrest programmes in the USA has met with surprisingly little resistance. Significantly, resistance to the adoption of electronic monitoring has emanated from two camps. On one side right-wing groups and judges have condemned it for not being sufficiently punitive; while on the other side civil libertarians have objected to its use on the basis that it erodes basic rights of freedom and movement. In Britain, however, the response has been more varied and certainly more hostile. The principal agency expected to be responsible for implementing these options — the probation service — has formally stated through its union that

> This union is totally opposed to tracking or electronic monitoring of offenders. This A.G.M. instructs the N.E.C. to campaign vigorously against such a proposal or practice. N.A.P.O. will not cooperate with electronic tagging schemes at any stage and instructs its members to withdraw from existing tracking schemes. (NAPO, 1988)

The National Association of Probation Officers had also, at the previous AGM, expressed opposition to the imposition of curfews and is therefore equally unlikely to cooperate with sanctions based on home confinement. For the probation service these policies are seen to run counter to the purposes of probation; they believe that the existing methods of personal supervision ought to be strengthened and that these approaches are in essence more effective than tagging or tracking systems.

This overt level of resistance, however, does not seem to have dampened the government's enthusiasm for tracking and tagging. They have clearly indicated that if the probation service refuses to operate such schemes they will consider the possibility of using private security agencies or other private organizations who might operate in conjunction with the probation service:

> One possibility would be for the probation service to contract with other services, and private and voluntary organisations, to obtain some of the components of punishment in the community. The probation service would supervise the order but would not itself be responsible for providing all the elements.
>
> Another possibility would be to set up a new organisation to organise punishment in the community. It would not in itself supervise offenders or provide facilities directly, but would contract with other services and organisations to do so. (HMSO, 1988b: 17)

Setting up new agencies to administer these sanctions may be more expensive and time-consuming than the use of electronic monitoring would warrant. Also, setting up a national agency would probably only serve to generate more hostility within the probation service, as well as in other agencies. However, where the role of the agency is predominantly one of monitoring and surveillance, rather than counselling or case work, private sector involvement would be easier to mobilize (Lindquist, 1980).

Technical problems

Finally, a number of technical problems have been reported in relation to electronic monitoring devices. In some of the early programmes there were problems in making the bracelets and anklets tamper-resistant and in preventing faults with the telephone system registering erroneous violations. In one project in Michigan, for example, it was found that 'eight of the 37 transmitters had to be replaced. There were replaced because of tearing straps, two were replaced because of false tamper alarms, one was replaced because of a false tamper alarm and torn strap, one stopped signalling and one was replaced because of a rattle' (Hatchett, 1987: 18).

Although much effort has been made to improve the technology and minimize faults there still remain some serious problems with the equipment. Each time a faulty signal is transmitted it has to be checked by the monitor. This is very time-consuming and causes continuous and unnecessary intrusions into the home of the controlee. Del Carmen and Vaughn found that about 15 per cent of the equipment developed faults, and that

> The system is reported to be accurate 85% of the time in monitoring violations. Inaccurate reports can be generated, according to one user, by power failures or severe thunderstorms that interfere with the telephone line transmissions. One operational problem has been discovered in the system itself. If a person places his body in a fetal position, as sometimes occurs during sleep, and his body mass is between the ankle device and the receiver, the signal is blocked and a false alarm is sent to the computer indicating that the user has left home. When the user rolls over and his body mass is no longer blocking the signal the receiver will indicate that he has returned. (Del Carmen and Vaughn, 1986: 6)

As these systems are becoming more widely used there is growing pressure on the manufacturers to provide more reliable equipment. Currently, almost all of the effort is being put into the system linked to house arrest rather than the cell net system. This is no doubt because manufacturers see the former system as more immediately marketable, adaptable and profitable. The development of an effective cell net system would require a considerable capital outlay. Although such a system could be extremely useful in addressing some of the more serious forms of violent crime it cannot be so immediately rationalized in terms of reducing the prison population. Developing a cell net system requires centralized coordination as well as some clear indication that it can provide a mechanism for addressing problems like interpersonal violence.

Conclusion

These are still early days in the development of house arrest and electronic monitoring. But the expansion in the use of these systems over the last two years in the USA alone suggests that they could become a pronounced feature of the criminal justice system in many countries in the very near future.

To date, the focus has largely been on electronic monitoring used in conjunction with house arrest, but it would seem that the potential application of this system is limited. Depending from which point in the criminal justice process controlees are drawn, these sanctions only appear to be currently relevant to a narrow range of offenders. The two groups of offenders who have been singled out as being most appropriate candidates for this punishment (drunk drivers and juveniles) turn out on examination to be largely unsuitable, either because they are unlikely to abide by the conditions of the curfew or because the deterrent effect of home confinement is less than a short mandatory prison sentence. Because of the general restrictions that apply to those selected it is already being seen by some as a 'white collar' sanction and as a 'soft' option. On the other hand, some critics see it as an inappropriate distraction from the main problems within the criminal justice system.

Its most effective usage is likely to be in conjunction with work release schemes or with early release if it can be used more widely and if it is generally the case that a significant number of inmates can be decarcerated on this basis who previously would have remained in prison. The same kinds of consideration apply to sentencing options. Given the problems of net widening it is incumbent upon those who propose electronic monitoring and house arrest as a sentencing option that they clearly demonstrate that it acts as an alternative to custody rather than as an alternative to existing alternatives. This in turn raises questions about sentencing reform and the establishment of a rational and consistent sentencing process.

It seems possible that it may well be in relation to the spread of HIV infection and AIDS that electronic monitoring and house arrest could have their greatest value. Managing the growing number of prisoners who are seropositive is likely to become a major problem for prison authorities and governments in the next few years, and some form of home confinement with a monitoring programme may prove an effective way of handling a proportion of this population.

But as we have suggested, it is also important to consider the alternative ways of employing these sanctions and to evaluate them not only conjointly but also separately. House arrest may in some cases be more effective by itself than when used with electronic monitoring. Similarly, electronic monitoring used in conjunction with work release, for example, may be viable without being linked to house arrest. Also, in general, we have suggested that is may be beneficial to develop those forms of monitoring and surveillance based on the cell net system which might allow us to intervene effectively in regulating some of the more serious forms of crime.

References

Ackerman, J. (1986) 'Applying Electronic Surveillance Systems to Probation and House Arrest in New York State', *Journal of Probation and Parole*, 17: 5–9.

Ashworth, A. (1983) *Sentencing and Penal Policy*. Weidenfeld & Nicolson.

Association of Chief Probation Officers (ACPO) (1988) *Electronic Surveillance*. London.

Austin, J. (1986) 'Using Early Release to Relieve Prison Crowding: A Dilemma in Public Policy', *Crime and Delinquency*, 32 (4): 404–503.

Austin, J. and Krisberg, B. (1981) 'Wider, Stronger and Different Nets: The Dialectics of Criminal Justice Reform', *Journal of Research in Crime and Delinquency*, 18: 165–96.

Austin, J. and Krisberg, B. (1982) 'The Unmet Promise of Alternatives to Incarceration', *Crime and Delinquency*, 28 (3): 374–409.

Ball, R., Huff, C. and Lilly, R. (1988) *House Arrest and Correctional Policy*. Sage.

Ball, R. and Lilly, R. (1988) 'Home Incarceration with Electronic Monitoring', in J. Scotland and T. Hirshi (eds), *Controversial Issues in Crime and Justice*. Sage.

Berry, B. (1985) 'Electronic Jails: A New Criminal Concern', *Justice Quarterly*, 2 (1): 1–22.

Berry, B. (1986) 'More Questions and More Ideas on Electronic Monitoring', *Justice Quarterly*, 3 (3): 363–70.

Blomberg, T., Waldo, G. and Burcoff, L. (1987) 'Home Confinement and Electronic Surveillance', in B. McCarthy (ed.), *Intermediate Punishments*. Criminal Justice Press.

Cohen, S. (1985) *Visions of Social Control*. Polity Press.

Corbett, R. and Fersch, E. (1985) 'Home as Prison: The Use of House Arrest', *Federal Probation*, March: 13–17.

Cullen, F. and Gilbert, K. (1982) *Reaffirming Rehabilitation*. Anderson Publishing Co.

Currie, E. (1985) *Confronting Crime: An American Challenge*. Pantheon.

Del Carmen, R. and Vaughn, J. (1986) 'Legal Issues in the Use of Electronic Surveillance in Probation', *Federal Probation*, 50 (2): 60–9.

Faugeron, C. (1988) 'Prisons in France: An Irresistible Increasing of the Detained Population'. Paper presented to the European Colloquium on Research on Crime and Criminal Policy in Europe.

Flynn, L. (1986) 'House Arrest: Start it Right or Quit', *Journal of Probation and Parole*, 17 (Fall): 1–5.

Fitzgerald, M. and Sim, J. (1979) *British Prisons*. Basil Blackwell.

Fitz-Maurice, J. and Pease, K. (1982) 'A Comparison of Some European Statistics', *Justice of the Peace*, 146: 575–9.

Gable, R. (1986) 'Applications of Personal Telemonitoring to Current Problems of Corrections', *Journal of Criminal Justice*, 14: 167–76.

Graham, J. (1987) 'The Declining Prison Population in the Federal Republic of Germany', in *Home Office Research Bulletin*, no. 24. HMSO, London.

Greenberg, D. (1975) 'Problems in Community Corrections', *Issues in Criminology*, 19: 1–34.

Harding, T. W. (1987) *AIDS in Prison* (Study Sponsored by the Council of Europe). University Institute of Legal Medicine, Geneva.

Hatchett, P. (1987) *The Home Confinement Programme: An Appraisal of the Electronic Monitoring of Offenders in Washtenaw County, Michigan*. Michigan Department of Corrections.

HMSO (1987) *Prison Statistics, England and Wales 1986*.

HMSO (1988a) *Private Sector Involvement in the Remand System*. Cm 434.

HMSO (1988b) *Punishment Custody and the Community*. Cm 424.

Ingraham, B. and Smith, G. (1972) 'The Use of Electronics in the Observation and Control of Human Behaviour and its possible use in Rehabilitation and Parole', *Issues in Criminology*, 2 (2): 35–53.

Jones, F., Maclean, B. and Young, J. (1986) *The Islington Crime Survey*. Gower.

Lindquist, C. (1980) 'The Private Sector in Corrections Contracting Probation Services from Community Organisations', *Federal Probation*, March: 58–63.

Lilly, R., Ball, R. and Wright, J. (1987) 'Home Incarceration with Electronic Monitoring in Kenton County Kentucky: An Evaluation', in B. McCarthy (ed.), *Intermediate Punishments*. Criminal Justice Press.

Lowman, J., Menzies, B. and Palys, T. (1987) 'Transcarceration and the Modern State of Penalty', in J. Lowman, B. Menzies and T. Palys (eds), *Transcarceration: Essays in the Sociology of Social Control*. Gower.

McCarthy, B. (ed.) (1987) *Intermediate Punishments: Intensive Supervision, Home Confinement and Electronic Surveillance*. Criminal Justice Press.

Marx, G. (1985) 'I'll be Watching You', *Dissent* (Winter): 26–54.

Matthews, R. (1987) 'Decarceration and Social Control: Fantasies and Realities', in J. Lowman, B. Menzies and T. Palys (eds), *Transcarceration: Essays in the Sociology of Social Control*. Gower.

Matthews, R. (1988) 'Reassessing Informal Justice', in R. Matthews (ed.), *Informal Justice?* Sage.

Ministry of Attorney General, British Columbia (1987) *Electronic Monitoring System for Offender Supervision*. Discussion paper. Vancouver.

Morris, N. (1974) *The Future of Imprisonment*. University of Chicago Press.

NACRO (1988) *The Electronic Monitoring of Offenders*. NACRO, London.

NAPO (1988) *Annual General Meeting Report*. London.

Nelken, D. (1988) 'Social Work Contracts and Social Control', in R. Matthews (ed.), *Informal Justice?* Sage.

Offenders Tag Association (1988) 'Cellular Radio'. London: Offenders Tag Association.

Palm Beach County (1987) 'Palm Beach County in House Arrest Work Release Programme', in B. McCarthy (ed.), *Intermediate Punishments*. Criminal Justice Press.

Peck, K. (1988) 'High Tech House Arrest', *The Progressive* (July): 26–8.

Peters, T. (1988) 'The Problems of Imprisonment, including Strategies that Might be Employed to Minimise the Use of Custody'. Paper presented to the European Colloquium on Research, Crime and Criminal Policy in Europe. Oxford, July.

Petersilia, J. (1986) 'Explaining the Option of House Arrest', *The Progressive* (July): 26–8.

Petersilia, J. (1988) 'Probation Reform', in J. Scott and T. Hirschi (eds.), *Controversial Issues in Crime and Justice*. Sage.

Pitts, J. (1988) *The Politics of Juvenile Crime*. Sage.

Prison Reform Trust (1988) *HIV, AIDS and Prisons*. Prison Reform Trust, London.

Santos, B., (1985) 'On Modes of Production, Law and Social Power', *International Journal of Sociology of Law*, 13: 299–336.

Schmidt, A (1987) *The Use of Electronic Monitoring by Criminal Justice Agencies*. National Institute of Justice. 2–87.

Schmidt, A. and Curtis, C. (1987) 'Electronic Monitoring', in B. McCarthy (ed.), *Intermediate Punishments*. New York: Criminal Justice Press.

Shapiro, M. (1972) 'The Uses of Behaviour Control Technologies: A Response', *Issues in Criminology*, 7 (2): 55–92.

Siltanen, J. and Stanworth, M. (1984) 'The Politics of Private Woman and Public Man', in J. Siltanen and M. Stanworth (eds.), *Woman and the Public Sphere*. Hutchinson.

Skovron, J. (1988) 'Prison Crowding: The Dimensions of the Problem and Strategies of Population Control', in J. Scott and T. Hirschi (eds), *Controversial Issues in Crime and Justice*. Sage.

Smith, S. (1986) 'Neglect as Control: Prisoners' Families'. Paper presented at the 14th Conference of the European Group for the Study of Deviance and Social Control, Madrid.

Stone, C. (1988) *Bail Information for the Crown Prosecution Service*. Vera Institute of Justice, London.

Timko, F. (1986) 'Electronic Monitoring — How it all Began: Conversations with Love and Goss', *Journal of Probation and Parole*, 27 (Fall): 15–17.

Vaughn, J. (1987) 'Planning for Change: The Use of Electronic Monitoring as a Correctional Alternative', in B. McCarthy (ed.), *Intermediate Punishments*. Criminal Justice Press.

Wilson, J. Q. (1983) *Thinking about Crime*. Basic Books.

6 THE VOLUNTARY SECTOR'S ROLE

Following the Wolfenden (1978) Report, the term 'mixed economy' is used to describe the balance of State, private, voluntary sector, and informal and community based services that might be called on to meet welfare needs. In this chapter by Rob Mawby, the term is used in the context of the criminal justice system as the basis for a discussion of the balance between voluntary and private alternatives as governments have sought to constrain public sector developments. Moreover, given the priority of 'law and order' for the current British government, greater voluntary sector involvement may be considered a more acceptable alternative to privatization of criminal justice. This is particularly the case where volunteers are incorporated within State agencies, and where the advantages of the voluntary sector appeal to a wider constituency.

Bearing these issues in mind, much of the chapter is concerned with questions of definition. It is argued that the distinction between the private sector and voluntary organizations is by no means clear, especially where consumer choice is restricted, and that the voluntary sector embraces an enormous variety of organizations, some of which find more favour with the government than others. Thus voluntary agencies might anticipate more government support if they have close, harmonious relationships with statutory agencies, if they prioritize service provision rather than pressure group activities, and if their clients are considered deserving (or, if not, the client-helper relationship is formalized).

In this context, government enthusiasm for increased voluntary effort is not to be understood merely in financial terms, or even with regard to the advantages associated with many voluntary service initiatives. It has to be considered as a *political* response. A shift towards the voluntary sector, which receives considerable public support, has wider public appeal than does privatization. It provides the additional advantage — from the government's perspective — of allowing for greater central control. In consequence, while in some respects the greater involvement of voluntary agencies in the provision of penal services may be only marginally different from privatization, in other respects it allows the government to scale down its involvement in the *provision* of services while at the same time tightening central control. It is in this context that the role of the voluntary sector in a mixed economy of criminal justice must be assessed.

The Voluntary Sector's Role in a Mixed Economy of Criminal Justice

R. I. Mawby

The last decade has seen a dramatic shift of emphasis in government's definitions of the appropriate level of State involvement in social and public services. Despite the very different levels of State welfare provision in the United States (Weddel, 1986), Canada (Guest, 1984) and Britain, in all three countries conservative governments have attempted to roll back the boundaries of State provision, and look to 'non-public' sectors for the provision of a variety of services. The age of 'anti-collectivism' (George and Wilding, 1985) has arrived with terrifying suddenness.

That said, however, a number of alternatives to State-run services exist. The Wolfenden (1978) Committee, for example, in the context of social welfare provision, identified three other service providers: the informal system of social helping, the commercial system, and the voluntary system. The last can be further subdivided into *voluntary organizations* and *volunteers* — who may be utilized by voluntary organizations, the statutory system or indeed the private sector. However, combined these alternatives make up what has been termed 'the mixed economy of welfare', preferable — according to Wolfenden — to State monopolization since it allegedly increases the range of services and consequently the choice available.

Ten years on, Wolfenden's fight to preserve a foothold for the voluntary sector appears somewhat quaint. Rather, the prospect of a range of State welfare services as available on a universal basis, to those who so choose, is under more of a threat. However, while clearly the role of the State in providing welfare services is under attack, the extent to which the State can be substituted, and the nature of the substitute provided, vary by country and by the type of service provided. Thus in Canada, where universal welfare services are less widespread, State services may be more vulnerable than in Britain, where universal provision (at least in theory) means near-universal support for some services. Equally, while the British government has been active in de-nationalization programmes in the industrial sector, rhetoric has (thankfully) outweighed action in the sphere of welfare, and even rhetoric has been restrained as far as the criminal justice system is concerned.

The criminal justice system is of note because, despite the *origins* of State provision in both the private and the voluntary sector, Britain does not have the same level of non-State provisions as is for example the case in North America. Police, prisons, probation service and the court system are all public services, even though they may depend to varying extents on volunteers. While some policing services and all crime insurance are provided by the private sector, and other non-State agencies do traditionally have franchise arrangements *vis-à-vis* the provisions of services or the according of responsibilities, such involvement is on a relatively small scale. Perhaps the most notable exceptions are recent development with regard to services for crime victims, where — given the inadequacy of statutory agency responses — the 1970s saw the emergence of Victims Support Schemes, Rape Crisis Centres and Refuges for Battered Women (Mawby and Gill, 1987).

Certainly there has been a much greater reluctance within the government to encourage moves towards privatization of criminal justice, although, encouraged by the Adam Smith Institute (Pirie and Young, 1987), and mindful of a decade of labour-relations problems, increased involvement of the private sector in the prison system seems likely.

In other respects though, alternatives to privatization have been sought. One of these, civilianization, as it has occurred within the police will not be considered further here. Instead the focus will be on efforts to involve informal and voluntary systems of helping.

Here, a number of initiatives can be cited. The Home Office, both directly and through individual forces, has prioritized the development of Neighbourhood Watch and urged an expanding role for the Special Constabulary; Victims Support Schemes have, since late 1986, been subject to central funding via the Home Office; the DHSS, following the initiatives of the 1969 Children and Young Persons Act, has increased funding available to the voluntary sector for Intermediate Treatment under the Local Authority Circular of 1983.

Elsewhere, my colleague Martin Gill and I have concentrated on developments in voluntary sector provision in three areas — police, the probation service, and victim services (Gill and Mawby, 1990; Mawby and Gill, 1987). In the context of the police, the use made of volunteers (the Special Constabulary) by a statutory agency may be considered and compared with the role of volunteers (Probation Voluntary Associates) within Probation Services. Victims Support Schemes are somewhat different, in that volunteers are utilized within voluntary agencies.

Here, this research will be discussed, but within a wider context.

First, in the next section, the nature of voluntary organizations will be analysed, drawing comparisons with the private sector. Second, voluntary agencies will be considered in detail, distinguishing between different types of agency, since clearly government enthusiasm for the principle of voluntarism does not extent to *all* such agencies. Third, the use of volunteers by a range of different organizations will be assessed. Finally, and in summary, the advantages and dangers of a shift away from State provision will be drawn together.

Voluntary agencies and the commercial system compared

To Wolfenden (1978) the distinction between the voluntary and commercial systems was self-evident. Later writers appear to agree, at least as far as can be assessed from the difficulties of commission an the sins of omission. Thus, while most academics writing about voluntary bodies have at least *attempted* a definition, most writers on the private sector, including its critics (LeGrand and Robinson, 1984) have tended to avoid one.

Possible reasons for this are hinted at in definitions of voluntary organizations. Put crudely, we all 'know' what a voluntary agency is, and what we 'mean by' the private sector, but mutually exclusive definitions are illusive. Indeed, one is tempted to follow the example of some American writers and pretend that the terms 'non-State' and 'private' are synonymous.

What, for example, is a voluntary body? Academics appear to have avoided the restrictions of a definition by specifying an 'ideal type' (Brenton, 1985; Hatch, 1980; Johnson, 1981). That is, such bodies tend to conform on five criteria:

1 they are initiated independently of the State;
2 they are not controlled or directed by the State, for example *vis-à-vis* the type of service provided or the choice of client;
3 they are not financed exclusively by the State;
4 in terms of motive they are non-profit-making;
5 finally, acceptance of clients is not based on ability to pay or membership.

There is, however, a range of problems associated with such an approach. For example, some agencies we consider voluntary may *not* fulfil all these criteria: the National Association for the Care and Resettlement of Offenders (NACRO) is a case in point, since it was *not* initiated independently of the State. Moreover, where do we draw the line? If a service is not financed *exclusively* by the State, how exclusive should its finance be to prevent its qualification? As will be shown in the next section, a number of agencies, like hostels for the single homeless or ex-prisoners, are practically speaking funded exclusively by the State, but far from this barring them from the voluntary bodies club they may actually be categorized as a distinct type of voluntary agency.

Further problems emerge if we attempt a similar ideal type of private sector provision. Clearly the first three criteria are equally applicable. That is, private services are initiated outside the State, are not controlled or directed by the State, and are not financed exclusively by the State. What then of the final two criteria?

On the surface, we associate the profit-motive with the private sector. However, not all private welfare services are profit-making, or indeed are designed to be so: many public schools, for example, achieve charitable status through their exclusion of the profit-goal, and BUPA, clearly a private agency, is non-profit-making.

What then of the final criteria, the basis for accepting clients? Here a number of problems exist. First, clearly, State welfare services do not accept clients indiscriminately — gatekeeping is a regular procedure (Foster, 1983) and for selective services, many clients may be expected to pay. Equally, as Blacher (forthcoming) demonstrates for the Plymouth Nightshelter, voluntary agencies may also reject clients on judgemental criteria and operate so as to maximize agency goals rather than to solve clients' needs. The archetypal private service is of course distinct from this. There two alternatives predominate. The consumer may choose to pay for a service privately, if and when the need arises. Unwilling to queue for my hernia operation, for example, I may pay to queue-jump. Alternatively, I can choose private insurance, so that I can receive private treatment for my future, anticipated hernia.

Even here, though, the voluntary/private boundary is fragile. Some voluntary agencies are constructed on a self-help principle; for example, where services are only available to those who are members — that is, those who have paid in advance through service rather than money. In contrast, some agencies considered 'private' may accept some clients at nil-fee because services are available and underused. For example, I am currently involved in the evaluation of a private short-term residential hostel for chemical dependents that routinely accepts residents who cannot afford the fees. Some of the fee is recouped from DHSS allowances for residential treatment; the rest is owed by the client, and a contract is drawn up whereby repayment takes place in instalments over a number of years. However, the system is operated in such a way that very little money is recouped in this way, and indeed little or no attempt is made to contact former residents for outstanding fees (Mawby, 1989a). For these clients, the unit provides a service akin to that of a voluntary agency.

This situation is further complicated where government money is used for subcontracting purposes, particularly prevalent *vis-à-vis* the criminal justice system where few clients *choose* the services. Continuing the previous example, DHSS money was made available for the Health Authority to pay the fees of a limited number of local patients considered suitable for residential drug treatment by the private unit. Similar arrangements have been made in other contexts, within both the private and voluntary sectors — for example, local authorities have long bought in places at voluntary run agencies such as Barnados, and more recently in some privately run residential homes (Laurance, 1983), and non-State bodies running intermediate technology (IT) projects may be funded on an intake basis. In these circumstances the extent to which choice of clients provides a basis for distinguishing between State, voluntary and private services is limited.

One must take care not to overstate the degree of overlap. Rather, I am concerned here to make two related points. First, in some circumstances it may be better to look on private sector and voluntary sector provision as variations within a category which is distinct from that of State-controlled services. In this context, the role of government in funding such services deserves special consideration. Second, with a government committed to a dismantling of social and public services, the blurring of boundaries may be useful where the rhetoric of an expanded voluntary sector is used to present the acceptable face of welfare pluralism. For example, the value of voluntary commitment, the preference for bilateral rather than unilateral help, and the benefits of community involvement and the representation of the lay public alongside bureaucrats and professionals, receive support from across a wide political spectrum.

Nevertheless, it should not be assumed that *all* voluntarism receives government applause. The following two sections concentrate on the degree of variation within the voluntary sector.

Variations within the voluntary sector

The fact that the voluntary sector is nowhere near a single entity has been noted, both in the distinction between *voluntary organizations* and *volunteers* and in the vagueness which permeates the private/ voluntary divide. The point is made more forcefully if we consider variations *between* voluntary organizations. Perhaps the most useful dichotomy has been developed by Hatch (1980).

Hatch subdivided organizations firstly according to whether the work is carried out primarily by volunteers or paid staff. He then distinguishes, for the former, between those that serve their own members ('mutual aid associations') and those that provide a service for others ('volunteer organizations'). Then, considering agencies dependent upon paid staff, he separates these according to source of funding. Those that depend to a large extent on government grants he terms 'special agencies'; those that depend on donations and fees he defines as 'funded charities'.

Mutual aid associations, so called, represent one of the major initiatives for growth in the 1970s and were indicative of the rebirth of the voluntary sector prior to current government enthusiasm (Rose, 1976). They are indicative of critiques of the over-bureaucratization or over-professionalization of welfare services, best illustrated in the work of Illich (1973; Illich et al. 1977), and as such draw support across a broad political spectrum. In the context of the criminal justice system, they are perhaps best exemplified, in somewhat contrasting ways, by Neighbourhood Watch (Bennett, 1987; Hourihan, 1987), the prisoners' rights movement and services provided by and for those with alcohol and drug problems, including AA or NA and more recently self-help groups formed to provide support for the families of drug-users (Donoghoe et al., 1987).

However, these examples illustrate the difficulties raised by Abrams (1977), namely that within Western industrialized societies such groupings rarely emerge spontaneously. Rather, they tend to be initiated, moulded, and perhaps nurtured by organized State agencies, which thus tend to create a service that if not exactly in their own image, is at least no threat to that image. This is particularly the case with Neighbourhood Watch where, as a number of recent studies have shown, schemes tend to emerge in middle-class areas according to a police-based definition of the crime problem and acceptable solutions, direct influence on policing roles and behaviour, much less police accountability, being minimal (Donnison et al., 1986; Kinsey et al., 1986). In contrast, in Britain PROP minimized its links with its supporters and sympathizers who were *not* current or ex-prisoners, and chose a purer, but more limited, base, on which it became quickly marginalized.

The second category defined by Hatch, volunteer organizations, is perhaps the most readily identified with the criminal justice system. Most especially as regards services for crime victims, as has been discussed at length elsewhere, the 1970s saw the emergence of Rape Crisis Centres and Women's Aid Refuges — each inspired by the growing feminist movement — and in complete contrast, and more akin to voluntary organizations *par excellence*, the Bristol victims support scheme heralded what subsequently became a mushrooming of individual schemes, coordinated by the end of the 1970s by the National Association of Victims Support Schemes (NAVSS)

(Mawby and Gill, 1987). Also within this category it is perhaps appropriate to mention pressure groups such as Radical Alternatives to Prison (RAP) and the Howard League. These are also run, in the main, by volunteers, but are distinct from PROP in that they are not, in intent at least, run by offenders or ex-offenders as officially defined.[1]

The final two categories distinguished by Hatch incorporate agencies which depend on paid staff, differing according to the principal source of funding. They can perhaps be most usefully dealt with together here because the balance between them illustrates one of the key findings of much of the literature on voluntarism, namely that when one is dependent upon public support — through finance or the commitment of time and effort — the public tends to be highly discriminating in its choice of who or what merits support. It is notable that the rapid growth within the volunteer organization category is among agencies formed to help *victims* rather than *offenders*. Equally, in the context of the giving of money, just as Wolfenden (1978) notes greater public support for charities which help 'good cause' groups like the elderly, so any funded charity providing help for deviant groups is based on insecure financial foundations. Indeed even the NAVSS has experienced difficulty raising money from the general public: its first BBC television public appeal raised only about £3000.

Thus, where voluntary bodies are dependent upon funds for the payment of staff, those within the criminal justice system are more likely to be found in Hatch's 'special agency' category than as funded charities. Nightshelters and other hostels for deviant groups are, in fact, examples *par excellence* here. As Hatch notes, these allow for government indirect support for 'unpopular causes' — unpopular both in the sense that the government itself would not wish to justify direct responsibility and in their being able to survive on public donations alone. However, one consequence of this is that such organizations tend to be government funded 'on the cheap': staff are relatively poorly paid, grants are generally periodically renewed, and agencies consequently are subject to considerable covert political control.

Clearly Hatch's model provides a useful basis for categorizing various voluntary agencies, and allows us to distinguish different categories among alternatives within the criminal justice system. Nevertheless, it suffers a number of weaknesses. For example, it does not distinguish between agencies which provide a direct service for those with specific problems, and pressure groups which provide a vaguer public service. Moreover, organizations that are very different in numerous respects, such as Rape Crisis Centres and Victims

Support Schemes (Mawby and Gill, 1987) are found within the same category.

A final difficulty evident to such a categorization relates to the problem of where to draw the boundaries. For example, the category 'mutual aid associations' excludes agencies such as Rape Crisis Centres, since most volunteers in such Centres have not themselves experienced rape, but one could argue that the helper/helped relationship in these agencies is based on philosophical principles more akin to mutual aid than to unilinear helping relationships. Moreover, many agencies incorporate features of different categories. Thus, Victims Support Schemes employ some paid staff — more since the 1986 Government funding initiative — but depend heavily on volunteers: where they do receive income, some comes from the Government, some from the public and other income from private corporations (NAVSS, 1987).

An alternative form of categorization, which has been used elsewhere to distinguish between different victim services in Britain and North America (Mawby and Gill, 1987), identifies agencies according to four separate issues. Clearly the issues are neither mutually exclusive nor do they incorporate all the essential features of every voluntary organization, but they do nevertheless allow us a more detailed comparison for present purposes. The four issues are, respectively, the relationship between the voluntary agency and conventional State agencies; source of funding; goals; and the relationship between helper and helped.

Taking first the relationship between the voluntary agency and conventional State agencies, we find at one extreme voluntary bodies that work in close cooperation with one or more State organizations, at the other voluntary bodies that provide very different services and/ or base their *raison d'être* on a critique of state agencies. In Britain, examples of the latter include PROP, RAP, Rape Crisis Centres and Women's Refuges, all on the political left. Slightly less oppositional is NACRO, with the Howard League (Ryan, 1978) and the NAVSS 'enjoying' much closer and more cooperative relationships with government, and Neighbourhood Watch being initiated by the police. Agencies at the 'opposing' end of the spectrum are not necessarily on the left, however. In the United States, for example, the voluntary body MADD (Mothers Against Drunk Driving) finds itself in opposition to most State agencies, but in advocating stiffer sentences for offenders is perhaps best identified with the political right.

The second issue, that of funding, is closely related to the first, for the reasons noted earlier. Thus, in North America, Rape Crisis Centres and Women's Refuges have tended to lose much of their radicalism as they have competed for government funding (Amir and Amir, 1979; Gornick et al., 1985), and MADD has remained largely self-supporting as it has continued its opposition to State policies and the interests of the alcohol industry (Mawby and Gill, 1987). In Britain, organizations such as Rape Crisis Centres, Women's Refuges, and radical pressure groups have tended to remain largely self-sufficient, and consequently continue their opposition to government policies. NACRO, more dependent on government monies, has nevertheless maintained an independent voice. Neighbourhood Watch, while dependent upon self-help groups, can also be located here given its reliance on police organization for survival. The NAVSS is an interesting example here because it is currently in a state of transition. Early schemes were heavily dependent upon volunteer effort, with State funding coming to local schemes by way of Urban Aid or MSC monies and central funding limited to support for the National Association. As a result, local schemes retained a degree of independence, and indeed their own idiosyncrasies, and both local and national bodies were independent of the state, even though levels of cooperation — particularly with the police and probation services, were endemic to the organization (Maguire and Corbett, 1987; Mawby and Gill, 1987). In late 1986, the funding situation was altered by the infusion of £9 million from central government, over a three-year period, allocated centrally through the NAVSS to individual schemes. The immediate consequence of this is that Victims Support Schemes more commonly employ salaried staff, at least as coordinators. The more indirect consequences *might* involve a lessening of the independence of individual schemes or the central organization, as the need to secure funds provides an impetus to follow the 'party line'.

Funding, of course, impinges on the third issue in the model, namely the goals of the organization, and specifically the balance between social movement and social provision goals, to use Pahl's (1979) terminology. Clearly some voluntary organizations — like PROP, RAP and the Howard League — exist primarily as pressure groups, attempting to influence the policies and practices of government and State bureaucracies. Other organizations, like Rape Crisis Centres, Refuges for Battered Women and NACRO, also prioritize political/educational goals, but consider the provision of a direct service to those in need as of equal, if not more, importance. Thus, for example, NACRO has since its inception initiated a number of action research projects in addition to its political/educational role. In contrast, other organizations, like the NAVSS, have tended to prioritize social provision goals, although as has been noted elsewhere this is at least partly an awareness of the dangers of following

North American cousins into policy debates that incorporate sentencing/offender-focused issues (Mawby, 1988; Mawby and Gill, 1987). At the extreme, Neighbourhood Watch has no more than a limited (security consciousness) political goal.

The final issue in our classification refers to the relationship between the helper and the helped. At one extreme are those agencies that Hatch (1980) terms 'mutual aid associations', at the other those where the helper/helped divide is extreme, exemplified by the professional/client relationship. Within the criminal justice system, clearly PROP lies to the left of the spectrum, as does Neighbourhood Watch.[2] However, a number of other agencies, while not exclusively recruiting ex-consumers as their volunteers, do consciously prioritize the minimization of barriers between helper and helped. RAP, Rape Crisis Centres and Refuges for Battered Women, in general, conform to this pattern, following the wider principle of fellowship, or, in the case of the feminist — inspired alternatives, sisterhood. In contrast, NACRO and NAVSS do not explicitly create a barrier between helper and helped, in the way for example that some North American victim services do, but they do provide a contrasting set of relationships.

The distinctions made here are summarized in Figure 1. Clearly this is only an approximation, and there may be marked variations between, say, different Women's Refuges (Gill, 1986). However, it not only provides a convenient way of distinguishing between agencies, but also allows one to consider government initiatives in the context of *political* preferences within the model. For example, all other things being equal, one might anticipate considerably more government support, including funding for organizations that

1   in terms of their relationship to conventional statutory services fall at the 'appeasing' end of the spectrum;
2   in terms of goals are to be found towards the social provision rather than the social movement end of the spectrum;
3   where the group to be helped are identified as deviant or undeserving, epitomize professional-client relationships.

Of the agencies discussed, recent government funding of Victims Support is a case in point. The problem of rape victims, in contrast, while widely recognized, has not led to widespread State support for Rape Crisis Centres. Rather, funding has been geared towards services provided by statutory bodies (extra training and facilities for the police) and Victims Support Schemes which are encouraged to widen their brief to include rape victims.

In the context of voluntary agency provision, then, government support can be understood on a number of levels. Not only is money

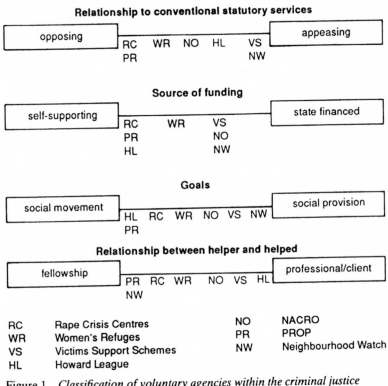

Relationship to conventional statutory services

opposing		appeasing
	RC WR NO HL VS	
	PR NW	

Source of funding

self-supporting		state financed
	RC WR VS	
	PR NO	
	HL NW	

Goals

social movement		social provision
	HL RC WR NO VS NW	
	PR	

Relationship between helper and helped

fellowship		professional/client
	PR RC WR NO VS HL	
	NW	

RC	Rape Crisis Centres	NO	NACRO
WR	Women's Refuges	PR	PROP
VS	Victims Support Schemes	NW	Neighbourhood Watch
HL	Howard League		

Figure 1   *Classification of voluntary agencies within the criminal justice system*

saved, and the power of statutory services constrained: in fact, State funding of voluntary bodies allows greater State political power through the control and direction of funding. This issue will be reconsidered later. Here, however, it is appropriate to consider the use of volunteers by all agencies, where financial savings are particularly appealing to government.

Volunteers and the criminal justice system

While volunteers may be incorporated within the commercial system[3], in most respects volunteers are utilized by either statutory or voluntary agencies. Clearly, as was indicated in the last section, some voluntary bodies make limited use of volunteers, others are highly dependent upon them. Equally, some statutory services give greater priority to use of volunteers than others. Holme and Maizels (1978), for example, show in their national survey how Social Services Departments have traditionally given less priority to volunteers than have the Probation Services.

Within the criminal justice system, public participation is endemic to the system through the part played by the jury and the lay magistracy. Moreover, many State services emerged from routes within the voluntary sector. The role of the public in the maintenance of order, for example, preceded the establishment of public police systems, and the Probation Service developed from the work of Court Missionaries, later incorporating the Discharged Prisoners' Aid Society (Gill and Mawby, 1989).

In each of these cases, however, the importance accredited to volunteers has varied. The Special Constabulary, established during the childhood of public policing and nurtured through the special conditions of two world wars, rapidly lost membership in the post-war period and despite two internal committees set up to inspire new initiatives (Police Advisory Board, 1976 and 1981), has only recently received a concerted degree of political support.[4] The use of volunteers within the Probation Service has been subject to even greater fluctuation. Professionalization and increased assessment and report-based work led the service away from its voluntary roots. Incorporation of prison welfare work encouraged a re-examination of the potential for volunteers (Reading, 1967), illustrated for example by Barr (1971). However, arguably most impetus has come from the Barclay Committee (1982) Report on the Personal Social Services and the subsequent Home Office (1984) Circular on the community role of the Probation Service. Unquestionably, though, both police and probation services are being encouraged by the government, through the Home Office, to expand their use of volunteers.

In this context, it is useful to pause to consider what use is currently made of volunteers, and what impediments there are to further developments. First, in terms of actual numbers, police specials far outnumber probation volunteers. However, looked at in relation to paid employees, the position is reversed. For example, there are over 15 000 police specials in England and Wales; that is approximately 31 per 100 000 population, but this is only on average 13 per 100 regular officers. Given that specials work no more than four hours per week the balance between volunteers and regulars is heavily weighted towards the latter. In contrast, while the number of probation volunteers is far less, our national estimates suggest that the number of volunteers is roughly equal to that of probation officers: even allowing for the less efficient use of volunteers in probation (Stockdale, 1985), this still means that volunteers contribute relatively more of the work within the Probation Service than within the police (Gill and Mawby, 1990).

Even then, however, it would require a quite dramatic expansion of voluntary effort to shift the balance significantly. But there are other problems associated with a greater dependence on volunteers. One, identified by Wolfenden (1978), is the imbalance between volunteers and need. This applies equally to the criminal justice system. With regard to police, specials are less readily available in high crime rate metropolitan areas, most evident in low density, low crime rate areas; in probation a similar if weaker pattern exists; finally, the patchy development of Victims Support Schemes has resulted in underused volunteers in rural schemes and over stretched volunteers in metropolitan schemes (Gill and Mawby, 1990).

Another issue surrounds the question of who becomes a volunteer. Since Aves (1969) it has been well recognized that volunteers are scarcely typical of the population at large, and Humble's (1982) more recent analysis of national data confirms the overpredominance of the middle-aged, the middle classes and women. Our own local research, while generally supporting this, demonstrates considerable variations between volunteers for work with different agencies. This is to a large extent a combination of pull and push factors, with agencies recruiting volunteers they define as suitable and the public volunteering to work in agencies of which they approve. The cosy, not unexpected, result is that police specials tend to be respectable working/lower middle class males, highly supportive of the police and the need to uphold law and order, attracted to work which incorporates action and excitement; by way of contrast, probation volunteers tend to be middle class females, or potential future probation officers, more supportive of treatment ideologies (Gill and Mawby, 1989). Far from introducing a new, radical, or even mildly critical dimension, volunteers provide the rubber stamp of approval to the role of statutory agencies (Gill, 1987).

One final and somewhat different point can be added here, regarding the work carried out by volunteers. This is indeed varied. In probation, for example, while some concentrate on limited service tasks like driving, most work with offenders, on a one-to-one basis, with groups, or in clubs (Holme and Maizels, 1978; Mawby, 1989b; Stockdale, 1985; Ward, 1984). In the police, many specials are assigned to organize event duty (at carnivals or sports events for example), others patrol with another special or more commonly a regular officer (Gill and Mawby, 1990). However, in most cases volunteers provide support for paid, trained staff. They do not provide equivalent or comparable services: they are not trained to do so (Brenton, 1985), nor would paid staff be willing to accommodate volunteers who replenished unfilled posts or took away their over-time. Indeed, one of the most frequent criticisms of the use of volunteers, common to both probation and police, is the fear that volunteers might be used in a cost-cutting exercise (Gill and Mawby, 1990). Even given the political will, moreover, the legal accountability of both police and probation is a constraint on any extensive shift between volunteers and 'professionals'.[5]

There are, of course, enormous advantages in the use of volunteers, and the above should not be taken as an indictment of voluntary agencies or volunteering in general. Elsewhere the very positive role of the voluntary sector has been covered in some detail (Gill and Mawby, 1990), aspects of which can be mentioned here.

First, provision and variety of services may be extended through the use of volunteers, especially where the agency consciously plans a service which makes best use of volunteers' strengths. Second, and related to this, volunteers or voluntary agencies are often associated with pioneering schemes; many of today's welfare services emerged from voluntary initiatives and recent developments, for example regarding Victims Support Schemes, Rape Crisis Centres and Refuges, are in response to apathy from many statutory agencies. Third, the voluntary sector may provide pressure 'from without' which influences government policy (or lack of it). It is thus no part of this chapter to argue that voluntary involvement is irrelevant or without value. However, in a context where governments are placing more reliance on voluntarism, I have attempted to spell out some of the dangers of this shift towards increased dependence on the voluntary sector *at the expense of* State services and 'professional' employees. Bearing this in mind, it is appropriate here to draw together some of the issues raised, in the wider context of this volume.

Discussion

In one sense, a shift towards voluntarism is a cost-cutting exercise. Volunteers are free resources, at least if we ignore the costs of training, supervision and other operating expenses. Increased funding for voluntary agencies is less evidently a part of such an exercise, and has other advantages for government (see below) but where staff in voluntary bodies work longer for less pay, less well protected by unionization, it certainly warrants Cabinet brownie points.

There are, however, constraints on the extent to which *volunteers* can substitute for 'professional' staff. As noted in the previous section, there are limits to the numbers who offer themselves for voluntary work, and even more limits when their geographical distribution is matched with need. There are also restrictions on work that volunteers can do, such that while they could be used to substitute for ancilliaries — in probation or social work, for example — where work incorporates the need for training and the requirement of accountability the role of volunteers is necessarily limited. In this context, the amount of time 'professionals' spend training or supervising volunteers may protect them from any cost-cutting exercises. As one probation representative wrote to us,

> We should never use a volunteer primarily to save money ... Volunteers are not an unpaid substitute for a Probation Officer or Assistant and it is important for management to be clear where lines are drawn ... Volunteers bring many additional skills to the Service gained through life experience or because they are members of the local community rather than having the 'professional', 'social work' or 'authority' label. The most important contribution of volunteers, therefore, is the added dimension which they bring to the work of the Service. (Mawby, 1989b: 9)

This raises the possibility that voluntarism's appeal lies elsewhere, that there is something intrinsically superior in using the public: to Beatle-quote, 'Money Can't Buy Me Love'. To a large extent this is true. The notorious case of Kitty Genovese raised the very real concern that the community might abdicate its responsibility for social problems and assume that the mess will be swept away, tidily and quietly by paid specialists (Mawby, 1985). Despite the Foucaultist nightmare of an all-pervasive State where community becomes the ultimate means of repression (Cohen, 1985; Foucault, 1977), well illustrated in accounts of Maoist China (Cohen, 1968; Lubman, 1967), public participation should be a source of enrichment. In the present context, however, the distinctive role which the public might contribute is stifled by the fact that those who become involved, as volunteers or as community representatives (Morgan, 1987), are scarcely representative of 'their' community. Partly as a result, and excluding the distinctive contribution of services which minimize barriers between helper and helped, there is a limit to the extent to which the service provided by volunteers or voluntary agencies is distinctive.

One might, then, consider more cynically how a shift to voluntarism benefits the present government in a more narrowly conceived political context. Here two advantages come to mind. First, ironically, central funding for voluntary bodies allows more central government control than does support for State services. It allows the government to control the day-to-day operation of the agency to a greater extent, first by removing the local authority 'middleman', second because short-term funding provides the carrot and stick with the result that agencies may adjust policies to operate in approved ways in order to retain grant aid. Given the variety of alternatives within the voluntary sector, as was stressed earlier, government funds can be directed at those which provide more 'appropriate' services and are less critical of State policies. The potential independent voice of the voluntary sector is thus effectively curtailed, at least to some extent.[6] Where a number of voluntary agencies find themselves competing for limited State resources, control is further strengthened.

The political significance of the voluntary sector is also relevant on a more general level. Extra finance may be provided — for the police to develop Neighbourhood Watch, for voluntary bodies to run IT schemes, to finance additional places in private or voluntary residential homes for the elderly — which implies an *increase* in State welfare spending. Cost is thus not the crucial factor. Rather, it is a matter of political preference that where spending is increased, it should not contribute to an increased public welfare sector. Under Thatcherism, giving money — and limited power — to non-State agencies at the expense of State services is a fundamental political priority, irrespective of any financial implications.

It is within this framework that the place of private and voluntary services, within welfare state or criminal justice system — must be viewed. The last few years have seen a concerted effort to shift the balance towards a North American model where the welfare state as a central feature of society is replaced by welfare services that are part of the private market structure. While voluntarism has much to commend it, I have argued that partly because of this it contains the danger that it becomes the velvet glove hiding the iron fist of a society in which market forces rule. Private services for the fee-paying thus lie alongside a marginalized State welfare sector, which, with subcontracted private and voluntary provisions, provides charity and control for those who merit nothing better. The assumption that the voluntary sector will continue as a just and humane alternative may in general be a reasonable one, but as Blacher (forthcoming) well indicates in the context of nightshelters, it comes without guarantee.

Notes

1 Given the extent of the dark figure of unrecorded offending, however, it would be rash to suggest that the typical Howard League member is a non-offender.
2 Since Neighbourhood Watch is essentially a community resource to pre-empt problems, rather than a service which helps those who have been victimized, this is so by definition. In other respects, though, research indicates both clear distinctions *within* schemes between activists and more passive members, and clear demarcation between scheme members and *outside* 'professional experts' (the police).

3 For example, private schools may encourage parents to help in the classroom, and private drug clinics incorporate voluntary provisions from lay people and outside specialists (such as the clergy).
4 See, for example, the Conference called by the Home Secretary to 'look for ways of strengthening the Special Constabulary to the benefit of the police service and the community' *(Police*, 20(4), December 1987: 6–7 — see also Hogg, 1988).
5 'Professionals' is included in inverted commas here because while the police may consider themselves to be professionals, and it distinguishes them from less well trained volunteers, they are not such by an sociological definition.
6 It would, however, be ridiculous to suggest that the government refuse funding from all agencies which criticize it. Nevertheless, as the case of CAB illustrates, even generally respectable, uncontentious agencies may incur government disapproval at times!

References

Abrams, P. (1977) 'Community Care: Some Research Problems and Priorities', *Policy and Politics*, 6: 125–52.
Amir, D. and Amir, M. (1979) 'Rape Crisis Centres: An Arena for Ideological Conflict, *Victimology*, 4: 247–57.
Aves, G. (1969) *Voluntary Workers in the Social Services*. London: Allen and Unwin.
Barclay Committee (1982) *Social Workers — their Roles and Tasks*. London: Bedford Square Press.
Barr, H. (1971) *Volunteers in Prison After-Care*. London: Allen and Unwin.
Bennett, T. (1987) 'Neighbourhood Watch: Principles and Practice', in R.I. Mawby (ed.), *Policing Britain*. Plymouth: Plymouth Polytechnic.
Blacher, M. (forthcoming) 'Living on the Margins: Nightshelter Use, and Single Homelessness in a British City'. Ph.D. thesis, Plymouth: Plymouth Polytechnic.
Brenton, M. (1985) *The Voluntary Sector in British Social Services*. London: Longman.
Cohen, J.A. (1968) *The Criminal Process in the People's Republic of China, 1949–1963*. Cambridge, Mass: Harvard University Press.
Cohen, S. (1985) *Visions of Social Control: Crime, Punishment and Classification*. Cambridge: Polity Press.
Donnison, H., Skola, J. and Thomas, P. (1986) *Policing the People*. London: Libertarian Research and Education Trust.
Donoghoe, M. et al. (1987) 'How Families and Communities Respond to Heroin', in N. Dorn and N. South (eds), *A Land Fit for Heroin*? Basingstoke: Macmillan.
Foster, P. (1983) *Access to Welfare*. London: Macmillan.
Foucault, M. (1977) *Discipline and Punish: The Birth of the Prison*. New York: Pantheon.
George, V. and Wilding, P. (1985) *Ideology and Social Welfare*. London: Routledge.
Gill, M. (1986) 'Wife Battering: A Case Study of a Women's Refuge', in R.I. Mawby (ed.), *Crime Victims*. Plymouth: Plymouth Polytechnic.
Gill, M. (1987) 'The Special Constabulary: Community Representation and Accountability', in R.I. Mawby (ed.) *Policing Britain*. Plymouth: Plymouth Polytechnic.
Gill, M.L. and Mawby, R.I. (1990) *Volunteers and the Criminal Justice System: A Comparative Analysis*. Milton Keynes: Open University Press.
Gornick, J., Burt, M.R. and Pittman, K.J. (1985) 'Structures and Activities of Rape Crisis Centres in the Early 1980s', *Crime and Delinquency*, 31: 247–68.

Guest, D. (1984) 'Social Policy in Canada', *Social Policy and Administration*, 18(2): 130–47.

Hatch, S. (1980) *Outside the State*. London: Bedford Square Press.

Hogg, D. (1988) 'A "Special" Relationship', *Police Review*, 19 February: 378–9.

Holme, A. and Maizels, J. (1978) *Social Workers and Volunteers*. London: Allen & Unwin.

Home Office (1984) *Probation Service in England and Wales: Statement of National Objectives and Priorities. London: Home Office.*

Hourihan, K. (1987) 'Local Community Involvement and Participation in Neighbourhood Watch', *Urban Studies*, 24: 129–36.

Humble, S. (1982) *Voluntary Action in the 1980s: A Summary of the Findings of a National Survey*. Berkhamstead: Volunteer Centre.

Illich, I. (1973) *Deschooling Society*. Harmondsworth: Penguin.

Illich, I. et al. (1977) *Disabling Professions*. London: Boyars.

Johnson, N. (1981) *Voluntary Social Services*. Oxford: Blackwell/Robertson.

Kinsey, R., Lea, J. and Young, J. (1986) *Losing the Fight against Crime*. Oxford: Basil Blackwell.

Laurance, J. (1983) 'Is Big Business Moving into Caring?', *New Society*, 10 Feb: 211–14.

LeGrand, J. and Robinson, R. (1984) *Privatisation and the Welfare State*. Hemel Hempstead: Allen and Unwin.

Lubman, S. (1967) 'Mao and Mediation: Politics and Dispute Resolution in Communist China', *California Law Review*, 55(5): 1284–1357.

Maguire, M. and Corbett, C. (1987) *The Effects of Crime and the Work of Victims Support Schemes*. Aldershot: Gower.

Mawby, R.I. (1985) 'Bystander Responds to the Victims of Crime: Is the Good Samaritan Alive and Well?', *Victimology*, 10: 461–75.

Mawby, R.I. (1988) 'Victims' Services: British and North American Models', Plymouth Polytechnic, Department of Social and Political Studies (CJS), *Occasional Papers*, 2.

Mawby, R.I. (1989a) *Dealing With Drugs: Evaluation of a Rehabilitation Centre*. Report to the DHSS, Plymouth Polytechnic.

Mawby, R.I. (1989b) 'The Probation Service and Volunteers: Final Report of a National Survey', Plymouth Polytechnic, Department of Social and Political Studies (CJS), *Occasional Papers*, 3.

Mawby, R.I. and Gill, M.L. (1987) *Crime Victims: Needs, Services and the Voluntary Sector*. London: Tavistock.

Morgan, R. (1987) 'Consultation and Police Accountability', in R.I. Mawby (ed.), *Policing Britain*, Plymouth Polytechnic.

NAVSS (1987) *Seventh Annual Report, 1986/87*. London: NAVSS.

Pahl, J. (1979) 'Refuges for Battered Women: Social Provision or Social Movement?' *Journal of Voluntary Action Research*, 8: 25–35.

Pirie, M. and Young, P. (1987) *The Future of Privatisation*. London: Adam Smith Institute.

Police Advisory Board for England and Wales, (1976) *Report of the Working Party on the Special Constabulary*. London: HMSO.

Police Advisory Board for England and Wales (1981) *Report of the Second Working Party on the Special Constabulary* London: HMSO.

Reading, Lady (1967) *The Place of Voluntary Service in After Care*. Second Report of the Working Party. London: HMSO.

Rose, H. (1976) 'Participation: The Icing on the Welfare Cake', in K. Jones and S. Baldwin (eds), *The Year Book of Social Policy in Britain*. London: Routledge.

Ryan, M. (1978) *The Acceptable Pressure Group: a Case Study of the Howard League and RAP*. Aldershot: Gower.

Stockdale, E. (1985) *The Probation Volunteer*. Berkhamstead: Volunteer Centre.

Ward, K. (1984) 'Voluntary Associates with the Probation Service', in G. Darvill and B. Munday (eds), *Volunteers in the Personal Social Services*. London: Tavistock.

Weddell, K. (1986) 'Privatising Social Services in the USA', *Social Policy and Administration*, 20(1): 14–27.

Wolfenden, J. (1978) *The Future of Voluntary Organisations*. London: Croom-Helm.

7 JUVENILE JUSTICE AND THE VOLUNTARY SECTOR

In Great Britain there has been a long history of provision for young offenders which is ostensibly 'outside the State', emanating largely from the same philanthropic and religious bodies who were concerned with orphaned and neglected children. In the nineteenth and early twentieth centuries reform schools, 'probation officers', probation hostels and the plethora of boy's clubs were all the creation of what has now come to be called the voluntary sector. From the outset, none of these initiatives was wholly independent of the State in that they were in varying degrees financed and regulated by either local or national government, and in the course of the twentieth century many of them came to be incorporated within the State or displaced by the State's own provision.

This process advanced most in regard to the probation service, especially when it began to focus more on adult offenders. It advanced much less in the field of residential care for young offenders, where many of the 'child-saving' organizations founded in the nineteenth century — Dr Barnardo's, the Church of England Children's Society and National Children's Homes, as well as a host of bodies that remained locally based — retained a strong presence well into the 1970s. It was, however, a presence almost totally dependent on local government finance, and one whose projected image sought to minimize its work with delinquents in favour of a more general, and more publicly acceptable, concern for deprived youngsters. When, for a variety of economic, humanitarian and ideological reasons, residential responses to young people's offending began to become unfashionable, these particular voluntary bodies were faced with a crisis of identity and purpose. They found they had little choice but to respond to new patterns of State funding and become involved in the provision of the more community-based approaches to offending — loosely called 'intermediate treatment', and mainly, though not exclusively, provided by statutory agencies — which they had once seen as rivals and to which they had initially been resistant and disdainful.

It is with this process that the following chapter by Mike Nellis is concerned, as it occurred in England and Wales, as a result — not entirely intended — of the government initiative outlined in Local Authority Circular 83(3) (DHSS, 1983). (In Scotland, the juvenile justice system in general and intermediate treatment in particular — not to say the voluntary sector itself — have evolved differently, and the conclusions may not hold good there, LAC 83(3) did not apply in Scotland.

The chapter describes the origins of LAC 83(3) and attempts to relate it to the Conservative government's apparent but questionable concern to shift intermediate treatment away from its base in low-key preventive social work, which is what it had mainly consisted of since its introduction in the Children and Young Persons Act, 1969, towards high intensity alternatives to residential care and penal custody. It examines the ways in which the larger, better known, national voluntary childcare organizations took advantage of the circular and became involved in intermediate treatment, and assesses the possible significance of this for the future direction of juvenile justice *policy*, rather than its immediate effects on practice. It also looks at the work of the Rainer Foundation, the only nineteenth-century philanthropic organization to have focused specifically on young offenders — it was one of the pioneers of probation — and to have welcomed rather than opposed the development of community-based approaches.

Juvenile Justice and the Voluntary Sector

Mike Nellis

The involvement of the voluntary sector in the administration of juvenile justice in England and Wales is a relatively unexplored subject, although there is in fact a history of such involvement dating back at least to the nineteenth century, most notably in the sphere of residential provision. The vast general literature on the voluntary sector is mainly written from the (pro-voluntary) standpoint of welfare pluralism, and typically leaves a number of key issues — political accountability and shifting patterns of State intervention — unexplored. The critical literature on the voluntary sector in Britain is quite small — Brenton, 1985, is a key text — and so far no attempt has been made to look at recent developments in juvenile justice in the light of that literature. This chapter is a preliminary attempt to do so.

It will focus on intermediate treatment (IT) — a term of convenience, given the steady decline in its use[1] — and concentrate particularly on the unexpected impact of the LAC 83(3) Initiative (DHSS, 1983) on the major national childcare voluntary organizations — Dr Barnardo's, the Church of England Children's Society, National Children's Homes (NCH), and Save the Children Fund (SCF).[2] It was around this Initiative that the role of the voluntary sector in IT was first seriously debated, ostensibly as a new development, although voluntary organizations had in fact been associated with IT from its inception. As well as ordinary youth clubs, the various facilities of 'the character training industry' (both voluntary like the National Association of Boy's Clubs, and commercial like Outward Bound) were to be incorporated in regional schemes of IT, and of the 5648 officially approved IT facilities that had come into being by early 1974, '1,556 ... [were] provided by local authorities and 4,345 by voluntary organisations' (DHSS/Welsh Office, 1974).

Although little use was made of these particular schemes (as IT became more of a Social Services Department (SSD)-based activity), nine of the showpiece projects promoted in *28 Choices* (DHSS, 1977) were run by voluntary agencies, and two of them, the Pontefract Activity Centre (taken over from the Quakers, as a 'one-off', by Dr Barnardo's) and the Hammersmith Teenage Project (established by

NACRO), helped significantly to define the public image of IT in the mid-seventies. The departure of the latter's first director to a senior post in SCF, an organization not hitherto concerned with young offenders, triggered the latter's first involvement in IT, in the form of the Junction Project in London and the Hilltop Consultancy in Yorkshire. Service provision and consultancies to local authorities have been the two main ways in which the voluntary sector has contributed to IT's development in the 1980s.[3]

The Rainer Foundation warrants special mention. Alone of the nineteenth-century philanthropic organizations involved with young people, albeit with more of an offender than a childcare focus, it sought immediately to capitalize on the new opportunities created by the 1969 Act, selling off its one Approved School in order to devote itself to the development of IT (see Wills, 1970, for an account of this). At the time, none of the national childcare voluntaries showed much interest in IT, and, like the residential sector in general, tended to doubt the compatibility of community-based approaches with the values, style and image of their organizations.

Throughout the seventies the projects established by the Rainer Foundation mirrored the changing definitions of IT. As a complement to its service provision, it was asked by the DHSS in 1978 to broker a fund aimed at developing IT in the voluntary and informal sectors, in the hope that this would help local authorities to move away from reliance on residential facilities. Although unsuccessful as a means of providing 'bridging finance' — because it concentrated on the low and medium intensity facilities which were then being deemed inadequate as alternatives to care — the IT Fund established itself as the flagship of IT in the voluntary sector, moving away from the passive distribution of grants to encompass an advocacy role as well, albeit for the kind of 'preventive work' which is harshly criticized by those who see alternatives to care and custody as the only worthwhile legacy of IT (*Ajjust*, April 1986: 28).

In this chapter I will be more concerned with the growing involvement of the voluntary sector in the provision of alternatives to care and custody than with prevention, though I will have occasion to refer to it again. The Rainer Foundation was intimately associated with this former development and rapidly adopted the ideas and techniques that had been developed by Thorpe et al. (1980) at the University of Lancaster. Its Woodlands Centre in Basingstoke, while by no means the first alternative to care and custody centre — there were others in the statutory sector — was one of the early approximations to Lancaster ideals, as well as being a model for later Rainer projects (see Rutherford, 1986: 136–47). In view of its innovative tradition the involvement of the Rainer Foundation in this area is unsurprising; what is significant is that as a result of the LAC 83(3) Initiative the major national childcare voluntaries now followed suit.

The LAC 83(3) Initiative

This Local Authority Circular, and its Welsh Office counterpart, WOC 48(83), issued in January 1983, was the last major government initiative in the field of IT, the repercussions of which have not yet worked themselves out. It announced that from April £15 million would be made available over three years to aid the development of intensive intermediate treatment schemes. Ostensibly it aimed to remedy three areas of perceived difficulty. Firstly, to shift IT away from its preventive base towards the provision of alternatives to care or custody for the more serious or persistent offender. Secondly, to facilitate inter-agency liaison at local level, among all concerned with juvenile offending — a coordinating task which had hitherto fallen loosely, and largely ineffectively, on either SSDs or the police. Thirdly, to provide 'bridging finance' that would enable IT projects to be set up prior to the closure of institutions, thereby facilitating a transfer of resources from the residential to the community-based sector of SSDs.

From the outset, the operation of the Initiative was to be monitored by the Juvenile Offenders Team (JOT), in the National Association for the Care and Resettlement of Offenders (NACRO), and apart from individual project reports themselves, it is from this unit that most of the information on the Initiative has come.

Although some of the ideas in the Circular had been in gestation for several years within the DHSS, its precise form and scheduling was determined by the emphasis given to alternatives to custody in the Criminal Justice Act, 1982. The LAC 83(3) funding sought to capitalize on the climate it created. However, the 1982 Act was not unambiguously opposed to custody for juveniles, and there were many who believed — rightly as it turned out — that the restrictions on its use, designed to make it an option of last resort, would be ineffective (Burney, 1985). The Act had in fact restructured custodial sentencing as assiduously as it had toughened IT, and it had actually repealed the section of the 1969 Act which would once have permitted the replacement of detention centres by IT schemes. The Government's promotion of alternatives to custody was thus embedded in a policy framework which still permitted the use of custody. Among practitioners, however, a strong commitment to the abolition of penal custody was emerging, and their understanding of the purposes of alternatives differed sharply from that of the Home Office (and the DHSS). The term 'replacement for custody' seems gradually to be developing among professionals to distinguish the abolitionist position.[4]

The prominent place which LAC 83(3) gave to voluntary organizations in the provision of alternatives to care and custody was not described as an aim, but was treated in the Circular as if it were merely a means to other ends, in particular to the transfer of resources from one sector of SSDs to another. The main aim, even more so than with the IT Fund, was to help local authorities, but because of 'rate capping' and restrictions on the Rate Support Grant imposed by other government departments it was not possible to give the £15 million directly to them.[5] However, by giving grants to 'particular voluntary bodies sponsored by a local authority' (DHSS, 1983: para. 5) these financial restrictions could be circumvented.

The relative unimportance of the established voluntary sector to the DHSS decision-makers is further indicated by the type of voluntary organization they primarily had in mind. According to the Circular 'the voluntary bodies so sponsored could be an existing local voluntary organisation, or a local offshoot of a national voluntary' (ibid.: para. 6), but 'a further possibility that authorities might find *particularly helpful* to consider is that a new voluntary body might be set up specifically for the purpose' (ibid.: para. 7, emphasis added). Archie Pagan, one of the key civil servants involved in the Initiative, explained:

> We wanted the local authority to take a major role in this voluntary organisation ... because in this way we felt that this would encourage them to continue funding the voluntary organisation, to run the facility, once the DHSS funding had stopped ... One of the good models was Coventry, for instance. To a large extent it was a voluntary organisation spawned by the local authority ... (Personal communication, 4 November 1987)

Two further examples of this latter type of voluntary body were included in the appendices to the Circular: Leicester Action for Youth Trust (LAYT) and Norfolk Children's Project (NCP). These particular projects were given prominence as a result of development work which the DHSS had been involved in, without much significance being attached to it, since the late seventies. Largely at local authority request, they had financed a number of demonstration alternative to care and custody projects through statutory/voluntary 'partnerships' under s. 64 of the Health Services and Public Health Act, 1968. NACRO's Community Alternatives for Young Offenders (CAYO), LAYT, NCP, the Doncaster Intermediate Treatment Organisation (DITO), several Barnardo's projects and the SCF Junction Project were all examples of these. It was, however, only the independent voluntary agencies, created from scratch such as

LAYT, NCP and DITO, rather than offshoots of established organizations, to which the DHSS gave specific encouragement.

Let us take a closer look at LAYT. The circumstances of its establishment bear out Hatch's (1980: 92) general observation that 'the type of trigger to which the creation of the largest number of [voluntary] organisations can be attributed are the staff of statutory organisations acting in an official or semi-official capacity'. LAYT began as an attempt by the Director of Leicestershire Social Services to remedy his authority's poor track record in IT provision during the seventies. He persuaded the local Council for Voluntary Service (CVS) to help set up an independent voluntary organization which would undertake the bulk of work with young offenders. CVSs nationally were at this time being encouraged to involve themselves in IT, and the Development Officer which their parent body (then called the National Council for Social Service (NCSS), now the National Council of Voluntary Organisations (NCVO) had recently appointed to undertake this (see Hope, 1977) became actively involved in establishing what became LAYT in 1981 (Unell, 1981).

The 'partnerships' created by s. 64 were not always intended to be permanent — the Junction Project was initially funded for three years — and plans for future funding and management varied between projects. The LAC 83(3) Initiative had tighter rules. One hundred per cent funding was to be available for only two years, with an option of part funding by local authorities in any third year that might be agreed. Somewhat vaguely, it was specified that even at the time of the original application 'the local authority will be expected to say what their plans for the funding of the facility will be after the expiry of grant aid from DHSS' (DHSS, 1983: para. 10). There was in fact a strong expectation that they would be taken over by local authorities, and funded by the 'savings' on residential care that the projects had enabled them to make. This was a further reason why the DHSS preferred specially created local voluntaries to offshoots of national organizations, with their long traditions of independence, their distinctive values and their imperative to survive. The former seemed intrinsically more manageable.

None the less, there were undoubtedly ambiguities in the DHSS attitude to voluntaries, and some elements in the Circular did suggest that something more permanent was being brought into being, and that the £15 million was 'seed money' rather than mere 'bridging finance'. It did propose, for example, that the voluntary bodies providing alternatives should have a measure of independence to raise money of their own in traditional voluntary sector style:

> The voluntary bodies providing these facilities should be encouraged to supplement their departmental grant from other sources. Additional

financial support towards a longer or more extensive facility than that covered by the grant, or towards an additional or associated project could be provided by the agencies represented on the management comittee, or might be sought from outside agencies like philanthropic bodies or trust funds. The voluntary bodies would also be eligible for limited capital grants from the IT Fund either for the grant-aided facility or for associated facilities or projects. (DHSS, 1983: Annex A, para. 15)

It was suggestions like this, despite the apparent dominance of local authorities in the arrangements being mooted, that caused early concern among IT practitioners, local authority associations, the penal reform lobby and the voluntary sector itself about the possible 'privatization'[6] of alternatives to care and custody. Outright opponents of voluntary sector involvement were few, but it was immediately clear, even to observers within the sector, that in establishing the Initiative, the government was seeking only short-term advantages, merely 'to meet certain manifesto commitments and to pacify increasingly vociferous critics of outmoded policies of institutional care' (Bernstein, 1984). Furthermore,

> It is quite clear to see how, by using voluntary agencies in the way that it is, the government is deflecting the very limited resources of the voluntary childcare sector from its role as 'the extension ladder of the statutory agencies', as Wolfenden put it, to becoming a poor substitute for necessary statutory provision. (ibid.)

The Initiative[7] was further criticized for the absence of prior consultation by the government with the implementing agencies, for its allocation of funds on a 'first come, first served' basis (which was hardly likely to prioritize areas of greatest need), for providing insufficient time to establish and then demonstrate the viability of projects to potential future funders, and for failing to include resources for the training of staff to run such short-life projects.

Ironically, given the intention of the Initiative to circumvent the problem of rate-capping, the issue which, at the time, came to be seen as its greatest flaw concerned precisely its longer-term financial viability. To an extent this ran counter to the prevalent anxieties about wholesale 'privatization', in so far as it envisaged that the projects would simply peter out when central government funding expired:

> Another characteristic of the schemes is the relatively short term nature of the funding. Most typical is a three year life with vague indications of how such schemes might be funded thereafter (by local authorities, charitable sources etc.). They are pump-priming efforts. At the same time other policies are attempting to reduce local authority expenditure in the social services. Sceptics might observe some contradiction in policies which attempt to squeeze local government spending and yet encourage volun-

tary organisations to embark on schemes which will require local authority funding if they are to survive after three years. (Westland, 1984)

Given that the local authorities who were squeezed most tightly also tended to be the areas of greatest social need, Bernstein (1984) drew 'the inescapable conclusion ... that some local projects are being set up to fail'. On this interpretation, the entrusting of alternatives to custody to the voluntary sector had less to do with 'privatizing' *genuine* alternatives, and more to do with using 'privatization' as a means of devaluing alternatives:

> Whilst the Government's stated intention is to divert youngsters away from custody into the LAC 83(3) project there are good reasons for thinking the Government would be very pleased with a totally different outcome. (Davies and Williams, 1985: 25)

Such speculation accorded with Brenton's critical view of the circumstances under which the State involved voluntary organizations in certain spheres of activity. Echoing Bernstein, she wrote:

> they add an instant task force capability to the cumbersome machinery of government in a way that rapidly accumulates political capital for relatively small financial outlays, *particularly for policies which governments are not too keen on*. There may be other factors involved such as a governments wish to distance itself from certain groups or functions, or the desire to bypass potentially uncooperative interests such as local authorities or trade unions. (Brenton, 1985: 89; emphasis added)

In 1983, there was much to commend this interpretation of the LAC 83(3) Initiative (Mellor, 1985: 166), although the desperate financial need of some SSDs and the absence of any better way of pursuing alternatives to custody tended to obscure this and gave the Initiative a degree of popularity. Yet it had undoubtedly been hastily organized without consultation, at a time when restrictions on local government finance made it unlikely that short-term voluntary sector initiatives could be sustained. It emanated from the DHSS at a time when it had already lost influence to the more custodially inclined Home Office (Tutt, 1980). It was not part of any coherent strategy to prioritize areas of greatest need, or to avoid net widening and to ensure that alternatives to custody were properly targeted.[8] Above all, the type of voluntary organization it was most keen to involve seemed a little too makeshift to carry the burden of a major development in penal policy — if indeed it was considered a major development.

The consequences of the Initiative

Slightly more than half the local authorities in England and Wales exercised their discretion to respond to the Initiative. Apart from the local political factors which are known to affect willingness to work with voluntaries (Cousins, 1976; Hatch and Mocroft, 1977), some authorities did not take it up because they already felt they had sufficient provision in the alternatives field, others because they doubted if they would be able to take financial responsibility when the grant ran out after three years. The end result was that it was used to finance 110 projects in 62 local authorities, offering places to some 3000 youngsters (NACRO/JOT, 1986a). The funding ended in March 1986, although for administrative reasons a number of projects did not become operational until 1987.

As predicted, many difficulties were encountered in establishing, running and planning the future of the projects (Davies and Williams, 1985; John, 1985; NACRO/JOT, 1986b: 29–30), although definite reductions in local rates of custody in the project areas (NACRO/JOT, 1986a: 4) and improved inter-agency cooperation (Dartington Social Research Unit, 1985; Warner, 1987) took the edge off some of the earlier criticism. It is not my intention to comment further on these issues, important as they are, but rather to concentrate on the more neglected issue of the form which voluntary sector involvement took.

The types of voluntary organizations involved in the partnerships varied evenly between offshoots of national voluntaries on the one hand, and local voluntary organizations on the other. A survey of 57 Initiative projects (out of the 82 approved at the time) indicated that of the 29 local voluntaries in the sample, 17 had existed before the 1983 Circular had been issued, a further 2 had come into being independently of the Initiative, and only 10 had been created specifically to apply for the new funding (NACRO/JOT, 1986b: 5–6). Thus the type of voluntary organization considered most appropriate by the DHSS, by dint of the ease with which the local authority could control and absorb it, proved to be the least common:

> This Initiative does not appear to have led to the creation of large numbers of new voluntary bodies established specifically to take up funding. (NACRO/JOT, 1986b: 31)

The proportion of national voluntaries which had applied for funding was greater than the DHSS had expected, and arguably greater than they had considered desirable, but the reasons were not difficult to find. The DHSS had tended to think only in terms of the pressure which local authorities were under to shift the balance of their resources from residential to community-based facilities but, as Hadley notes,

> Similar pressures were also affecting the big voluntary child care organis-

ations such as the Save the Children Fund, National Children's Homes, Dr. Barnardo's. Expensive residential facilities and experience in working with socially deprived youngsters were being underused. (Hadley, 1983: 10)

These organizations, hard pressed by the ravages of inflation on their reserves, the decreasing use of their resources by local authorities, the declining numbers of 11 to 15 year olds in the population and the competition for available funds as voluntary sector facilities for children proliferated, badly needed to diversify into new fields. LAC 83(3) gave them the opportunity to do so. Despite the lack of prior consultation, the national child care voluntaries leapt at the offer of 'easy money' (Bernstein, 1984), even though it meant a rather sudden restructuring for many of them, and movement in a direction (alternatives to care and custody) for which few had campaigned or possessed specific expertise.

The large childcare voluntaries were not the only national bodies to be brought into the alternative to care and custody field by LAC 83(3). Others included Community Service Volunteers (CSV) and the Community Projects Foundation (CPF), both of which developed their own distinctive interpretation of what alternative regimes should consist of, according to their own values and styles. The rooting of alternatives to custody in the wider value systems of modern voluntary organizations — often with an explicit emphasis on compassion and empowerment, as well as on offence resolution — has had an important leavening effect on IT, reducing the impact of 'justice talk' (Pratt, 1987) and what Hudson (1986) has perceived as the penal orientation of many such alternatives.

The CPF Dewis Project in Clwyd, Wales, for example, 'would appear to be the only project managed by a national community development agency, though some have been set up by local community projects' (Phipps, 1988: 3). It offers an individualized programme in a rural area for both sentenced and remanded youngsters who are at risk of custody, but also works with school nonattenders, youngsters 'beyond control' and 'the youngster's family or friends on a negotiated basis' (Project publicity). The Children's Society Gerard Avenue Project in Coventry (see Holman, 1988: 133–43) and two of Barnardo's' pre-Initiative projects were similarly broad-based, aware of the potential for net-widening (Barnardo's, 1985: 1) but confident that they were being managed in ways that minimized the risks.

In addition to the involvement of more national bodies than the DHSS had expected, there were other ways in which the outcome of the LAC (83)3 Initiative has diverged from DHSS expectations. JOT's 1985 Project Development Survey showed that take-over by the local authority was not what the projects themselves were anticipating:

> The majority of voluntary organisations are indicating that they expect to continue to manage projects after the DHSS funding expires, either by attracting grant aid from the local authority or other funding sources. This points to the fact that the voluntary sector will be making a significant contribution to the management of alternatives to custody and care schemes in the longer term. They do not appear to see their role as being short-term development bodies, (NACRO/JOT, 1986b: 31)

What this meant was that many of the projects were, in the future, going to be financed (in whole or in part) by local authorities, as the DHSS had envisaged, but would retain their independent management body and their 'voluntary' status. In that sense they were not being 'taken over' by the local authority — a new arrangement which had, in several respects, become mutually advantageous.

The advantage of remaining independent for the national voluntaries was the simple fact that it aided their survival. They were concerned to find a new and durable role for themselves in an environment which no longer favoured residential care, and working with young offenders in the community, although not the only option pursued, was attractive because of the likelihood of continuing government funding for it. Although, as Bernstein (1984) had noted, the voluntary childcare sector would have preferred to undertake innovative and developmental work in spheres of its own choosing, the collapse of residential care led all the major bodies in this field to incorporate IT (in both its preventive and alternatives to custody form) as mainstream rather than experimental work. It became part of their new philosophies of support for families in the community, alongside work with the young unemployed, homeless youth, runaways and drug abusers and alongside initiatives in youth training, divorce conciliation, homefinding, leaving care schemes, family centres and youth and community work in general.

The advantage to local authorities of voluntary organizations retaining their distinct identity stemmed from the growing importance of 'purchase of service contracting' (POSC) in the delivery of personal social services (Judge, 1982; Etherington, 1983). Throughout the eighties there has been strong government pressure for local authorities to become coordinators and procurers of social services from the informal, voluntary and commercial sectors rather than service providers themselves (see Walker, 1988), on the grounds of the latter's alleged cheapness, flexibility and capacity to innovate compared to the moribund bureaucracies of local government. In the rhetoric of welfare pluralism there is a tendency to dignify all such arrangements as 'partnership', but that term implies a greater degree of collaboration and joint planning than exists in many cases. At present there are still — to use Locke's (1981) terms — 'complementary' and 'augmentation' models of statutory/voluntary relationships in the IT field, as well as full partnerships at local level, and the general arrangement is better described as contractual rather than collaborative. Many of the larger voluntary organizations understandably prefer to think of themselves as partners rather than mere contractees, but significantly it is 'the juvenile crime projects run by the Rainer Foundation; the family centres run by the Children's Society and the paid organiser schemes of Community Service Volunteers' (Holroyd, 1983) that have been cited, from a local authority perspective, as key examples of POSC.

Demand for services to young people increased as the eighties progressed. Even before the end of the Initiative the national voluntaries were setting up new projects — although it is also the case that some Initiative projects were not refunded and did close.[9] The new projects covered the entire range of IT provision, from prevention and community support through to alternatives to custody, and in that sense the voluntaries might be said to have unified the legacy of IT — without ironing out the tensions — after a period of determined professional effort to prise it apart.

While it had been distinctly unfashionable, for a number of years in IT, to defend or engage in preventive work, there had in fact been a variety of political pressures on local authorities and voluntary organizations to expand it on all fronts, even in regard to young offenders. The work of the IT Fund, the attention which the 1981 and 1985 'riots' focused on inner-city deprivation, especially among black youth (Pitts, 1988), the Social Services Select Committee Report on 'Children in Care' (1984) and the growth of 'social crime prevention' (Blagg, 1988) all helped to resuscitate work of a kind which would once have been called IT, even though that term was now rarely used for it, for example, in Barnardo's Wakefield Action for Youth project (Siddal, 1988). However much the national voluntaries may have isolated their juvenile justice projects for administrative reasons (and even this is variable), all now engage in preventive work in some form or another, by some name or another (community support, family support, etc.), and their work in the alternatives to custody field is presented as an expression of the same concerns and the same values, rather than an expression of penal values.

None the less, the most remarkable development in the eighties has clearly been the extent to which the rhetoric and ambition of the abolitionists in juvenile justice (as opposed to the Home Office exponents of 'alternatives') has been fully incorporated into the national voluntaries core philosophies. 'The future direction and objectives for the Children's Society', for example,

> are to work towards the abolition of custody for juvenile offenders; to promote policies and practice which divert young offenders from the criminal justice system; and to contribute to debates about the raising of the age of criminal responsibility, family courts, child care reform, advocacy and greater priority for crime prevention and provision of youth services. (De'ath, 1988)

It should not be assumed, however, that the voluntaries' adoption of abolition will necessarily make its achievement any easier, not least because such a stance may diminish their credibility with policy-makers and lose them public support. In this connection it is interesting to note that a recent Children's Society advisory comittee which put forward a detailed and convincing strategy for abolishing custody for juveniles has so far failed to generate significant debate, despite having been chaired by a junior government minister (Children's Society, 1988). All that one can say at this stage is that calls for abolition are now voiced by more powerful bodies than hitherto.

Discussion

The growth of voluntary sector involvement in juvenile justice is beset by paradox, but from a purely professional point of view it has — so far — worked out better than expected. The LAC 83(3) Initiative had not intended to involve the established voluntary sector in any major way, but merely to augment, temporarily, the services provided by local authorities. However, once it became involved the opportunities it presented were welcomed by many juvenile justice practitioners, and a number of the more prominent among them subsequently pursued their careers — and their campaigns — within it. Despite the government's attempt to deprioritize alternatives to custody, the reverse has happened and the high profile that the voluntaries have given to abolitionist policies has meant that the early anxieties about 'privatization' have been substantially weakened. It has arguably been their greatest achievement to have incorporated ideas that were once the preserve of small and socially invisible professional bodies (the AJJ and NITFED) in organizations which, because of their associations with 'childsaving' rather than penal reform, still occupy the moral high ground and enjoy broad public support.[10] Even more so than NACRO, because many of them are household names and have powerful friends in the most illustrious elites in the land, they have become a major pressure group for a custody-free juvenile justice system, although the impact of this, not least on their own reputations, remains to be seen.

Having said this, it is important not to overplay the practical gains that have been made so far. The merits of voluntary sector involvement are more mundane than those traditionally proclaimed by the rhetoric of welfare pluralism. Apart from cheapness, the key merits — the capacity of voluntaries to be more innovative and flexible, and to get in closer touch with communities — are only discernible in the contemporary IT field (and then only to an extent) because the Government's onslaught against local authorities and its denigration of much statutory social work has weakened the latter's capacity to match the voluntary effort. Had local authorities been funded properly, and had the government prioritized alternatives to custody to the same extent as, say, child protection, the administrative topography of juvenile justice in the eighties may have looked very different.

Current voluntary sector involvement in IT has, in any case, less to do with innovation and more to do with the 'consolidation' of developments which began in the seventies (Bernstein, 1984), and while there have in the past been a number of innovative voluntary IT projects, one might reasonably argue that almost the entire history of IT has been a history of successful innovation — building up new facilities from scratch — in SSD settings. Since 1970 there have been few developments in the voluntary sector in approaches to work with young offenders, apart from the consultancies, that were not either paralleled or preceded in local authorities.[11]

On the basis of recent research, Holman (1988) does suggest that voluntary community projects are more adept at using local resources (including residents), at offering help without stigma and at promoting their values than are their local authority counterparts. Given the traditionally bureaucratic image of local government, it is less obviously the case than with innovation that this could be otherwise: certainly some — though not all — municipal attempts at decentralization and 'community social work' have been criticized for their somewhat cosmetic approach to participation (Beresford, 1985). Yet it remains the case that even this judgement of local authority performance is made against a background of failure to develop a strong tradition of participative local democracy in the country as a whole. The channelling of 'goodwill' through the voluntary sector has to an extent been a substitute for it.

It is in terms of the traditional limitations and recent weakening of local government, that one needs to examine the most common criticism of voluntary sector involvement in IT (and social services in general), namely its independence from direct electoral control. This was raised early and made repeatedly throughout the history of the

LAC 83(3) Initiative. According to Peter Westland, Social Services Under Secretary of the Association of Metropolitan Authorities, the new management bodies that were to be created would introduce 'an unnecessary and unaccountable level of bureaucracy' (quoted in *Community Care* 16 December 1982). In their 'Manifesto for Management', Tutt and Giller (1987) insisted that the provision of alternatives to care and custody was a statutory responsibility: 'No local authority', they wrote, 'should be dependent upon voluntary or experimental projects to carry out a sentence of the court', lest an uneven distribution of facilities leads, as so often, to 'justice by geography' (Richardson, 1987) and a sense of alternatives being makeshift and marginal compared to custody. More recently it has been emphasized that the welfare of young people

> is not a state asset to be hived away to the private sector (as it is in the states) nor to large voluntary organisations working to central government contracts. The provision of any service to young people demands a level of public accountability obtained through local democratic process. Let us be on our guard that this fundamental and hard fought for principle is not placed under threat. (*Ajjust*, 11, January 1987)

The relevance of this latter line of argument to provision for young offenders has regrettably to be questioned. The principle of local democracy ought indeed to be defended, but 'the local state' in Britain, in general, has never been especially democratic (Dearlove, 1979) and, more to the point, penal reform and services for offenders have never been an electoral asset. While there are isolated examples where members rather than officers of local authorities have initiated progressive practice in juvenile justice,[12] it has more often been lay people and professionals who have had the freedom to disregard electoral opinion, who have most advanced offenders' (as opposed to 'deserving' childrens') welfare. It is idle to pretend that the magistrate-packed management bodies of the LAC 83(3) projects (NACRO/JOT) 1986b: 7–12) are any kind of ideal, but it has to be admitted that in general they have done an effective job in reducing the use of custody, and that many magistrates (and some clerks) have, as a result of them, been persuaded of the merits of 'custody-free zones' (Gibson, 1986). True, the geographical distribution of alternatives to custody is uneven, but the reasons for that are complex and it is difficult to believe, given economic constraints, that local authorities alone could have acted in unison to remedy this, not least because custody (as opposed to residential care) is financed by central government and is not therefore part of any expenditure from which they might make savings; *ergo*, they have had no real incentive to provide alternatives. In principle, central government could perhaps have enforced universal provision, but such directiveness is not 'the British way' (yet?) and it is precisely because reducing custody is of low priority in central government (if not to all people who work within it) that this has never been seriously considered.

To have shown that the voluntary sector's achievement in IT stands out only because of the flatness of the local authority landscape is not to invalidate that achievement. As noted above, it made good use of the LAC 83(3) Initiative and has exploited its limited independence to co-opt and pursue an anti-custodial policy with far greater vigour than the DHSS ever envisaged or (probably) than the Home Office ever wished.

But how real is this independence, and can it last? The fact remains that although a number of the long-established voluntary organizations are independently wealthy the expansion of the voluntary sector in Great Britain in the seventies and eighties was financed largely by a system of central and local government grants. Most of the voluntaries referred to in this chapter are dependent, not for survival itself, but certainly for the scale of their operations, on statutory funding. Should they wish to undertake initiatives for which they do not receive such funding, they are dependent on reserves, private finance, trust funds, charities and the ingenuity of their admirers, and if the State withdrew its support that is all that would remain.[13] So how far can the voluntary sector pursue its own goals and inclinations, according to its own values and priorities.

Not far. The extent of State funding, both in general terms and specifically in relation to juvenile offending, in fact renders problematic the whole notion of 'a voluntary sector' and the concomitant notions of 'voluntarization' and 'privatization' in their usual meanings. The organizations that have proliferated since the LAC 83(3) Initiative began are more accurately described as 'quasi-statutory organizations' (Brenton, 1985: 70); they are forms of State organization, not something wholly distinct from it. They are different forms, admittedly, from those which have pertained hitherto, not least in the degree and type of their managerial independence and their explicit stance on values, which patently does give them some room for manoeuvre. In the end, however, they are doing work whose importance (or otherwise) has been determined by the State, to a level only slightly in excess of what the State itself is prepared to fund.

The autonomy of 'quasi-statutory organizations' is thus ultimately conditional, not so much on the extent of funding — although the Rainer Foundation (1986: 5) says it 'does not receive the support it needs' — but on the very pattern of funding, the limited and shifting range of areas in which grants are made available. It is this which channels, directs and redirects voluntary sector activities, and it is difficult to see how the juvenile justice voluntaries, even the bigger ones, can be immune to this process in the long term. As Brenton puts it,

> In this symbiotic type of relationship, one may discern a factor which the sceptic might describe as 'the bandwagon effect', where voluntary bodies energetically subscribe to the policies upon which finance is currently contingent. Government social policies characteristically exhibit ad hoc and short term enthusiasms and 'we must be seen to be doing something' political reflexes. Voluntary bodies, trading on a reputation for flexibility and innovation, and short of money, tack and turn expertly in relation to them . . . [they] become increasingly adept in the fine art of grantmanship, changing direction or sprouting new projects to fit the label attached to whatever grants are available. (Brenton, 1985: 89–90)

The next field of criminal justice in which we can already see the voluntary sector tacking and turning in order to secure funding is that of young adult offenders (17 to 21 year olds). Over the past few years a number of voluntary organizations traditionally involved with juveniles have considered this, and three — Rainer, NCH and LAYT (which has now abandoned its work with juveniles) — have already embarked on projects. The reasons are largely to do with the contraction of demand for the organizations' original services — whether consultancy or service provision — the declining number of juveniles in the population and the need to find both alternative avenues for their expertise and alternative means of survival. Two of the main organizations (NCH and Rainer) have recently joined forces with the Association of Chief Probation Officers, the Association of Directors of Social Services and NACRO to form 'Action on Youth Crime', an umbrella organization which will campaign for the reduction of custody for young adult offenders. According to NCH's Director of Social Work this was 'a logical next step' (White, 1988).

The policy framework in which these developments are now taking place was set by the green paper 'Punishment, Custody and the Community' (Home Office, 1988), which demands of the Probation Service that it replicate, with the 17 to 21 year olds, some of the methods which have reduced the use of custody for juveniles.[14] Each Probation Service has been told to develop an Action Plan for young adult offenders, and £1.3 million has been made available over three years to fund voluntary sector participation in this work. It remains to be seen which voluntary organizations respond to this, not least because of grassroots opposition to their encroaching on the work of the Service (Greater Manchester NAPO, 1988). Smaller, independent voluntaries, such as LAYT, which lack a specific childcare tradition, and the Rainer Foundation, which has a long association with probation hostels, may find it quite easy to move into work with older age groups, but for any of the national childcare voluntaries this is likely to require alterations to their constitutions, names and images more far reaching than anything they have yet considered.[15]

Notes

1 The term 'intermediate treatment' (IT) was introduced in England and Wales by the white paper 'Children in Trouble' (Home Office, 1968) to refer, somewhat vaguely, to a wider range of provision for young people at risk and in trouble. In the early seventies it took the form of low intensity preventive social work, but towards the end of the decade, and in the early eighties, a group of researchers from the University of Lancaster (Thorpe et al., 1980) led a successful but controversial attempt to restrict it to high intensity alternatives to (residential) care and custody schemes. From the mid-eighties its lack of specificity was considered too serious an impediment to good public relations (Stevens and Crook, 1986), and a number of areas — by no means all — abandoned it, without there being any clear consensus as to what it should be replaced with.

2 The three national childcare voluntaries all had their origins in the evangelical and philanthropic movements of the nineteenth century and still call themselves Christian organizations. The eponymous founder of Dr Barnardo's began a Mission for poor children in the East End of London in 1866 (Wagner, 1979); it evolved to become the second largest charity in Britain and has branches in Australia and New Zealand. Neither the National Children's Homes nor The Church of England Children's Society are as large or as well known, although they also have some branches abroad. The former was founded by a Methodist, Dr Stephenson, in 1869; the latter (originally called Waifs and Strays) by Edward Rudolph in 1881 'to make sure that destitute children were reared in the teachings of the established church' (Bowder, 1980). The Save the Children Fund had somewhat different roots; it was founded as an international relief organization in 1919 and its childcare work in Britain is still a relatively small part of its total work (see note 3 below). The Rainer Foundation was also not a childcare charity as such but, as the London Police Court Mission (founded in 1876), was one of several organizations which pioneered probation work in Britain. Its current projects are mainly in London and southern England.

3 The neglect of the consultancies in this paper is due only to limitations of space, and not to any sense of their unimportance. They have undoubtedly been influential, and represent the most genuinely innovative contribution of the voluntary sector to IT. Most of them originated within SCF: Hilltop in 1980 (whose precise function has changed since then — see Jepson, 1985); Contact (in Newcastle) in 1984 and a contribution to the statutory/voluntary consortium which set up the Scottish IT Consultancy Unit, The Children's Society has run the The Wales Centre for Juvenile Justice since 1985.

4 The term 'abolition' is not used in the politically sophisticated manner suggested by Mathiesen (1974) or, specifically in connection with IT, by Pitts (1988). Some practitioners may well have used it in this sense, but most used abolition simply to mean working for the ending of *penal* custody (as opposed to some secure accommodation, which was permitted), either by straightforward campaigning or by starving custodial institutions of customers — the 'eliminationist' position described by Tutt and Giller (1987).

5 Both measures were part of a central government strategy to curtail the expenditure of local authorities, especially those with whose social welfare policies it disagreed.

6 I use the term 'privatization' because that is how the process of involving the voluntary sector is usually described by its critics (Davies and Williams, 1985; John, 1985). It is in fact a misnomer, and in the welfare context at present it should be restricted to the displacement of statutory services by the *commercial, private enterprise sector* rather than the voluntary sector. That is not to deny that there can be overlap between the sectors, or that genuine privatization may not occur in the future, especially if voluntary organizations form companies to bid competitively for local authority contracts (see *Community Care* 20 October 1988: 1 for details of Barnardo's, *possible* involvement in such a scheme); it is merely to register that the term has been used inappropriately in connection with LAC 83(3).

7 LAC 83(3) was one of nine Government Initiatives in various areas of social welfare which were launched in the early eighties, and which made use of the voluntary sector. Westland (1984) called them 'ad hoc policies'. Most suffered from the same over-hasty preparation and the Under-5s Initiative virtually collapsed as a result of SSD reluctance to take over projects (*Community Care* 3 October 1985: 2).

8 The net widening potential of the Initiative remains unresolved, Davies and Williams (1985: 26) observed that 'the number of places provided for by the established social services, probation and voluntary bodies together with the projects initiated by LAC 83(3) exceeds the number of custodial sentences made in 1983' and warned that the Initiative projects 'will cater for children who would not otherwise have received a custodial sentence'. Jones (1987), on the other hand, suggests that because of proper targeting 'initial fears that projects would widen the social control net do not appear to have materialised'.

9 At the time of writing full details of what had happened to the LAC 83(3) Projects when the DHSS funding expired was not available. The late starting projects were still in receipt of such funding. The options for the rest varied between (a) takeover by the local authority; (b) recombination into something completely new, as with the inter-agency teams which evolved from the Initiative scheme in Kent (Warner, 1987); (c) assumption of full voluntary status; (d) voluntary status but with local authority grants for running costs; (e) voluntary status but with seconded local authority workers. I am grateful to Barry Anderson of NACRO for this information.

10 When Barnardo's first moved into community-based work with young offenders the then Director of Child Care opined 'this sort of work is less attractive to the giving public than some of the work we used to do with much younger children' (Barnardo's, 1982: 6), and for a while it played down the specific details. Nowadays, none of the voluntaries attempts to subsume this work behind a safe, traditional image of needy children and in October 1988 Barnardos (sic) relaunched itself, formally dropping 'Dr' from its name, and using a distinctive new logo to convey to the public the nature of the changes in its work (see *New Statesman/and Society* 21 October 1988: 23). In the course of a five-year campaign, it is determined to lose its Victorian orphan image once and for all' and its alternative to custody programmes now permeate its publicity, even its education pack for secondary school students (*Barnardos Today*, Spring/Summer 1987: 2–5). To take another example, NCH 'is well aware that its beliefs as to the best way of dealing with juvenile offenders runs counter to popular opinion' and

'therefore takes every opportunity to explain our work with juvenile offenders to the public' (NCH, 1987: 4), through factsheets, videos etc.

11 The use of 'new careerists' (ex-offenders as volunteers) in the Hammersmith Teenage Project and the importing of tracking from Massachusetts by The Children's Society PACE Project in Coventry are the two most innovative approaches to have been pioneered in the voluntary sector. The former was not deemed to have been very successful, did not survive the Project's transfer to local authority control (Covington, 1979) and has only ever been a minor feature of work in juvenile justice elsewhere. The latter, interest in which came first from the *statutory* rather than the voluntary sector (see Spencer, 1982), came in for a lot of criticism when PACE first adopted it, and only spread to other projects after PACE itself had abandoned it. The voluntary sector, whatever its reputation, cannot always innovate in uncongenial climates.

12 This appears to have happened in Leicestershire, in 1982–84, in developments that were, confusingly, unconnected with the establishment of LAYT. See Sue Ross's account of the AJJ Annual Conference (*Ajjust*, 7, Oct. 1985)

13 A news item recently appeared in *Community Care* (11 August 1988: 7) noting that a certain social work lecturer was participating in an attempt to climb a peak in the Himalayas: 'The team hopes to raise £8,000 for the Rainer Foundation's scheme working with young people on remand'. Is this a sensible way to fund alternatives to custody? There is also the issue of private funding. One aspect of LAYT's early work, a Neighbourhood Intervention Project, was eventually lost when funding was withdrawn, but a new project, the Job Placement Scheme, was established for a three-year period in 1983 with funds from the Prudential Assurance Company (LAYT, 1984: 5).

14 John Patten, the DHSS minister 'responsible for agreeing the 1983 Initiative' (*Probation Journal* Sept. 1988: 84), subsequently became the Home Office minister with responsibility for taking forward the green paper.

15 Although responsibility for the argument in this paper, and for any errors, is mine alone, the ideas in it developed over the years of the Initiative in conversation with a number of people, beginning with Tony Bottoms and Phillip Brown at the University of Cambridge. I would particularly like to thank Colonel Archie Pagan and Mr Chris Sealy (of the DHSS) for agreeing to be interviewed about the Initiative. In addition Norman Tutt (of Lancaster University), Celia Moore (of the IT Fund), Allison Skinner (of the National Youth Bureau), Alan Walker (of Sheffield University) and Chris Stanley and Barry Anderson (of NACRO) were all very helpful.

References

Barnardo's (1982) *Annual Review.* Ilford: Barnardo's.

Barnardo's (1985) *Yniscedwyn IT Project: Consumer Survey Report*, Cardiff: Barnardo's.

Beresford, P. (1985) *Patch in Perspective: Decentralising and Democratising Social Services*, London: Battersea Community Action.

Bernstein, M. (1984) 'Something Will Turn Up'. *Community Care*, 6 September.

Blagg, H. (1988) *Social Crime Prevention and Policies for Youth in England*. Research Bulletin No.24. London: Home Office Research and Planning Unit.

Bowder, B. (1980) *Children First: A Photohistory of England's Children in Need.* London: Mowbray.

Brenton, M. (1985) *The Voluntary Sector in British Social Services*, London: Longman.

Burney, E. (1985) 'All Things to All Men: Justifying Custody under the 1982 Act', *Criminal Law Review*, May.

Children's Society (1988) *Advisory Committee on Penal Custody and its Alternatives for Juveniles*, chaired by Virginia Bottomley M P. London: The Children's Society.

Covington, C. (1979) *Evaluation of the Hammersmith Teenage Project*, London: NACRO.

Cousins, P. (1976) 'Voluntary Organisations and Local Government in Three South London Boroughs', *Public Administration*, 54: 63–81.

Dartington Social Research Unit/University of Bristol (1985) *Services for the Adolescent; The Contribution of the CSV Local Partnership Scheme*.

Davies, T. and Williams, S. (1985) 'Privatisation and the LAC(83)3 Projects' *Ajjust*, 7, October.

Dearlove, J. (1979) *The Reorganisation of British Local Government: Old Orthodoxies and a Political Perspective*. Cambridge: Cambridge University Press.

De'ath, E. (1988) 'The Challenge of Diversion', *Youth and Society*, August.

DHSS/Welsh Office (1974) *Joint Memorandum on the CYPA 1969 in the Eleventh Report of the House of Commons Expenditure Committee*, Vol.2. Minutes of Evidence and Appendices (1975), London: HMSO.

DHSS (1977) *Intermediate Treatment: 28 Choices*.

DHSS (1983) *LAC 83(3): Further Development of Intermediate Treatment*.

Etherington, S. (1983) 'Community Wares on the Private Market', *Social Work Today*, 7 June.

Gibson, B. (1986) 'The Abolition of Custody for Juveniles, Parts 1 and 2', *Justice of the Peace*, 150 47–8.

Greater Manchester NAPO (Branch Executive Committee) (1988) 'Tackling Offending: A Reaction Plan?', *Probation Journal*, 35 (4).

Hadley, J. (1983) 'Hope at the Heavy End', *Voluntary Action*, 15 (Summer).

Hatch, S. (1980) *Outside the State: Voluntary Organisations in Three English Towns*. London: Croom-Helm.

Hatch, S. and Mocroft, I. (1977) 'Factors Affecting the Location of Voluntary Organisations', *Policy and Politics*, 6: 163–72.

Holman, B. (1988) *Putting Families First: Prevention and Child Care*. London: Macmillan.

Holroyd, D. (1983) 'Service Purchase — What it can do for a Department', *Municipal Journal*, 2 December.

Home Office (1968) *Children in Trouble*, Cmnd 3601, London: HMSO.

Home Office (1988) *Punishment, Custody and the Community*, Cm 424, London: HMSO.

Hope, P. (1977) *Intermediate Treatment; A Discussion Document for Voluntary Organisations*. London: National Council of Social Service.

Hudson, B. (1986) *The Incarceration of Young People: Custody, Alternatives to Custody, Alternative Custody in Probation; Engaging with Custody*. London: National Association of Probation Officers.

Jepson, N. (1985) *A Review of the Hilltop Project*. Leeds: Save the Children (Northern Region).

John, E. (1985) 'Does the Initiative lead to Schizophrenia?' *Initiatives: NACRO/JOT Newsletter*, 5 (Winter).

Jones, D. (1987) 'Recent Developments in Work with Young Offenders', in J. Coleman (ed.), *Working with Troubled Adolescents*. London: Academic Press.

Judge, K. (1982) 'The Public Purchase of Social Care: British Confirmation of American Experience', *Policy and Politics*, 10 (4).

Leicester Action for Youth Trust (1984) *Trust Report*.

Locke, T. (1981) 'IT and the Voluntary Sector', IT Mailing, May. Leicester: National Youth Bureau.

Mathiesen, T. (1974) *The Politics of Abolition*. London: Martin Robertson.

Mellor, H.W. (1985) *The Role of Voluntary Organisations in Social Welfare*. London: Croom-Helm.

NACRO/JOT (1986a) *Diverting Juveniles from Custody: Findings from the Fourth Census of Projects Funded under the DHSS Initiative*. London: NACRO.

NACRO/JOT (1986b) *Project Development Survey: DHSS IT Initiative*. London: NACRO.

National Children's Home (1987) *The 1987 NCH Review*. London: NCH.

Phipps, A. (1988) *Dewis: A Community-based Approach to Working with Young People in Trouble*. London: Community Projects Foundation.

Pitts, J. (1988) *The Politics of Juvenile Crime*, London: Sage.

Pratt, J. (1987) 'A Revisionist History of Intermediate Treatment', *British Journal of Social Work*, 17.

Rainer Foundation (1986) *Annual Report*. London: Rainer Foundation.

Richardson, N. (1987) *Justice by Geography*? Manchester: Social Information System.

Rutherford, A. (1986) *Growing Out of Crime*. Harmondsworth: Penguin.

Siddall, A. (1988) 'A Model of Discretion', *Youth Social Work*, 7 (June). Leicester: National Youth Bureau.

Social Services Select Committee (1984) *Children in Care*. London: HMSO.

Spencer, N. (1982) *P.A.C.E.: The First Interim Research Report — April to December 1982*. Coventry: Children's Society.

Stevens, M. and Crook, J. (1986) 'What the Devil is Intermediate Treatment?' *Social Work Today*, 8 September.

Thorpe, D. et al. (1980) *Out of Care: The Community Support of Juvenile Offenders*. London: George Allen & Unwin.

Tutt, N. (1980) 'Janus Pushes Back Justice', *Community Care*, 16 October.

Tutt, N. and Giller, H. (1987) 'Manifesto for Management — The Elimination of Custody', *Justice of the Peace*, 28 March.

Unell, J. (1981) *Voluntary Action and Young People in Trouble: Funding*. London: NCVO.

Wagner, G. (1979) *Barnardo*, London: Eyre & Spottiswoode.

Walker, A. (1988) 'Tendering Care' *New Society*, 22 January.

Warner, N. (1987) 'Out of the Blue', *Social Services Insight*, 2 October.

Westland, P. (1984) 'No Sense of Direction', *Community Care*, 17 November.

Wills, D. (1970) *Spare the Child*, London: Penguin.

White, T. (1988) 'In Consideration of Youth Crime — Anti-Custody Strategy for Young People' *Ajjust*, 17 (June).

8 PRIVATE PRISONS AND PENAL PURPOSE

Private prisons are already well established in America and are about to take off in Britain soon. In view of the actual and proposed development of private prisons the question facing all those concerned — both critics and advocates — is what kind of safeguards can be employed to ensure that private prisons operate as required. The problem of providing safeguards is complicated by the fact that there are a number of different functions associated with incarceration that have been identified as being suitable for privatization and that each of these particular functions may require different measures. Taylor and Pease argue that the critical question is not so much whether prisons are run for profit but whether acceptable, relevant standards are applied to the provision and administration of prison facilities.

Can we prevent private prisons from absorbing those who otherwise would have received non-custodial sentences? How can controls be formulated so as to ensure that the required standards are maintained? Could more effective rehabilitative programmes be encouraged, making incarceration not only a more humane but also a more constructive sanction? What is the basis for appeal for unfair treatment in prisons? Could the private prisons be designed to save money or even make money? These are the questions currently being raised by penologists and to which Taylor and Pease address themselves.

Against a background of mounting criticism of how State prisons operate, the movement towards privatization cannot be easily discounted. Nor are existing methods for monitoring and evaluating how State agencies operate considered adequate. There is a growing feeling that the State might be more vigilant when monitoring private organizations than when regulating itself. As in other areas of 'privatization' there is the perennial danger that the regulating agency may be 'captured' by the regulator. Also, it may prove difficult to enforce standards, terminate contracts, or improve prison conditions beyond the minimum standard (Ascher, 1987).

However, State administrators do have a wide variety of methods available for ensuring that private contractors meet reasonable standards and respond to changing imperatives. The means are also potentially available for encouraging private agencies actually to improve performance and the delivery of services (Gandy, 1985). Through a mixture of licensing, fiscal measures, legal constraints, systematic monitoring and increasing public access and accountability, privatization could conceivably serve to overcome the inertia and secrecy that have become associated with incarceration. If such regulatory mechanisms are fully developed and implemented, Taylor and Pease suggest, decline can be avoided and the penal system itself could become more responsive and constructive.

Private Prisons and Penal Purpose

Max Taylor and Ken Pease

In the course of the 1983–84 Conservative administration, private prisons have moved from being a wild idea to probable existence by 1995. The possibility of privatization of prisons was apparently recognized quite suddenly. Nowhere is the road to Damascus experience more evident than in the remarks made in 1986 by the then Chair of the Home Affairs Committee, Sir Edward Gardner. He announced his conversion in a preface to his committee's examination of the Earl of Caithness, then Minister of State at the Home Office, on 19 November. Sir Edward described the visit of members of the Committee to private prisons in the USA and opined 'I had in mind the possibility that they were more absurd than realistic. However, ... [f]ar from thinking that these prisons might be something in fantasy rather than something we could use in practice, I think we all felt that they were in fact institutions of a very high standard indeed' (Third Report from the Home Affairs Committee, Session 1986–7: 22). It is impossible not to feel sorry for Lord Caithness, faced with a paeon of praise for this novel idea: 'I have only been in the job some 10 weeks' (ibid.: 22).

Others have been as enthusiastic in their opposition as Sir Edward was in his support. In an information sheet of the Howard League for Penal Reform issued on 12 January 1987, we read 'There are very many urgent issues to be resolved in Britain's penal policy, and the Howard League argues that the important opportunity offered by the Home Affairs Committee investigation should not be wasted by diverting attention to marginal considerations of privatization, away from substantive problems'. Perhaps because the debate is further advanced in the USA, or perhaps because it is operating against a different political background, the attitudes expressed are more circumspect. The public information coordinator of the National Prison Project of the American Civil Liberties Union stops short of outright condemnation. Writing in 1985, she argues only that 'we oppose privatization unless and until we are assured that adequate safeguards are in place' (Elvin, 1985: 50). In similar vein, but from the opposite side of the political tracks, the American Bar Association House of Delegates urged merely that jurisdictions that are considering the privatization of their prisons should not proceed until the complex constitutional and other issues are resolved. Borna (1986) provides an admirably even-handed account of the issue from his base in Indiana.

It is to be regretted that in the United Kingdom the response to the private prison issue has tended to be predictable on party political lines. The present government's programme of privatization of, *inter alia*, British Gas, British Airways, British Telecom and Rolls-Royce, and its encouragement of local authority departments to tender for services in the private sector, has changed the climate fundamentally. Organized labour opposes privatization in all its manifestations (see, for example, Hastings and Levie, 1983). Criticisms of privatized monopolies permit the privatization programme as a whole to be described as a 'Tory dream turning sour' (Young, 1987: 23). The advocacy of private prisons in Britain has its origins in work done for the Adam Smith Institute, typically referred to in the press as a Tory think-tank. Thus, from this side too, the discussion of prison privatization is conflated with general issues of privatization rather than considered as a distinctive exercise. This conflation is subtly demonstrated in the title of the Prison Reform Trust's debate on the issue of 3 November 1987. The title was 'Privatization *and* the Prisons' (emphasis added), rather than 'Privatization *of* the Prisons'. The title thus suggests the application of a general process (privatization) in a particular context (prisons), rather than a process specific to prisons. The more considered commentaries on privatization stress the *variety* of possible outcomes of the process. The prior adoption of any ideological position means that the fact of privatization will be emphasized and its form neglected. This is to be regretted for two reasons. First, some services within prisons are already provided by private concerns (see Camp and Camp, 1985). Privatization is not an all-or-nothing process and the ideologically generated preclusion of debate about which services are best supplied in that way is as unfortunate as any other premature closure of options. Savas (1980) distinguishes four general types of function in respect of prisons: their finance; their construction; their operation; and their provision of work and services. Within each of these, many particular functions may be considered separately.

The second reason for regret about the premature adoption of a stance on private imprisonment is the one we regard as central. There is a political head of steam pressing towards privatization. There are some attractions for penal reformers in even a wholly privatized prison system. However, these are contingent attractions. They depend upon a firm specification of how each of the parts of the system is to be privatized and on what terms. Without Governmental choice and firmness, it is clear that the sectors of the system privatized will be those containing prisoners who should not be locked up at all. This will lead to spurious claims of economy for the privatized part, based upon the costs of imprisoning those for whose containment the cost is lowest.

Those who believe that the use of imprisonment should be as low as possible, and prison regimes as constructive as possible, may absent themselves from the debate if they have taken a prior ideological position. This will have readily predictable consequences on the form and manner in which privatization takes place. There is, in short, a window of opportunity for those wishing to exert influence. The window will soon close. Too many people with reformist ideals have been looking away and sulking.

In our view, the approach to prison privatization taken by the American Civil Liberties Union is the right one. That is to say, the crucial question is not whether a prison is run for profit, but whether acceptable and relevant standards are applied to the establishment and administration of private facilities. Prisons are acceptable or not on the basis of the application of those standards. The single most contentious issue identified by US opponents is the application of force, typically thought of as a monopoly of the State through its agents. Can this properly be derogated to private citizens? We argue that it often is (*vide* the role of Securicor at Heathrow airport and the bouncer at any nightclub), and that this is in principle acceptable. It should be stressed that we do not necessarily regard current practices at Heathrow as satisfactory. We merely point out that private security is already carrying out custodial duties. How they are carried out may be taken as an illustration of the consequences of allowing a drift into private provision. In general, what should be ensured is effective redress against the improper use of force, by whoever that force is applied, public or private employee. This is the central responsibility which cannot be shuffled off. Yet this standard is not consistently achieved by public employees. This is neither more nor less acceptable than the same shortcomings of private employees. The point is well put by Logan:

> In a system characterised by rule of law, state agencies and private agencies alike are bound by the law. For actors within either type of agency, it is the law, not the civil status of the actor, that determines whether any particular exercise of force is legitimate. The law may specify that those authorised to use force in particular situations should be licensed or deputed and adequately trained for this purpose, but they need not be state employees. (1987: 1)

We believe there to be some advantages in a private system in regard to the control of the exercise of power by prison staff. Current discipline arrangements are flawed by the lack of opportunity for a prisoner to present his side of the argument adequately (Ditchfield and Duncan, 1987). To redress this, any offence at a private prison should be triable at an outside court, rather than by a Governor or Board of Visitors. This would avoid the difficulty of the position of those who have to try issues between their subordinates and other people. Such an arrangement would, however, have to be put firmly in place by Government. The alleged remark by the warden of a private facility in Texas that 'I am the Supreme Court' is a salutary reminder of this. Specifically, the crucial provision that would need to be made is a routine channel of communication between prisoner and court.

Since the Prison Medical Service would presumably not operate in private establishments, and local GPs would undertake the work, there would also be a less acute conflict of interest here, leading to a greater tendency to report prison abuses to authorities outside. Neighbourhood Law Centres could have (perhaps be required to have) access to the prisons, and Parliament may introduce a prison equivalent of place of safety orders, to remove prisoners from prisons where they may suffer intimidation. We are not wedded to the particular form of protection suggested above, but a channel of communication would be required. Even if very modest, such a channel would represent a real improvement on the current position.

Other problems concern the power of private agencies to order discretionary early release and to intrude into local politics (Borna, 1986). While these difficulties will have to be confronted it is difficult to imagine why they are regarded as so destructive of private corrections as to prevent their further consideration. This is not to minimize the problem, although it is not specific to private arrangements. As concluded later in the chapter, determination of length of time to be served should be kept out of private hands, and the relationship between contract terms and length of time served is crucial. It would be naive to suppose that the building industry would not make its views known to government, but there is no reason to suppose that government would readily cave in.

To restate: we have concluded that the application of agreed standards, not a particular form of ownership, is the road to penological propriety. That said, our belief is that there are features of private ownership which could facilitate the achievement of penal purpose. The effects of privatization can be various (LeGrand and Robinson, 1984; O'Higgins, 1987). The distinctive features of the prison, we contend, may well mean that private institutions will enjoy some advantages in operation.

The distinctiveness of prison privatization

In terms of physical plant and poverty of regime, prison provision in both the United Kingdom and North America is almost universally dire. If one were to search for an instance of a State monopoly which has failed, one would not need to look beyond the Prison Service. It confines citizens and aspires to direct them towards a good and useful life. In fact conditions give the lie to the aspiration. They are more likely to brutalize than to improve. It is against the backcloth of this failure that we must consider privatization. If our starting point were a humane system, most of the arguments which follow would be less compelling. The starting point is, in fact, a disastrous mess.

The alleged basic problem with public provision has been its inability to change (Savas, 1980; Klein, 1984). The central reasons for this are well stated by LeGrand and Robinson — although they do not accept the argument in its simple form:

> Individuals in state organisations pursue their own interests in the same way as individuals in private ones do; they all want jobs that are rewarding (in terms of money, status and power), satisfying and as secure as possible. However, in their pursuit of those ends, public employees are not faced with the same constraints as private ones; in particular, their firms cannot be driven out of business or be taken over, even if they provide an inefficient service. Hence they will engage in practices that serve their own ends at the expense of their clients. Hours of work will be reduced, work practices will be inefficient, wages will be too high, other elements of remuneration such as pension schemes will be too generous, and so on. Generally, resources will be wasted because the public sector lacks accountability. (1984: 7–8)

One could be forgiven for regarding this as a precise account of the development of working practices in the Prison Service, up to and including the Fresh Start initiative. However, as noted earlier, we are not suggesting that the defects of prison administration are a simple effect of State monopoly, nor that privatization has uniform benefits and problems across contexts. We adopt instead the approach of O'Higgins, in a closely argued paper concluding that

> While the motivations underlying privatisation initiatives (and the responses to them) may be characterised as either instrumental or ideological, their evaluation must be strategic and contextual. This allows fewer clear-cut answers (particularly *ex ante*) of the general implications of privatisation initiatives, but provides a better basis from which to assess the probable impact of particular proposals at particular junctures. (O'Higgins, 1987)

One should think of prison privatization as instrumental and specific to its context rather than ideological and just another instance of a uniform policy. What, then, is the problem with public prisons? One is the lack of any pressure to innovate, which may be coupled with the powerful position of the Prison Officers' Association. Prisons as we know them mock the aspiration of the first Prison Rule, to enable prisoners to lead a good and useful life. The rhetoric of 'humane containment' has come to signify the limits of what is hoped for, and itself is belied by the reality of warehousing of prisoners. A casualty of the process has been the hope of rehabilitation. Pessimism prevails. The research evidence on alleged rehabilitative inefficacy was never as conclusive as it purported to be. The assertion that 'nothing works' (Martison, 1974) seems less certain now than in 1974 (see, for example, Cullen and Gilbert, 1982), and indeed, there may even be grounds for modest optimism (Gendreau and Ross, 1987). Even if the evidence had been conclusive, there is a case for saying that the rehabilitative ideal is the only bulwark against the erosion of the quality of prisoners' lives towards which economy and pragmatism press. The run-down of prison workshops announced in 1985 is only the most obvious sign of this. The emphasis in the prison building programme is on new establishments rather than the provision of the necessities of decency, notably the provision of integral cell sanitation. This is not consistent with the aspiration to change people. It is consistent with a tolerance of their degradation. As for the Prison Officers' Association, what are the costs of failure? If treatment in prison increases the rate of return to prison, the only consequence is more work opportunities. The inexorable and expensive rise in the number of prison officers per prisoner detained since World War II (see the Annual Reports of the Work of the Prison Department) may have something to do with increasing security requirements. But it has at least as much to do with the powerful position of the Prison Officers' Association. The development of powerful interest groups is one of the traditional reasons for opposing State provision of service.

The penal reform lobby is, paradoxically, part of the prison problem. It is Janus-faced, advocating both the improvement of prison conditions and the greater use of alternatives to custody. The latter advocacy has tended to predominate in recent years and seems to have usurped aspirations to reform. This emphasis may well have paradoxically contributed to the pessimism about the positive possibilities of prison. Its arguments in favour of alternatives to custody become more compelling the worse prison conditions become. At worst, the penal reform lobby has a perverse interest in keeping prison conditions bad. An emphasis on overcrowding misses the central point that the conditions in which prisoners are kept are inappropriate. Changing overcrowding in prisons will merely change the problem, rather than solve it. A similar argument has been

advanced about the probation service (Chapman, 1987), and generally about non-State, non-profit agencies by Ericson et al. (1987),
who hold that the work of such agencies

> thrives on a discourse of failure, an assertion that what went before is
> inefficient and wrong and can only be corrected and improved through
> progressive alternatives. In a 'cognitive passion' that they are more
> efficient with a 'righteous passion' that they are more humane, non-state
> agencies are able to ensure their 'success' without attention to the facts of
> the matter. (1987: 368)

Most recently, this has manifested itself in opposition to the current
prison building programme. We hold no torch for the priorities
enshrined in the prison building programme. Nor should the danger
that the courts will fill whatever prisons the Home Office provides be
disregarded, although the evidence for this is less impressive than has
sometimes been contended. Despite all the dangers, Sir Leon Radzinowicz's assertion that 'building prisons today is a measure of penal
reform' (on the BBC Radio 4 programme 'Law in Action', 24 January 1986) should not be dismissed. We would prefer to put the same
point another way. *If* the pattern of court sentencing cannot be
changed dramatically, not building more prisons would be an act of
folly. To say that sentencing is part of the problem of prisons is only
partly true. It is true that if the courts had less recourse to prison the
state of the prisons might be better — at least less overcrowded. But
the use that the courts make of prison cannot, in the aggregate, be
'wrong'. It is a choice made under a particular set of pressures.
Change the pressures and the use of imprisonment will change in
response. This is clear from a variety of penal innovations (see Pease,
1983). If a court buys in to private facilities, their cost is brought
home much more forcibly to those making the decision to incarcerate. The likely effect of this would be to reduce the total amount of
imprisonment handed down.

A final, neglected, paradox lies in the relationship between prison
training and employment prospects. From the history of prisons, as
far back as the Rasphuis, public prison labour in the West has
studiously avoided offering competition in outside markets. The side
of the equation which has traditionally been emphasized has been the
need to avoid putting people outside prison out of a job. The other
side of the equation is much less often mentioned. It is that prisoners
gain expertise in prisons that is irrelevant to their employment prospects outside. Only if prison industry *does* compete with firms outside
will an ex-prisoner reliably have relevant work skills upon release.
The advantages (and possible problems) of private work provisions
have been well set-out by Lightman (1982).

Having presented an outline view of what is wrong with prisons as we know them in the UK, it is necessary to outline the problems. Before doing so, we must address the difficulties in directly copying US practice, as has been somewhat uncritically advocated, notably by Young (1987).

The US example

There are reasons other than xenophobia for being cautious about the adoption of US practice in prison privatization. On the evidence of recorded US experience (an excellent bibliography of US work on the topic is provided in Immarigeon, 1987), the approach is severely flawed, and we must learn from the mistakes rather than reproduce them. That some of the private agencies in the USA lack relevant experience is beyond doubt. That some oversell their product and employ people with unappetizing backgrounds is clear. Most worryingly, the low cost of private operations may be spurious because it is being achieved through private provision being limited to those groups of offenders who should not be in custody in the first place, leaving public provision for 'hard-end' offenders. This, as Borna (1986) notes, distorts costings, making the private facilities look better value. This is all the more worrying as being precisely the same dynamic as is familiar in the provision of private health care, with the difficult groups (like psychiatric and geriatric patients) continuing to fall to the State's responsibility. Discussing the probable first British contract for a private penal institution, an executive of a building contractor said 'These places do not have to be secure. People sent there may not have paid their rates or something like that. Anyone charged with multiple rape would probably be sent elsewhere' (Helm, 1987). Young (1987) argues that private facilities are expanding up the security classification. His examples and Immarigeon's (1987) review suggest that if this is so, it has not yet progressed far. The work of Ericson et al. (1987) gives reasons why it will not go far. The further up it goes, the less attractive will be the cost differentials between public and private provision. It is premature to conclude that they will disappear altogether. One possibility is that early private facilities with good operating standards will generate a 'halo effect' (Champion, 1988). This is easier to create the more biddable the prisoners. It is also more misleading. This is an area in which the enthusiasm of Sir Edward Gardner and his colleagues on the Home Affairs Committee should have been more qualified than it was.

Another difficulty was raised in a letter by Thomas Goodman to the *Guardian* on 31 October 1986: 'Private contractors, being paid per head per day, will wish to see full prisons.' However, in our view the recognition by the sentencer that there *is* a cost, will substantially outweigh the effects of private contractor lobbying.

The particular case of remand

We must interrupt the flow of the narrative to discuss briefly the case of remand. Lord Windlesham (1987) speaks as a former Home Office Minister and Chairman of the Parole Board, and a respected and influential commentator on penal matters. In January 1987 he elaborated on the privatization of remand facilities. He opines that

> [T]he description 'remand prisoner' obscures an all-important distinction between the punishment of convicted offenders and the pre-trial detention of persons accused of a criminal offence punishable with imprisonment; that the conditions in which persons on remand are confined are now indistinguishable in most essentials from the restrictions on liberty imposed in the name of punishment; and that separate provision for as many as possible of those remanded in custody by the courts is not simply desirable in principle, but is the only reform which is capable of resolving the acute and continuing crisis of prison overcrowding. (1987: 11)

He advocates the establishment of New Remand Units (NRUs), with private sector companies supplying operational staff under contract, and Home Office managers. The arguments have apparently so influenced the government that a green paper on the issue was published in July 1988.

The argument is powerful because remand conditions are a disgrace (the penal reform lobby stands accused here too of collusion, in so far as it advocates that people so detained should be bailed instead, rather than humane conditions of custody established). It is also true that in the decade up to 1985, the remand population was the fastest growing part of the prison population. The very power of the argument creates a problem for us. On the one hand, should we make the remand centre the exception in what would otherwise be a clear requirement of replacement of long imprisonment by private facilities, because the Windlesham proposal addresses a real problem? On the other hand, success in this arguably less difficult custodial area will generate spurious economic comparisons with the remainder of the prison system, and thus lead to the state of affairs earlier held to be undesirable, in which the least tractable prisoners remain the State's responsibility. Our fears in this direction are such that, on balance, we would prefer other means of dealing with the remand population. Electronic tagging of some form would be cheaper and less restrictive than remands in custody, even custody in the New Remand Centres. The presumption in favour of unconditional bail should of course continue to apply, and any evidence that tagging was being substituted for straight bail addressed promptly. Evaluation of technological alternatives to prison seems to be as constrained by ideology as in the notion of private prisons. Rational and systematic analysis of these technologies may well reveal them as important elements in prison reform (see Berry and Matthews, this volume).

The organization of private prisons in the UK

We have examined some of the issues that seem to us to cloud the debate about private prisons. To develop that debate further, we present below the outlines of one possible form of organization of the UK prison systems under private ownership. In doing so we recognize that any change would be piecemeal, either by the privatization of individual functions within a prison (*à la* National Health Service) or by the operation of one or two 'test bed' prisons runs by private concerns. This is undoubtedly prudent. The former process in particular will move institutions closer to the world outside, in ways for which liberal commentators have clamoured for decades. However, even these first steps should be taken with an awareness of the overall framework of a penal system within which private facilities would operate. After writing them, we came across Cullen (1986), which contains some similar ideas. The following outlines a potential framework.

(1)   Private agencies, local authorities, the Home Office and other Ministries would be invited to submit bids direct to the Lord Chancellor's Department. It would be made clear that any contract issues would not be for a period in excess of five years, after which competitive tender would recur. It is clear that competitive tendering is not a wholly satisfactory process, since it favours the largest private organizations. Ericson et al. (1987) entertainingly compare private prisons with hamburger franchises (McPrisons, Burglar King). However, McAfee (1987) describes the most extensive safeguards which the State of Tennessee has instituted to protect itself from the abuses and unhappy consequences of such an arrangement. Thus it is a defensible approach — more defensible, we assert, than its rivals. Bids would be required to specify the range of offenders whom the proposed facility would house, maximum numbers, plans of the facility, regime details including staffing levels, and the proposed charge per unit time which the agency would impose. All bids for facilities for less serious offenders must be dismissed out of hand, for fear that the facility would draw people from non-custodial sentences. No prisoner whose sentence was less than 18 months would be eligible for placement in a private facility. The risk of

private facilities drawing from those now sentenced to non-custodial alternatives is so great that such a restriction must remain in place for many years. If private prisons do prove themselves with longer-term prisoners, there is no reason in the distant future why their benefits should not be extended. The arithmetic of imprisonment (see Fitzmaurice and Pease, 1985) is that longer-term prisoners (assuming sensible use of prison space) cause the crisis of overcrowding, so the proposed initial restriction addresses the central problem of prison overcrowding. The bidding agency must satisfy the Treasury that it has enough resources to settle any claim from members of the public in respect of offences committed by those escaping from the facility. Inevitably, claims by prisoners arising from mistreatment will occur, and should be dealt with like those from any other citizen, with the private agency responsible for settlements. The Treasury should not indemnify against such costs.

(2) The Lord Chancellor would select from among the schemes remaining those which he or she was willing to approve. The decision would be informed by advice from a Penal Services Audit Unit which would assess regimes and nominated senior staff and analyse costings. Approval would not entail that any prisoners would be sent to the facility, merely that the courts could choose to send offenders to the facility if they so wished and the sentence band involved was appropriate to the facts of the individual case. Contractors would no doubt commission market research before injecting capital, just as they would in any other uncertain market. The capital cost of high security prisons would be prohibitive if they were built by conventional, (that is inefficient) means. We should not extrapolate costs or designs of private prisons from those of their public rivals; potential contractors are well aware of the danger of this. A spokesman for a British consortium claims 'It takes six to eight years to build a [public] prison. We would be able to do it in a year' (Helm, 1987).

(3) Contracts would be issued. These would incorporate statements of willingness to submit to regular inspection, and to agree to a rigorous statement of institutional standards, whose breach would entail the immediate withdrawal of approval. The absence of Crown immunity from private prisons would make them subject to national and local health, safety and other requirements. If this spurred the removal of Crown Immunity from State-run prisons, so much the better. Contracts would require terminal objectives to be identified for each prisoner at the point of reception, as well as general objectives of the regime itself.

(4) Whatever prisoner-specific objectives are specified, a conviction-free period after release will be a tacit objective and will form the basis of part of the payment. The size of the 'no reconviction' bonus

element would depend on a priori probability of reconviction. A suitable instrument could readily be developed from the work of Nuttall et al. (1978). This is a vital element of the procedure to provide an incentive to generate truly rehabilitative programmes in prison — an incentive which does not now exist. Reduction in rates of reconviction, constrained only by humanity of means, is the *only* measure of effectiveness by which prisons should be judged. That such rates are not a perfect reflection of offending behaviour is beside the point. The escape by the probation service in particular into quality of life indices of penal effectiveness is wholly misconceived, and is a result of its failure to achieve uniformly good reductions in rates of reconviction. As Logan remarks,

> In addition to due process, justice requires clarity as to the purpose of punishment. It is the state's job to ensure that private prisons pursue a proper penology. This may be difficult, since the state itself is rarely clear and consistent in penal philosophy. (1987: 2)

(5)   Prisoners would find their way into private facilities either directly by court sentence or upon transfer from the public system. If they are sentenced directly by the court to a named institution, the court would have available the per diem costs and the statement of objectives (and in due course the reconviction record) of both public and competing private facilities. Appeal against sentence would be to a judge who did not know whether a private or public facility was involved, so as to avoid the development of a twin-track system. Costings would always be on the basis of release at the earliest date. Parole decisions would remain in the hands of a publicly appointed Parole Board operating on information provided by persons who were *not* prison employees. Such an arrangement would give private facilities an incentive to produce quick results, since no further money would be paid for detention beyond the earliest date. If a prisoner were to be transferred from a public to a private system the Prison Department of the Home Office would be appropriately charged. In a mixed system of this kind, private provision, if effective, would tend to increase.

(6)   Half of all savings achieved by the scheme (based on a formula which includes an element to reward a reduction in total use of custody) would be earmarked for schemes to support crime victims.

(7)   Contract and inspection procedures would absolutely prohibit the subcontracting of prison labour. It is of fundamental importance to avoid the abuses which the chain gang represented — although there of course the corruption was of *public* employees. Within that restriction, imaginative employment programmes would

be encouraged, and artificial restrictions on rates of prisoner pay removed.

The advantages

Looking at our analysis of what is wrong with prisons alongside the scheme proposed, it will be seen that the scheme does address the problems quite precisely. What we see to be the important characteristics and consequences of the scheme proposed are as follows:

(1) Most fundamentally, an incentive to rehabilitate is introduced. The provision of a commercial incentive to develop programmes which really change people would constitute a welcome development. Reviewing the research literature, it is difficult to resist the view that the possible techniques for change identified in that literature (and interestingly they are all acceptable from a humanitarian standpoint) have by and large not been tried in prisons. This is perhaps in part because of the institutional inertia of public prisons, rather than for reasons of principle.

(2) Related to the first point, it is a matter of common observation that few penal sanctions die. They fade only to be revived when the climate comes full circle. Ineffective penal sanctions ought to die. New options and improvements ought constantly to be sought. One of the characteristics of good private systems is that, not without social cost, they allow change in response to measures of effectiveness.

(3) Certain prisoner groups cause disproportionate difficulties. For them, a private alternative on the lines set out would be particularly desirable. We have in mind prisoners who are HIV positive and those segregated for their own protection (Rule 43 OP prisoners). These would be obvious groups for an early trial of private provision.

(4) The powerful position of the Prison Officers' Association would be undermined.

(5) By linking a reduction on prison cost to an increase in victim support, a wholly new pressure would be exerted on judges. By merely making the costs of custody visible at the point of sentence, more would be done to reduce prison use than any amount of good sentiment.

(6) The dual role of the Home Office in prison management would be eliminated. While the Home Office serves both as an adversary of the prisoner and adjudicator of the conflict in which the prisoner is involved, the private prison separates the two functions.

(7) Adherence to a set of standards of operation would constitute a term of the contract, whose monitoring would be an explicit cost within the contract. Inspection of prisons is now undertaken by an

arm of the Home Office. The Home Secretary is invited to act against his or her own employees in cases of severe criticism. With an inspected private system, the same difficulties would not apply. This is not to underestimate the difficulties of maintaining standards in private institutions. They may, in the right context, be less than is the case with other controlled groups (notably the old and mentally impaired) where residents are more passive.

Mixed emotions

Our vision chimes with that of Borna, who writes:

> Nowhere in the literature of penology is mention made of one state competing with another to provide a higher level of care for its inmates. Nor do institutions in the same state compete with each other. The concept of competition is, at best, foreign to the field of corrections. The privatisation of the prison industry may witness the introduction of competition and result in a general upgrading of inmate custody, care and treatment. (1986: 333)

Our view that the introduction of private prisons may offer a much needed opportunity for the re-introduction of aspirations to reform in committal to prisons is also broadly consonant with the views expressed by Cullen (1986). Yet we are conscious of the warning of O'Higgins. He notes, that, while privatization may have a variety of effects, 'the context within which it is currently being advocated and implemented in the UK makes it unlikely that it will generally advance progressive social welfare aims' (1987). If prison privatization takes place as an unthinking copy of North American practice, the situation in the UK will probably become worse. If it takes place without strong insistence on standards and on rewards for success in reconviction terms, the situation will probably become worse. If it takes place with no restriction on the triviality of offences which consign one to a private prison, the use of imprisonment will increase, and the private facilities will gain a spurious reputation as offering value for money. In short, the potential advantages which private prisons offer are specific to a narrow range of possible schemes. Our advocacy of such schemes is therefore a high-risk strategy. If all the right elements are not in place, privatization will have entered our penal system to no good effect. We will have opened our gates to a particularly unpleasant Trojan Horse. Our fear is that liberal and radical lobbyists will oppose privatization *per se*. The scheme introduced would then be a primitive and unsatisfactory version, and an opportunity would have been lost. Anyone who thinks that criticism of privatization in principle will delay its introduction to our prisons is misguided.

Note

We are grateful to Paul Wilding for his most helpful comments on a first draft of this chapter, and to Roger Matthews for equally helpful advice about the second draft.

References

Ascher, K. (1987) *The Politics of Privatisation*. Macmillan.
Borna, S. (1986) 'Free Enterprise goes to Prison', *British Journal of Criminology*, 26: 321–34.
Camp, C. and Camp, G. (1985) 'Correctional Privatisation in Perspective', *Prison Journal*, 62: 14–31.
Campion, M. (1988) 'Jail Inc. is Popular but Doesn't Make a Cent', *Independent*, 1 July.
Chapman, T. (1987) 'Let's Bury Black, not Praise it', *Lynx*, 32, October: 14.
Cullen, F.T. (1986) 'The Privatisation of Treatment: Prison Reform in the 1980s', *Federal Probation*, 50: 8–16.
Cullen, F.T. and Gilbert, K.E. (1982), *Reaffirming Rehabilitation*. Santa Barbara: University of California Press.
Ditchfield, J. and Duncan, D. (1987) 'The Prison Disciplinary System: Perceptions of its Fairness and Adequacy by Inmates, Staff and Members of Boards of Visitors', *Howard Journal*, 26: 122–38.
Elvin, J. (1985) 'A Civil Liberties View of Private Prisons', *Prison Journal*, 654: 48–52.
Ericson, R.V., McMahon, M.W. and Evans, D.S. (1987) 'Punishing for Profit: Reflections on the Revival of Privatization in Corrections', *Canadian Journal of Criminology*, 29: 355–87.
Fitzmaurice, C.T. and Pease, K. (1985) *The Psychology of Judicial Sentencing*. Manchester: Manchester University Press.
Gandy, J. (1985) *Privatization of Correctional Services for Adults*. Report to Ministry of Solicitor General of Canada.
Gendreau, P. and Ross, R.R. (1987) 'Revivification of Rehabilitation: Evidence from the 1980s', *Justice Quarterly*, 4: 349–407.
Goodman, T. (1986) 'If the Corrections Corps get a Foot in our Prison Door', *Guardian*, 31 October: 12.
Hastings, S. and Levie, H. (1983) *Privatisation?* Nottingham: Spokesman.
Helm, S. (1987) 'Consortium Aims at 'Free Hand' over Private Jails', *Independent*, 18 November
Home Office (1988) *Private Sector Involvement in the Remand System*. Cm 434.
Howard League (1987), *Prisons for Profit?* London: Howard League.
Immarigeon, R. (1987) 'The Private Financing and Management of Jails and Prisons in the United States: A Bibliography', *Criminal Justice Abstracts* 19 (1): 123–39.
Klein, R. (1984) 'Privatisation and the Welfare State', *Lloyds Bank Review* (Jan.): 12–29.
LeGrand, J. and Robinson, R. (eds) (1984) *Privatisation and the Welfare State*. London, Allen & Unwin.
Lightman, E.S. (1982) 'The Private Employer and the Prison Industry', *British Journal of Criminology*, 22: 36–48.
Logan, C.H. (1987) *Privatising Prisons: The Moral Case*. London: Adam Smith Institute.

McAfee, W.M. (1987) 'Tennessee's Private Prison Act of 1986: An Historical Perspective with Special Attention to California's Experience', *Vanderbilt Law Review*, 40: 851–65.

Martinson, R. (1974) 'What works? — Questions and Answers about Prison Reforms', *Public Interest*, Spring: 22–54.

Nuttall, C.P. et al. (1978) 'Parole in England and Wales', *Home Office Research Study No. 38*. London: HMSO.

O'Higgins, M. (1987) 'Privatization and Social Welfare: Concepts, Analysis and the British Experience', in S. Kamerman and A. Kahn (eds), *Privatisation and Social Welfare*. Princeton: Princeton University Press.

Pease, K. (1983) 'Penal Innovations', in J. Lishman (ed.), *Research Highlights*, 7. Department of Social Work, Aberdeen University.

Savas, E.S. (1980) *Privatizing the Public Sector*. Chatham NJ: Chatham House

Windlesham, Lord (1987) 'Punishment and Prevention: The Inappropriate Prisoners'. Lecture given at Earlham Hall, University of East Anglia, 3 December.

Young, P. (1987) *The Prison Cell*. London: Adam Smith Institute.

Index

Printed in the United States
132077LV00001B/23/A

9 780803 982413